Biological Time

Dear,

It's all about
the night I think

Bill [?]

Biological Time

Bernie Taylor

The Ea Press
www.TheEaPress.com
Oregon

Biological Time

Copyright © 2004 by Bernie Taylor

ISBN 0-9749932-0-4

1. Nature — Non-Fiction,
2. Biological Clocks — Non-Fiction,
3. Astronomy — Non-Fiction,
4. Salmon — Non-Fiction,
5. Native — Non-Fiction,
6. Oregon— Non-Fiction,

Illustrated by Kit Richards

Cover and interior design by Tightline Advertising

The Ea Press
www.TheEaPress.com

Printed in the United States of America
First U.S. Edition

Table of Contents

This book is dedicated to all those
who have questioned what is known
in order to find new answers.

Acknowledgements

Special note needs to be given to Ron Newman, whose careful record keeping brought me to first consider the biological time hypothesis. To Ken Kenaston and Tim Dalton from the Oregon Department of Fish and Wildlife whose ears were always open and helped to retrieve some of the key salmon data used in this work. To Dr. James Fenner who reminded me that just because we are not aware of something today doesn't mean that it was not known before. And, to Berne McNelly who helped to bring the wisdom of the ancients and mysteries of the skies to within reach.

There were many other individuals who contributed to this book. They include Gil Bergen from the Connetquot River State Park, Richard Price, Bob Richards, Dr. Keith Jones, Caleb Zurstadt from the U.S. Forest Service, Dave Teppola from Laurel Ridge Winery, Al McDonald from Chemeketa Community College, Dr. James Hall, Dr. Carmo Vasconcelos and Dr. Norman Anderson from Oregon State University, Dr. John Palmer from the University of Massachusetts at Amherst, Keith Braun, Kirk Schroeder and Gary Susac from the Oregon Department of Fish and Wildlife, David Vogel from Natural Resource Scientists, the Reverend Ralph Hamlet, Dr. Christian Zimmerman from the USGS, Dr. E.C. Krupp from the Griffith Observatory, Dr. Ruston Sweeting from the Pacific Biological Station at Nanaimo, Dr. David Mackas from Fisheries and Oceans Canada, Steve Dolan and Dan Bishop from the New York State Department of Environmental Conservation, Stan Jones from the Tulalip Tribe, Frank Lake from the Yurok Tribe, Harold Blackwolf from the Warm Springs Tribe, Gary Vaughn, Carol Turcotte and Jack Tipping from the Washington Department of Fish and Wildlife, Susan Kosisky with the Allergy Immunology Service at Walter Reed Army Medical Center, Polly Owen from the Hazelnut Marketing Board, Dr. David Stone from University of Alaska Fairbanks, Gary Lewis, Scott Richmond, Arnie and Barbara Mitchell, Dr. Dick Ewing from Biotech, John Bell and Bruce Ward from the British Columbia Water, Land and Air Protection, Jerry Taylor, Jeff Fox and Timothy McKinley from the Alaska Department of Fish and Game, Michelle Workman from the East Bay Municipal Utility District, Sabrina Ford from TMI and Laith Jawad from the Museum of New Zealand. There are so many other contributors whose years of research appeared in the primary literature and are available to us all. Their names and contributions are listed in the bibliography.

Thanks to the Oregon State University and George Fox University who allowed me to utilize their libraries and the Newberg Public Library for their retrieval assistance. To Hank Hosfield, Jason Graham and Travis Huntington who smoothed out some of my sentences, Kit Richards who edited the complete text and provided the line drawings and Cameron Prow from Type-Rite II who did the final edit, Chris Johns, Scott Preppernau and Brandt Balgooyen who did the statistical work and James and Brian Flaherty from Tightline Advertising who designed the book and stunning cover. Finally, to my wife and daughter who were supportive throughout this process.

Preface

IT IS OUR CAPACITY TO DOUBT THAT WILL
DETERMINE THE FUTURE OF CIVILIZATION.
~ RICHARD FEYNMAN

I'm on my way to a favorite salmon river on the Oregon coast, just over an hour's drive from home. The main source of water for this river is the many springs that percolate up from great basins under the earth's surface. Combined with seasonal rainfall, otherwise known as the "Oregon Eclipse" (from October until June), the spring water cascades through a series of steep gorges into pools in the upper reaches where I like to fish. Downstream, a more gradual sloping gradient takes the flow through low-lying hills before meandering around pastured stretches on the way to tidewater.

To reach the river from Oregon's Willamette Valley, I must invariably put my engine to the test of climbing the winding one-lane highway up and over the Coastal Mountain Range. Although this may not seem like much work for the mechanized fisherman, I am reminded of first nation native peoples, also from the valley, who had for centuries climbed on foot up and over the pass and down along the winding river through rain soaked gorges in order to catch salmon and trade with coastal tribes. It wasn't until much later that Euro-American settlers and eventually civil engineers widened the path, reinforced the banks to support bridges, and coated the earthen track with asphalt so that a comfortable passage could be made within an hour. Even though the current road has significant advantages over the traditional first nation people's method of traversing, society in some capacity was still not satisfied. There was a time not too long ago when a movement to widen the road into two lanes was presented by local enthusiasts. However, the expanded highway concept was thwarted when environmental groups sued the agency in charge for the potential damage the road construction would cause Coho salmon spawning habitat. One has to wonder how much damage the first road inflicted on the salmonids. Can the injury still be seen today or was it short-term? Populations of salmon and other organisms appear to wax and wane in their own rhythms over 10-year periods, in spite of what we do for or against them.

As I crested the summit of this mountain highway, I considered these fluctuations in the number of returning salmon in recent years. Conventional wisdom suggests that this year will see resurgences in population, as we appear to be in an upswing from a long drought of fish, allegedly initiated by the El Niños of the mid-1990s. Similar weather arguments are made for virtually all organisms. More or less rain or snows are the usual suspects. However well intended, due to the erratic and almost immeasurable effects of the weather, no one can really dispute the claims—for the salmon or any other organism. There are also fluctuations in populations under similar climatic conditions. In my mind, these hypotheses have not been convincingly quantified. Down-shifting in response to the steeper grade, I considered the idea that there exists a better method of analyzing nature's design.

Traditionally, the river fishes best for steelhead (an ocean-going form of rainbow trout) from January through March, although the peak window within that period shifts from year to year. For most fishermen, these dates are often circled on calendars posted on shop windows or passed by word of mouth in coffee shops across the valley. But, how is it that native tribesman knew when to begin their trek? They did not use our calendar system and their journey would have taken days, which would have required them to gauge precisely their timing in the solar year. There are anecdotal stories of indigenous peoples timing the arrival of the salmon to plants, insects and birds, but the appearance of these organisms also appears to be earlier or later in some years. It's easy to assume that the slightest mistiming could have resulted in dire consequences for the whole tribe. So how did they know? What tradition has told us is that salmon synchronize their movements on an annual basis. We are pretty sure that these animals can't think or plan their movements as we do, so it must be a type of sensory response.

Assuming that the natives arrived at this section of the river as I did on this day, they would have observed that the most productive periods for salmon angling are generally at first light and around dusk. During this time of year the mornings arrive late and the evenings come early. On this afternoon, I pulled off the road at a bend and onto the sharp gravel that separates the asphalt from the wild grass. In one hand I gathered my rod and reel, and with the other stowed a few flies and spool of leader material in a breast pocket. Heading down to the river I carefully traversed the well-traveled, root-strewn path through overgrown nonindigenous Himalayan blackberry bushes. These plants have a distinctive habit of growing in the ground at both ends, suffocating lower growing plants from the sun. Unfortunately, it was these lower plant forms that were traditionally responsible for holding the stream banks intact. However, it is hard these days to know exactly what is native and what has been introduced. Thomas Jefferson's famous saying about a man having nothing greater to offer his country than to introduce a new species that will bear fruit comes to mind whenever I see these plants. Wild isn't always native or better.

The water in the river has a gin clear flow, almost sterile. There are no insect hatches this time of year and even algae growth is invisible to all but the trained eye. My right wading boot kicked over a rock on which clung a few snails. There is life in this water, but perhaps only a shade of earlier times when the river hosted tens of thousands of salmon, which spawned and died. The nutrients they once brought from the sea would have deposited a wealth of fertilizer for the algae that coated the rocks and the small invertebrates that fed on plant life. Steelhead trout and salmon juveniles would have eaten the protein-rich flesh and invertebrates, providing them with sufficient food to develop before making their inevitable ocean sojourn.

My fingers methodically ran the line and leader through the guides, and cinched down the knot on the fly in anticipation of a fish. The fly was made of red yarn and didn't actually resemble any form of insect. Such attractors are still called flies by anglers. The color incites a reaction in the fish, just as red signs, cars, dresses, etc., alert people. Clever marketers on Madison Avenue and anglers both take advantage of this trick of nature. My use of this artificial "fly" was considered fair since the steelhead wasn't feeding on its spawning run. Even if it were, there was an absence of insects to imitate.

I keyed into a deep slot just above a pool where all fish must pass through. This opening, flanked by two large boulders, has remained virtually the same since I started fishing it six years ago, providing a predictable avenue for fish passage and one on the line. Others appear to be rewritten with each passing storm. Keeping track of the edits as time marks each page is part of the game. The zone in this run is no wider than a yardstick under moderate flows. The line was flipped with the forearm and wrist into a roll cast over the water, and mended upstream once so that the fly would sink to the right depth before the lighter floating line would sweep it downstream. The line stopped on the first pass. Lightly lifting the tip I felt the subtle indistinguishable vibrations of a fish moving somewhere beneath. With a quick snap of my right wrist complemented by a sharp downward tug with my left, the wire hook set and the fight began.

The jig was up and the fish screamed down into the pool. My heart beat faster with the rush of the fish and I accidentally bit my lower lip. The steelhead leaped twice, screamed down further through the pool and turned. Any farther and the fish could have tumbled into the next pool and taken all the line off my reel. He then headed back in my direction faster than I could take up line. As a result, my line went limp, but only for a second. I now had the advantage, as the water's current and leverage were both working against the fish. The steelhead soon tired. I grabbed the leader with my free hand and led the steelhead in closer. A chrome buck of about 12 pounds was now in hand. Not the largest steelhead I had seen, but a good fish nonetheless. My forceps clasped the hook and gently released the steelhead into the flow—unharmed.

The adipose fin (on the upper back) was clipped, indicating that the steelhead had been raised to a juvenile stage in a hatchery and then released for a two-or-more-year ocean journey. There are no hatcheries on this river, but strays from a heavily stocked tributary nearby sometimes take a wrong turn at the intersection just downstream and find their way here, just as the wild fish sometimes end up in the hatchery river. Straying is a natural process. I could not tell if the fish was of hatchery origin at the time of the take or over the course of the fight. There does not seem to be a difference in behavior at this time in their lives. The fight for survival in the marine environment makes them all equal.

The fish could have been kept for the table but a fresh fillet wasn't what drew me to the river. This day, added to countless other such hunts around the globe, was fieldwork. We can study a fish in a tank in an attempt to understand the creature, but the story isn't the same as in its natural surroundings. The sterile laboratory environment lacks the interactions between predators and prey, the moods of the weather and the natural rhythms of light and darkness. Being among plants and animals in the wild can provide a different way of looking at them. Such hands-on research helped me to develop my first book (*Big Trout*, 2002) that was directed towards an angling audience. My primary area of interest in the trout book was the where and when of this fish, concepts that must have been crucial for indigenous peoples when they fished for salmon. My inquiries suggested that the primary connection among the rhythms of the fish was how they reacted to light and darkness. This force was tied to both chemical processes and conditioned behavior. I began to consider that light cycles affected the behavior of the ocean-going forms as well. This insight brought me to ask more questions and find answers that revealed the secrets of how they coordinate many rhythmic events. To better understand these concepts, a synergy of a wide range of fields, such as physics, ichthyology, marine biology, anthropology, endocrinology, biorhythms, astronomy and archeology, was required. The resulting book is quite different from the one originally envisioned. The answers have turned out a wealth of findings relating to the understanding and conservation of salmon and other species, ranging from the smallest invertebrates to the majestic elk. Also important, the findings draw conclusions about man's beginnings and the nature of our existence.

Thinking in Space and Time

From the dawn of history, man has looked to the heavens in search of his place in time and space. He charted the stars and planets, followed the path of the sun, timed the moon, and created astral, solar and lunar calendars to describe these celestial events, believing their movements dictated life on earth. Finding synchrony with their rhythms promised harmony with the natural world and offered hope for predicting the future. Thousands of years later, modern man has a much greater knowledge about the universe, but seems more out of step with its natural cycles. Why is this? We seem more conflicted than ever. If you asked a roomful of learned people to explain man's understanding of time and space, each would probably give you a different answer based on his/her background. For instance, to the physicist, time is relative, whereas to the Buddhist, time is eternal. The biologist measures time as the duration of life. And the Rabbi marks time from the beginning of creation. All are correct within the narrow constricts of their academic disciplines and/or religious teachings. There may even exist a common thread of truth running through all of them. Yet they are also in conflict with each other and, to a greater or lesser extent, somewhat incomplete explanations.

Discerning the nature of time and space is perhaps the most significant subject that man has pondered throughout the ages. The manner in which people of different cultures and eras have answered these questions defined their societies and their world—as well as their views of the afterworld and companion religious beliefs. Great societies were built upon the reading of calendars that calculated the cycles of a certain specific natural occurrence. The different theories on which these calendars were based led to battles between schools of science and religion, as well as real wars. The great irony about all of this is that, while at the highest level these calendars appear to differ greatly across cultures, at the most fundamental level they are measuring the same thing. Everything is actually based in *biological time*, a term I use to describe the natural lifecycles and events of organisms dictated by the presence or absence of light. Biological time is a unifying theory, linking the timing of ancient calendars with modern scientific research and historical records that show how the natural world is marching to a drumbeat that we are just now learning how to hear.

To gain a greater understanding of biological time, we need first to look back. Archeological evidence from prehistoric times illustrates how man looked to the skies for the answers. He followed the cycles of the sun, moon, stars and some of the more visible planets and, to him, these celestial bodies held power. The sun and stars appear to have governed the seasons and the moon shifted the oceans, all of which affected his daily well-being. The radiance of the sun provided warmth, even during the winter months, and at other times of the year seemed to help grow the plants that fed him and his game. Perhaps the most significant find of recorded time reckoning goes back to about 6,500 BCE when a hunter-fisherman named "Ishango," who lived on the shores of Lake Edward in Central Africa, carved patterns in bone tools that appear to monitor the phases of the lunar cycle. Alexander Marshack, author of *The Roots of Civilization* (1972), modeled the scratches and argued that this early man was concerned about the dark and light periods of the moon. He didn't know specifically why, but the lunar calendars were very precise. Marshack's studies of early human etchings on other animal bones, many of which also contained pictures of animals, demonstrated that there was a relationship with the lunar cycle, but the exact uses of the calendars were never unraveled.

Without knowing the significance of the animals, we can logically come to the conclusion that he was using the cycles of the moon as a calendar. The position of each cycle, perhaps signified by a New or Full Moon, in relation to the season (position of the sun in the solar year), would have told him what, where and when he should engage in any given activity. These cycles may have told him when and where he should search for game, migrate to more hospitable areas, and perhaps find wild fruits and nuts. Some modern-day calendars still show us the harvest, hunter and other moons, although these remnants from an earlier time mean little in our present technological age. But this information was vitally important to our ancestors. In order to keep track of intervals of time within each 29.5-day lunar cycle, early man could have marked the days by the lunar phases, counting the days from the time the moon disappeared at New Moon (day 29), or reappeared at the first Crescent Moon (day 1) to when this celestial body reached (waxed) toward its maximum illumination and brilliance at Full Moon (day 14) and then receded (waned) again to become the darker New Moon [Appendix 1-1]. In this book, I will refer to both the names of the phases and the numbers associated with them, as listed in Figure 1-2.

While archeo-astronomers have primarily focused on man's interpretation of the celestial bodies from the perspectives of how they influenced his storytelling and religion, there are other important relationships between these heavenly movements and the lifecycles of plants and animals. These

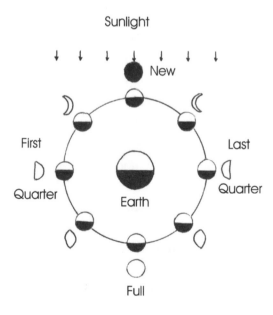

Figure 1-1: The moon's position relative to the earth and sun determines how much of its disk will be illuminated. It takes 29.53 days for us to see the same phase twice from earth.

Lunar Phase	Day
New	0
Waxing Crescent	1 – 6
Waxing Half	7
Waxing Gibbous	8 – 13
Full	14 – 15
Waning Gibbous	16 – 21
Waning Half	22
Waning Crescent	23 – 28
New	29

Figure 1-2: The phases of the moon can be numbered. In scientific circles the New Moon of each cycle begins on day 0.

organisms obey rhythms that are entrained by light. Sunlight has the greatest influence, but this star's reflection off the moon is also significant. There is also the darkness in the absence of these forces. Some animals, especially those in the marine environment, follow lunar/tidal rhythms. Early man was more cognizant of these controlling forces than we are since he held much closer contact with the natural world than we do today. They were hunters, farmers, fishermen and shepherds whose lives depended on understanding how specific movements of the celestial bodies coincided with the availability of food. They knew how to utilize these cycles, but over time this understanding has been lost. Few of us these days plan our activities by the moon. What do we have to gain by doing so? If we could regain this ancient knowledge, how could we apply it to benefit our modern world? We shall explore these themes throughout this book.

Timing to Life

While we don't have the ability to go back in time to interview early man to see how he thought, we still have indigenous peoples who use the celestial bodies to understand the activities of plants and animals as well as to measure time and plan events. One such people is a fishing tribe called the Yami that lives on Lanyu Island about 60 miles southeast of Taiwan. The Yami's calendar is unique. Their mechanism to gauge time is the arrival of a migratory flying fish, *Exocoetus*, which is present off their island for a few months each year in the spring.[1] These flying fish move along the Malay Gulf Stream to spawn in the cooler waters off the coast of Japan and the Aleutian Islands.[2] Yami fishermen head out into the ocean to hunt them during the darkest nights prior to New Moon, counting 12 lunar cycles since the last time the flying fish first appeared. The darker nights around the New Moon are the most productive fishing times for these flying fish, as they swim closer to the surface and can be readily netted under the light of a torch as it is swept next to the boat.

If the fish are present, many are caught, and the Yami have a feast (Flying Fish Festival) which enjoins the resetting of their calendar. If the fish are not present, the Yami wait one more lunar cycle, then head out to sea with their nets and torches to try it again. The fish always seem to be there by this second cycle. In years when this happens, the Yami reset their lunar calendar from 12 lunations (the period between two successive Full Moons) to 13. The Yami have no recognition of a solar year, but they know their fish and know when they can be caught. A Yami fisherman can identify almost 450 species of fish, 88 of which they have deemed taboo to eat.[3] Ethnologists have been keenly interested in the Yami because in addition to having no concept of the solar year, they don't truly have a lunar calendar either. Instead, the Yami time their lives to the fish, which appear to be influenced by the cycles of the moon. The Yami tribe's unique ability to set their calendars to the migration of the flying fish is of particular interest to biologists, as it demonstrates that movements of fish can be timed to the lunar cycle.

Closer to my home, the Tulalip Tribe of Washington historically used the appearance of the white pine butterfly (*Neophasia menapia*) to time the arrival of the Chinook salmon (*Oncorhynchus tshawytscha*) to Tulalip Bay. The white pine butterfly appears in the region from the middle to the end of June. The Tulalips saw it as the harbinger of fish to come, as it is present during the general window of time in the solar year (based on the position of the sun) when the first salmon arrive. The Tulalips also anticipated that the Chinook salmon would arrive at the highest tides of the lunar cycle, which occur around the New or Full Moons. Predicting the correct timing of the Chinook return was critically important to the Tulalips, so they strategically built their ceremonial longhouse just above where these high tides would reach. The position of the longhouse to the tide was crucial to the transportation of the heavy canoes off the beach and into the bay. At low tides, the Tulalips could not easily portage their canoes across the muddy flats. Once out in the canoes, tribal members paddled about a mile into the bay where they would net salmon. In the old days, the Tulalips gauged their preparation time by observing the encroaching higher tides. Today, as related to me by tribal member Stan Jones, the Tulalips use commercially printed tide tables to plan the event months in advance.

In addition to practical reasons for timing the return of the salmon, the advent of the first salmon was also spiritually important and celebrated by the Tulalips with a First Salmon Ceremony called "Kla-How-Yacq". The first Chinook salmon netted by the tribe was immediately brought to the longhouse to be honored. At the end of the ceremony, the first salmon's remains were placed in the bay facing the westward direction. The Tulalips believe that, if properly honored, the first salmon's spirit will swim back to the other Chinook in the ocean and invite them to return.

The Yurok tribe of Northern California also looked at the cycles of the moon to see the future, although they took it a step further than the Tulalips by monitoring their position in the solar year as well. Prior to the 19th century and for an unknown period of time, perhaps many centuries, the Yurok tribe built what they referred to as a fish dam, or a weir, about thirty-five miles up river from the mouth of the Klamath River, to catch summer steelhead trout (*Oncorhynchus mykiss gairdneri*). We know about this and have documentation of the Yurok traditions, thanks to anthropologists who interviewed tribal members about their history during the middle part of the last century.[4] This annual event took place at about our month of July. Yurok people from up and down the river met at a gathering point at the town of Ke'pel where they built a barrier constructed of poles, logs and small stakes that spanned the Klamath River entirely. In order to harness the rapid current, this ambitious project required hundreds of people, as well as huge amounts of material. Openings leading into small enclosures which the Yuroks described as "traps," "corrals" or "pens" were created at regular intervals along the course of this weir. The steelhead were caught in these enclosures and harvested with hand nets. They were then split and dried for consumption over the long winter.

The Yuroks' formula to build the dam was very precise and was carefully passed down from one shaman to the next. The complete instructions for its design and construction—perfected through many seasons of trial and error—included painstaking detail of timing, process and materials. The first two days of the lunar month *(Ixrivkixan)* were set aside to announce the upcoming event. A ten-day interval followed and the next ten days were required to build the dam. The dam was then used for ten days afterwards.

Let's examine the Yurok timing. From the New Moon (at day 0), the first three sets of numbers add up to 22, which means the harvest of fish would have begun on either the 21st or 22nd day (Waning Half) of the lunar cycle (depending on how they determined the New Moon) and continued through the darkest lunar phases. This schedule suggests that the Yurok anticipated that the salmon would arrive during this darker period. (The significance of this will be further explored in the next chapter.) The Yurok were closely attuned to the lunar rhythms of the animals. Tribal member Frank Lake related to me that even today they adhere to the wisdom of their age-old Yurok saying: "Hunt land by Full and fish water by New." There is much to be learned from native practices.

The Yurok calendar was both lunar and solar. Before we explore this, there are some important measurements and calculations that need to be understood. The solar year (the time it takes the earth to circle around the sun) is 365 days, 5 hours, 48 minutes and 45.5 seconds. Since 365 days do not equally divide into 12 months, our modern calendar manipulates the sum of the months to equal the days of a solar year. The solar calendar is an ideal system to measure years and divide the 365 days into well-defined increments for regulated societal purposes. It is rhythmic and unwavering in almost even multiples of 365—which also gives us an easy-to-count historical record of time.

The problem with using a lunar-solar calendar is that, since the 29.5-day lunar cycle does not divide equally into the 365-day solar year, events timed to the moon are not on the same solar calendar from year to year. This is best demonstrated with solar movement of the Christian Easter holiday, which Catholics and Protestants place on the first Sunday after the first Full Moon (day 14) that comes on or after the Vernal Equinox (~March 21),[5] as described in Figure 1-3. As a consequence of the lunar shift in the solar year, Easter moves in a 35-day window between March 25 and April 25. A lunar day only repeats itself on the same solar calendar date every 19 years. This is referred to as the Metonic cycle.

Back to the Yurok: How did they set their lunar-solar calendar to those of the fish? The Yami mark their new year in retrospect, sometimes adding

Year	Easter Day	Year	Easter Day
1995	April 15	2001	April 15
1996	April 7	2002	April 31
1997	March 30	2003	April 20
1998	April 12	2004	April 11
1999	April 4	2005	March 27
2000	April 23	2006	April 16

Figure 1-3: Easter is timed on the first Sunday that succeeds the first Full Moon after the Vernal Equinox. The lunar cycle of 29.5 days does not evenly divide into the 365-day solar year so the date moves around from one year to the next

a month, based on the late appearance of the flying fish. The Yami system of predicting their arrival had a fudge factor of an entire lunar cycle. The Yurok enjoyed no such slack. This would not have been possible due to the complicated construction of the Ke'pel dam. As there is no record of the Yurok building dams that didn't produce fish or starting second dams during following months, we can surmise that they were accurate in their initial calculations.

The Yurok owe their time-keeping success to their practice of recalibrating their lunar calendar against the solar year at the Winter Solstice. To be more specific, their lunar calendar began at the first New Moon after the Winter Solstice. The month of the salmon ceremony (*Ixrivkixan*) fell six lunar cycles later. This was their new year, their big event. And this arrival of the salmon at the dam directly determined what kind of year it was going to be. A poor run meant hard times. With prosperity so dependent on the run, it only made sense for the Yurok to time their calendar to this lifecycle. In this regard, they are very much like the Yami, only with more precise calibrations of the solar and lunar cycles. If this hypothesis about their greater understanding and utilization of the cycles of the sun and moon proves to be correct, as we will explore further in the coming chapters, then the Yurok knew something critical about the timing of the salmon migrations that today's scientists have yet to discover. That is, they grasped how the salmon navigated time and space. This is not to say that modern man doesn't know the salmon will arrive during a season or even in a specific month. The parking lots at boat ramps are full during the peak periods. The difference is that the Tulalip and Yurok tribes had the timing of the first salmon in the bays (before they could be seen in the rivers) and peaks in the rivers quantified to the day, months in advance. We will see throughout this book that many indigenous and ancient peoples were aware of critical biological insights that have been unknown by western science. Fortunately, we still have peoples such as the Yami and Tulalip, as well as information about the Yurok, to take us back in time to a hunter-gatherer period that probably resembles our own history.

The Solar Year

How important is the sun? Our sun makes life on earth possible! Its relative size, distance from us, intensity, stability, gravity and our own orbit and rotational axis around it combine to create ideal conditions for life on our planet. It is likely that in our universe only an infinitesimally small fraction among the billions of solar systems have planets that aren't hostile environments. We need to put the importance of the sun into perspective. Without it, we would not be here!

Let's start at the bottom of the food chain. Plants grow via the process of photosynthesis. Tiny insects and other invertebrates feed on these plants as well as decaying matter. Birds, amphibians and fish feed on these small animals, and so it goes further up the food chain. Animals tend to give birth during seasons when food is most plentiful—both for survival of their offspring and/or their own recovery. Understanding the timing of specific temperatures (seasons) over the course of a solar calendar helps us determine the correct time to plant crops, predict the rising of rivers and more.

The most significant points of reference during the solar year are the solstices and equinoxes. The term *solstice* means "sun stands still." The Summer Solstice and the Winter Solstice occur around June 21 and December 21, respectively, as described in Figure 1-4. At these times in the Northern Hemisphere, the sun changes little in declination from one day to the next

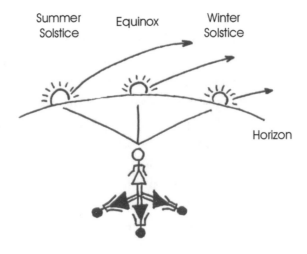

Figure 1-4: The sun's position on the horizon changes from day to day. This shift occurs because the sun's apparent yearly orbit lies at an angle of 23.5 degrees to the celestial equator. Ancient peoples typically used rocks and mountains or man-made structures to chart the transition. In the Northern Hemisphere, the calendar dates vary slightly. The Vernal Equinox occurs around March 21, the Summer Solstice ~ June 21, the Autumn Equinox ~ September 23 and the Winter Solstice ~ December 21.

and appears to remain in one place north or south of the celestial equator. The days are longer during the Summer Solstice, providing more heat. The sun is also higher in the sky; its rays are more vertical, offering more direct sunlight and less atmospheric cooling. The opposite is true around the Winter Solstice. Its days are shorter, the nights are longer and the sun sits low in the sky, seemingly distant and much cooler as its rays appear to lose intensity before they reach us.[6] The equinoxes are the two times of the year when the sun's position makes day and night of equal length in all parts of the earth. Equinox means "equal nights" in Latin. The Vernal Equinox marks the beginning of spring in the Northern hemisphere. The days succeeding the Vernal Equinox lengthen (in amount of daylight time) a little more each day until the longest day of the year at the Summer Solstice. Then the days begin to shorten a little more each day. But the days are still longer than the nights until the Autumnal Equinox, after which nights become longer than the days and the days continue losing daylight until the shortest day of the year at the Winter Solstice.[7]

Timing by the Stars

In the absence of having the technical ability to gauge the solar equinoxes and solstices, some ancient sky watchers charted the positions of the stars to keep their place in time.[8] Stars are useful for this purpose, as these heavenly bodies appear to move in a regular manner at predictable times of the year. There are more than 1,000 stars visible to the naked eye but some are brighter than others and those that are clustered and grouped in formations tend to be more noticeable. One early record of man charting the movements of stars, called the "sky disk," as pictured in Figures 1-5 and 1-6, dates back to more than 3,500 years ago. This bronze plate, embossed in gold, was recently found in eastern Germany. On the disk are depicted the star cluster Pleiades and the belt of Orion (the hunter) constellation as well as the Crescent and Full Moons, transiting from east to west. The three stars depicting the belt or waist of Orion are the only visible ones in the sky that are in a straight line. They also appear close to the horizon in the Northern Hemisphere. Betelgeuse (just below Pleiades) forms the right shoulder of Orion, and Rigel (to the right of his belt) his foot. Procyon is pictured just below the Crescent Moon. Other celestial reference points on the disk appear to be the three stars (in descending order) Capella, Aldebaran and Sirius, pictured transiting in the sky to the right of both the moon phases.[9] All of these stars appear in the Northern Hemisphere night sky in late autumn into early winter and can be seen without instruments. Sirius is on the horizon in late December and can be used to gauge the Winter Solstice. These stars are also bright enough to be clearly identified during the light of the Full Moon when dimmer stars are lost to the lunar luminance.

Orion and Pleiades are commonly associated with weather forecasting among ancient cultures. However, the appearance of the moon and stars together on this disk suggests that the people of this period thought both forces influenced their lives. What this meaning might have been has yet to be determined. They were probably not timing the runs of salmon or migrations of flying fish with these positions, as would have the indigenous peoples previously presented. Nevertheless, the timing of other animals and plants would have been just as important. The reference position for their purpose would have been established by when the stars were in view during the waxing of the moon to full. A clue to the riddle of the disk might be the ten symmetrical dots at the top. They have the appearance of a graph with years on the X-axis and quantity on the Y. The curve above them can be interpreted to represent the peak in cycle. Many organisms are known to have ten-year cycles with yearly rhythmic fluctuations.[10] What times these cycles is a matter of debate. My suggestion is that they are lunar-timed, as will be further explored in this book. The peak in cycle may also be a result of a period with greater rainfall or a plan for planting or harvesting crops. In any case, the combination of the moon and stars appears to be critical in the function of this device and an integral aspect of our distant heritage. Man can also find his place in the solar year with the aid of these stars.

Mesopotamian Wisdom

The ancient people of Mesopotamia (Sumerians, Babylonians and Assyrians) [Appendix 1-2] can be considered some of our earliest documented scientists, as they gave us the means to precisely measure and manage time which is a necessary component for the study of plants and animals. They were a progressive people from a region that is now the southern part of Iraq, sometimes referred to as the "children of Noah." Their homeland was situated between the Tigris and Euphrates Rivers, which is also the legendary birthplace of Abraham, father to both the Jewish and Arab nations. During the second and first millennia BCE, the city of Babylon, meaning "Gate of God," and the Biblical Babel[11] was a center of commerce and culture.

Mesopotamians created the first known calendar, recorded celestial movements and developed the mathematics for seconds, minutes and hours. We inherited the concept of the week from them, although originally this period was based approximately on four days of the moon (7th, 14th, 21st and 28th) evenly distributed within the 29.5-day synodic cycle. Observance of these dates included laws that forbid certain persons from engaging in certain activities during these days. These were ancient forms of blue laws that some municipalities and religions still practice today. Modern versions in Western societies include the prohibition of hunting or the purchasing of alcohol on Sunday.

Northern Sky

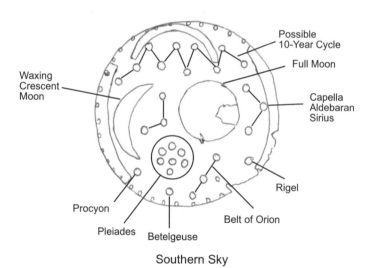

Southern Sky

Figures 1-5 and 1-6: This "sky disk" found in Germany dates back to more than 3,500 years ago. All of the stars pictured appear in the Northern Hemisphere during late autumn to early winter. The users likely relied on them in conjunction with the Crescent and Full Moon phases to fix the lunar cycles in the solar year and predict events or rhythms. The symmetrical series of dots at the top of the disk appear to make up a primitive graph, showing the yearly fluctuations and the ten-year cycle of organisms with a peak in the center. The peak in cycle may also be a result of a period with greater rainfall.

For these ancients, the beginning of each month was set upon the sighting of the first Crescent Moon (the first evening after New Moon) in the west. A vestige of this tradition was carried on by the Muslims' continued use of the crescent, an earlier symbol of the Babylonian moon god. Components of the Babylonian calendar were also passed on to the Greek and Jewish calendars and, to a lesser extent, the Christian calendar. The major difference with these successors was that they instituted mathematical mechanisms to readjust the lunar cycles to fit the solar year, while the early Babylonians chose a high priest who made the adjustment visually by referencing celestial patterns.

Such decisions, however, were not made haphazardly. The high priests had a firm understanding of the movements of the sun, moon and the five major planets. They even had the ability to predict lunar eclipses. Astronomy played a major role in Mesopotamian society. But this science wasn't just the study of the celestial bodies. The high priests also used cyclical celestial movements to interpret the fate of society. They believed time was cyclical, and therefore predictable. Since the fate of mankind was tied to these same celestial movements, it must be foreseeable as well. This concept of the relationship between the heavens and earth was brilliantly explained in a diviner's manual from the seventh century BCE.[12]

> The signs on earth just as those in the sky give us signals; [the] sky
> and [the] earth both produce portents, though appearing separately,
> they are not separate [because the] sky and [the] earth are related.

Some believe that the Babylonians, rivals of the Hebrews, charted the heavens to foresee the future from the Tower of Babel. The official account in the book of Genesis was that the Babylonians built a city and tower whose top reached unto the heaven and whose aim was to share glory with God.[13] While archeologists are divided about the existence of a specific tower called "Babel," the Babylonians built many pyramid-looking structures called *ziggurats*, which were essentially celestial observatories. The largest mound remaining in Babylon, E-temen-an-ki (*the House of the Foundations of Heaven and Earth*), is believed to be the tower referred to in the Bible. Archeologists estimate that it reached 298 feet high upon a square base of the same dimension.

This tower faced heavenly opposition. Isaiah warned: "You are wearied with your many counsels: let now the astrologers, those that prophesize by the stars, those that predict by the New Moon, stand up, and save you from what will come upon you."[14] In Isaiah's mind, the judgment of his god Yahweh made the reading of the signs in the celestial bodies obsolete. He held that if you were obedient to the will of Yahweh, then you would prosper. If not obedient, he would exhibit his wrath in the forms of earthquakes, floods, plagues and the like. It's easy to see why the Hebrew god Yahweh might therefore disapprove of this project. He is said to have interrupted construction by causing among the builders a previously unknown confusion of languages. The story tells us that he then scattered these people, speaking different languages, over the face of the earth. Interestingly, the word "Babhel" is actually a play on the name of the city made by Israelite priests, who told stories of the confounding of tongues.

Archeological evidence tells us the Babylonians listened to their god Ea (or A-e, as some scholars prefer) from this platform. Ea was said to have created all and knew everything. When he spoke of a thing, it would be made. With the aid of Ea, the high priests believed that they could predict the future. This forecast occurred during the New Year's festival, called *Akitu*, which began on the first Crescent Moon after the Vernal Equinox (around March 21), during which the priests told the king of what was to come.

We find Ea symbolized in a Mesopotamian cylinder seal (see Figure 1-7), dating between 2360-2180 BCE that depicts the New Year's festival. Fish, a bird, a lamb, and plants accompany him. As the god of water, it should be of no coincidence that Ea is involved with the fish. He also had a personal fisherman in his service, named Adapa, who received his advice about angling tactics. What is generally agreed upon among scholars is that the three celestial guardians of time depicted are Ea, Shamash (the sun) and Ishtar who has an uncanny angelic appearance; the time is the Vernal Equinox (as designated by Ishtar) and the scene is the ceremony when they predicted future events. The figure to the far left is the king, as designated with his symbolic lion. The king was annually reinstated at this ceremony as per the will of the gods and translated through the cleric.

I also believe that the depiction of Shamash, the sun god, rising through the peaks suggests that the calendar started at sunrise on the Vernal Equinox.

This is an important reference point, as the moon phase can be different at 8 in the morning from 8 at night. My own additional interpretation is that the presence of the plants and animals indicates the Mesopotamians were using these solar and lunar positions to predict whether the runs of fish would arrive and/or be strong, the birds numerous, the crops bountiful or when the lambs would drop. Their presence certainly signified meaning to these ancients. If this hypothesis turns out to be correct, then the basis of their religious and cultural beliefs were not tied to some archaic mythology but to the biology of time. Our interpretations of the archeological evidence may have been limited by our own scientific understanding.

In this vein of thought, let's try to identify the fish in the image and see if its presence represents something of value and not just ceremonial or mythical art. An inquiry in the region found that there are three strong candidates for the fish. One is the anadromous (freshwater to ocean migrating) anchovy. The Farsi people of Iraq celebrate their New Year, called "Nowroz", on March 21 with the arrival of two species of anchovies (*Thyrssa hamiltonii* and *T. mystex*). These anchovies are numerous and important to the economy. But their influence is also limited, as these fish only migrate in these rivers to a point around Basra, a city near the coast. They didn't go far enough to have mattered to ancient Mesopotamian cities much further north.

Another possibility is the carp (Family: Cyprinidae) that have an inland migration from the northern part of Iraq to the marshy areas in the south for reproduction. Migration starts in the middle of March and ends in May. In the present time, people set nets in the Tigris River during the springtime to catch large and mature carp, the most popular being the shaboot (*Barbus grypus*). The carp is also a draw to the marsh for people seeking abundant, low priced and tasty fish. We eat a similar form in fish fillet sandwiches at fast food restaurants. Iraqi ichthyologist Laith Jawad closely examined the taxonomy of the fish portrayed on the cylinder seal and came to the conclusion that the depiction is most representative of the shaboot. He also related that images of this fish are the dominant relief in Mesopotamian art.[15] The only problem with the shaboot being the one in the illustration is that it migrates downriver to the marshes. The picture shows the fish swimming upriver.

The other candidate is the Indian shad (*Tenualosa ilisha*), commonly referred to in the region as *sbour*. Estimates from the Food and Agriculture Organization

Figure 1-7: The angelic goddess at the center left is the chief goddess Ishtar. The god at the right with streams of water and fish flowing about his shoulders is Ea. The profile of the god Shamash, the sun, makes his dawn appearance between the peaks on the horizon. The figure to the far left is the king. Ea is the god of waters who knows everything. When he speaks of a thing, it will be made. This Mesopotamian cylinder seal (2360-2180 BCE) has been interpreted to symbolize the Vernal Equinox sunrise, when the ceremonial New Year readings of omens for the coming year took place and the reinstatement of the king was made. An additional interpretation is that the illustration represents when certain plants and animals would be present. (Illustration courtesy of Griffith Observatory.)

count 6,576 tons (over 14 million pounds) of sbour in the Basra fish market during 1990 to 1991. The total size of the run is unknown. The sbour ascend the Shatt Al-Arab River, formed by the confluence of the Tigris and Euphrates Rivers, during the early days of March.[16] These fish historically migrated from coastal areas inland as far as Baghdad, which is much further upstream from the Persian Gulf than the ancient city of Babylon. Jawad related that fishermen on the Tigris and Euphrates set their nets for sbour based on the phases of the moon. He successfully managed to correlate the onset of the sbour fish riverine migration to the lunar cycle. This suggests the calendar of the ancient Mesopotamians was similar in nature to those of the Tulalip and Yurok. One of the purposes appears to have been to time the arrival of the fish. There might have been another use for the calendar. The runs of sbour also have yearly fluctuations in strength. Certainly it would have been a great advantage for the ancients to be able to predict the sizes of these runs. Such a find would indicate the high priests could have predicted prosperous or lean years for the people via the celestial bodies. Could their calendar have achieved this as well? We will continue to explore these interrelationships and the possibility of predicting the behavior and success rates of plants and animals via celestial movements throughout this book.

Based on what we have learned thus far, we need to be open to consider that the practices of predicting the future based on celestial events were not astrology, as known in the present day, but rather some long-lost study of astrobiology. We may scoff at such an assertion in our age of genetic engineering and microchips. But the intentions of our science are not that much different. Modern scientists make observations and search for patterns that will help them predict future events. They test their theoretical models against reality, consult new information and modify them until they agree and are consistent with what happens in the real world. Mesopotamian methodology and those of the tribes were the best science of the times, and are still useful today. I found them helpful for positioning lunar-influenced animal behavior against a solar position to work out the biological time hypothesis that will be applied throughout this book. Their calendars helped me to better understand how to manage solar and lunar time.

Our Inheritance

Early Mesopotamian society inherited some of their celestial knowledge from more ancient societies, which would have likewise learned the foundations of heavenly timing from earlier nomadic groups who lived by fishing, fowling and collecting edible plants in the marshlands along the rivers. We similarly inherited much of our time management from the ancients although key information and benefits appear to have been lost. For example, we commonly believe that our current week is a religious increment of time taken from the creation epic in Genesis, and is not based on a natural phenomenon. However, as stated earlier, the concept of a *week* was originally derived from the Mesopotamian practice (and possibly an earlier tradition) of slicing up the 29.5-day lunar cycle into seven-day periods. The most important day from the perspective of Christian religions is Sunday, which is derived from the German name "Sonntag," with a Latin root "dies solis" (meaning "day of the sun"). This is followed by the day of the moon: "dies lunae." The remaining days of the week in Latin are named after our closest planets, although few of us consider them in those terms. The *month* is an imprecise delineation of a lunar cycle tailored to fit into the solar year. The word "month" is derived from the word "moon," and both are rooted in a word that means "to measure."

Our yearly reference is the standard wall calendar, often given to us by merchants to help us time our birthdays, holidays and tax return deadlines. The wall calendar is formulated from the solar year. This "Gregorian calendar," from Pope Gregory XIII who decreed it around 1600, bases its starting year as the assumed date of Christ's birth. In Western scientific circles, everything in the year before the birth of Jesus Christ is designated as BCE (before the common era) and all years after are ADE (after the common era). The mechanics of this calendar are worked out on the solar year. We only use the lunar to time Easter. The Nicene Council, convened by Constantine the Great, in 325 ADE fixed the date of Easter, as currently celebrated, against the 19-year cycle of the moon. As shown earlier, the placement of Easter moves with the moon from one year to the next. All other springtime Christian feasts and festivals are set with Easter as a starting point. We add other cultural and political dates in our modern age but, like Easter, they're not central to the yearly or monthly mechanics of the calendar. The Christian calendars were based on the Julian calendar, which was introduced by the Roman emperor Julius Caesar in 45 BCE. The Julian calendar established the order of the months and the days of the weeks, as they exist in our present-day calendars.

The Egyptians had earlier adopted a solar calendar based on the movement of the brightest star in the sky (Sirius), which also coincided with the flooding of the Nile. The Alexandrian sage Acoreus said to Caesar during a visit to see the lovely Cleopatra, "The Nile does not arise its waters before the shining of the Dog-star." This was and still is a big event to the people of Egypt, as the flooding of this great river deposits rich sediments along its banks, creating fertile farmland and determines when the crops can be planted. This event is as important as the sbour is to the people of Iraq and the arrival of the salmon to the Pacific Coast of North America. The Yami, Yurok, Tulalip, Egyptian, Julian and Babylonian calendars were different calendars for different uses. Most appear to have been designed to mark the movements and events of plants and animals—to observe biological time.

Summary

In this first chapter we've explored the questions of time and space and noted the cross-cultural, universal propensity of peoples to mark the passage of time by charting the positions of the sun, stars and moon. While doing so, we've also looked at the different methods man has used to keep track of the important events in his world and predict their recurrence. We've seen evidence that suggests our ancestors believed the movement of their prey was dictated by celestial cycles. And we've seen how these astral, lunar and solar cycles were commonly used throughout history across diverse cultures. We've seen the same stories repeated from advanced civilizations with written histories to aboriginal peoples, where lore is passed down through the ages by storytelling. A great deal can be learned from the practices of ancient societies, such as the ancients in Mesopotamia, and the Yurok, Tulalip and Yami hunter-gatherers—especially about the natural world. And we can use their knowledge to better understand the biological time of the animals.

We have seen how Egyptian, Julian and Babylonian calendars were different calendars for different uses. And we examined the origin of our modern Gregorian calendar and showed how it is useful for dividing the solar year into 12 months, offering greater convenience for commerce, collecting taxes and keeping societal order. But it is less useful for understanding the natural world. More and more as the clock rules our technological society, the gulf between our awareness of the lunar and solar is leading Western man to lose the entire concept of natural cyclical time and its relationship with space. While the solar year has a strong influence on plants and animals, as will be presented, this force does not fully explain the scope of their behavior. Nor does it aid our own self-discovery. Except for a few indigenous cultures, a more complete awareness of how the physics of time and space intertwine with biology has been almost entirely lost.

The Journey of the Salmon

According to Greek mythology, there was a monstrous god named Typhon, who was determined to overthrow Zeus and his entire group of gods. So terrifying and powerful was this evil deity that he caused the immortal followers of Zeus to flee into Egypt in exile. Zeus alone remained behind to do battle and eventually conquer Typhon. The Greeks tell us that one day Aphrodite and her son Eros were walking along a riverbank when they sensed Typhon's presence. The two quickly plunged into the river where they took the form of fishes and escaped. To this day, we see them as the constellation Pisces, symbolized by two fishes whose tails are bound together by a wavy band.

Pisces is a zodiacal constellation, which means that the formation is located along the ecliptic, the apparent annual path of the sun across the sky. These fish hold on the edge of that huge ancient region of the sky known as the Sea. Pisces does not include any notable stars, but does contain the point through which the sun passes at the Vernal Equinox, claiming the number one position of importance among the twelve constellations of the Zodiac. For many of the ancients, the cycles of time were reset when Pisces met the sun on its travels. Today the sun is within the boundaries of Pisces from March 13 to April 19, when the rapidly lengthening days carry us from winter into spring. This period is when many fish migrate. This solar window coincides with the arrival of the sbour and anchovies to Persian Gulf tributaries.

There are other zodiacal constellations that seem to look like the animals after which they are named. Pisces is not one of them, suggesting that the appearance of the animal came first and the story was pieced together to fit the prevailing constellation, perhaps to signal when certain fish would be present. The Greeks were not alone in observing this constellation. The Persians referred to the constellation as "Amhik" and the Turks "Balik"; in Syriac it was called "Nanu" and in Babylonia "Nunu"—all of these mean "fish."

Juvenile Out-Migration

In North America, we do not have the same fish that people in the Middle East harvest under the guidance of Pisces, though the concept of migrating to and from the salt at the seasonal shifting light of the sun might apply to other anadromous species. In the previous chapter, we learned that the Yurok and Tulalip tribes could time the arrival of salmon in the bays and rivers based on a combination of solar and lunar cues. While the phenomena may seem amazing, given our perceived scientific limitations of the tribes, this is a more extraordinary feat for the salmon, which need to have very precise timing for these people to have predicted their arrival. How could a fish that travels for thousands of miles have such accurate timing? Is Pisces a clue?

This question led me to plan a trip to the north fork of the Nehalem River in northwestern Oregon to view the springtime out-migration of the Chinook salmon fry and fingerlings on the first New Moon after a Vernal Equinox and under the guidance of Pisces. Fry are juvenile salmonids that have absorbed their egg sac, while fingerlings are those that are less than one year old. Oregon Department of Fish and Wildlife (ODF&W) biologist Tim Dalton and his crew allowed me to observe their juvenile salmon trapping operation that is part of a larger program studying the survival rates of the fish in a freshwater environment, from the in-migrating adults to out-migrating juveniles. With this data they can also monitor the survival rates in the marine environment. I had watched Dalton record and mark the adult Chinook salmon as they returned the previous fall. The juveniles we would observe could have been the offspring of those fish.

That New Moon day also turned out to be cloudy, wet and cold to the bone. Admittedly, the weather inhibited the observation of Pisces the previous evening, but I had viewed the constellation the week before, and the solar and lunar cues helped me to target the right window of time. The inhospitable conditions did not deter the crew. Their hands trembled as each fish was taken from a trap in the river and inspected in the frigid water to determine the species and stage of development before being marked for release. The catch for the morning was 205 Chinook fry. A three-day average that covered the day before and after yielded 280 fish. I visited the trap 13 days later on the Full Moon. The night before was easy to remember because the luminance from the moon had peeked through my blinds as the clouds passed and woke me up at 2 a.m. (Light has that effect on most day-active animals.) A three-day average around the Full Moon yielded only 16 fish, or less than 8 percent of the New Moon catch. One could suggest this reduction in catch was due to the run ending, so another dark phase of the moon was required to create the groundwork for a lunar light migration hypothesis. The results for the following New Moon period showed a three-day average of 309 fish. A review of out-migrating Chinook salmon and Atlantic salmon (*Salmo salar*) for a number of rivers flowing on two continents demonstrated similar lunar patterns. Salmon migrate more readily under dark than light phases of the moon.[1, 2, 3] [Appendix 2-1]

Light and darkness have an obvious influence on animal behavior. Indeed, previous work had shown that salmonids migrated during the less illuminated hours of the day.[4, 5] This behavior would be expected so as to avoid daytime predators, such as birds. The effect of the moon on salmon is a much less discussed—almost forgotten—topic. These lunar rhythms of light and darkness have a strong influence on the spatial distribution of salmon as indicated in Figure 2-1. This drawing is hypothetical and assumes that the Full Moon always falls in the center of each group. In the real world, the Full Moon separates the population into sub-groups, but the salmon are not evenly distributed within them. The distribution of the eggs may also be bimodal (with two peaks) partly based on how the lunar light influenced the spawning adults. This lunar mechanism distributes the salmon over a wide space-time that may benefit the survival of the species by not having all of their eggs in one basket.[6, 7]

When the juvenile salmon head down river to the ocean we call them "smolts." This nighttime migration may take days, weeks or months, depending on the species and distance to the ocean [Appendix 2-2]. Out-migration is initiated by shifts in the photoperiod[8] and the degree of illumination at night, and the speed is partly influenced by water temperature.[9] The salmon cannot think to make the choice of whether to stay or go and must rely on such environmentally induced processes to guide them through life. Some of these cues are hormonal. A key hormone, associated with illumination, that informs the salmon of when and where to go is prolactin. This hormone comes from the pituitary gland, often referred to as the master gland of vertebrates. Prolactin is associated with the fluctuations of another hormone—melatonin—which is synthesized by the pineal body (a part of the brain) in the absence of light. In humans, blood levels of melatonin are ten times higher during the night than during the light of day, and this tells us whether we should be asleep or awake.

Pharmacologists, endocrinologists and other scientists who study the biological rhythms of vertebrates have demonstrated that the pineal body acts as a photometer, measuring the amount of light in the environment. This gland then tells the body through a diffusion of melatonin whether the animal should be resting or active. The pineal body probably has an additional function for salmon and steelhead trout, serving as a photochemical transducer that influences the development of sexual organs. In laboratory experiments, decreasing

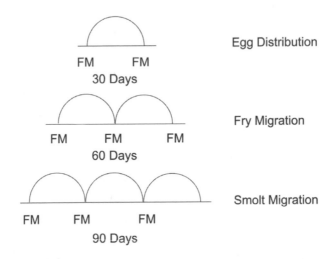

Figure 2-1: The lunar cycle separates the population of salmon into distinct sub-groups. This hypothetical model assumes that the Full Moon always falls in the center of each group. In the natural environment, the moon shifts along the path of the sun, so the division changes between years. This lunar mechanism distributes the salmon over a wide space-time that may benefit survival of the species by not having all of their eggs in one basket.

day length in a salmonid's environment can make this fish physiologically ready to spawn earlier than those in the wild.[10] Laboratory work has also shown that constant darkness, with accompanying increased melatonin synthesis, results in elevated levels of prolactin. Therefore, shorter days/longer nights should have a similar effect. Inversely, longer days/shorter nights could decrease prolactin levels.

The period between the Vernal Equinox and the Summer Solstice, when the days grow longer, is generally the period that the salmon juveniles out-migrate. If the fish are not physiologically prepared to depart in this window, they will wait until a succeeding year.[11] Prolactin is believed to be responsible for helping fish make the shift from fresh to saltwater.[12] Increased levels of prolactin (as a result of longer nights) make the anadromous fish more freshwater-acclimated while decreased levels make it more saltwater-comfortable. One hypothesis is that, as the nights become shorter in the spring, reduced prolactin levels impair the smolt's ability to respire (exchange oxygen) in freshwater and stimulates seaward movement,[13] as illustrated in Figure 2-2. This leads to other physiological changes that help the salmon to survive in the marine environment. One of these prolactin-related changes allows the kidneys to switch from retaining salt during the freshwater stage to one that excretes large amounts of salt in the ocean.[14]

Life in the Ocean

The timing of ocean entry is critical to the survival of the smolts. If there is an abundant amount of food present when the fish arrive or reach their destination, they will have the opportunity to grow quickly and avoid predators. The survivors need to build up energy stores to survive the less productive winter. In recent years, scientists have become more keenly interested in the ocean period of their lives, as the answer to the fluctuations in salmon stocks have not been adequately explained by their freshwater experiences alone. Such marine studies on salmon rarely come to the attention of the popular angling and conservation media since there is little that concerned individuals can affect. Local fish habitat restoration projects are more achievable than monitoring a school of fish out in the Gulf of Alaska.

Tracking specific stocks of fish is challenging due to the time and expense. However, we know that salmon generally stay on the continental shelf as juveniles and some become pelagic (open water) feeders as adults. The strategy to find salmon in the open ocean is to follow their roads, which are usually the contours of the ocean's bottom or the currents. The current systems in the ocean are like rivers that carry them around.[15] The boundaries between these masses of moving water form walls that trap nutrients and plankton rising up from the depths. Zones within these moving water masses can be tremendous feeding grounds for the salmon and the major predators, from sharks to seals and killer whales to birds, which are also aware of these boundaries.

How salmon and steelhead trout find their way through thousands of river and ocean miles and have the ability to return to their natal waters on time to spawn has stimulated the curiosities of scientists and naturalists for ages. The concept is really daunting if you consider it closely. We need road signs and maps to guide us just a few miles from our homes and still lose our way. We have clocks and calendars, yet we still wake up late and miss important

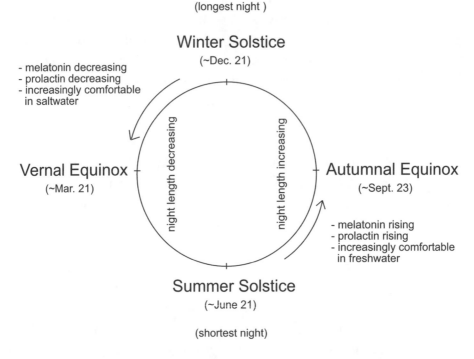

Figure 2-2: Length of day/night influences the out- and in-migrations of salmonids over the solar year. Reducing night length stimulates the juveniles to migrate out to sea while increasing night lengths result in the sexual development and ultimately the in-migration of these fish to the freshwater environment.

appointments. A fish without any capacity to reason can navigate time and space with more precision than we can. There are numerous hypotheses that explain how the salmon accomplish this feat. The most plausible navigational mechanisms to find their way are the rhythms of light and darkness, magnetism, tidal movements, current and scent [Appendix 2-3].

Daily Rhythms

Salmon are not tied just to light/dark cycles, as we have observed with seasonal migrations, but also daily to the shifting periods of illumination we call "dusk and dawn" [Appendix 2-4]. This is easily observed on any salmon river where the adults become active during these times of day, jumping around and splashing the surface of the water. These bewitching hours do not put the salmon on the feed, but make them more active. In contrast, during the day, these fish tend to remain down in the pools and appear to be sleeping. Fish do not sleep in the same manner as humans, but they do have equally important resting periods.[16] Scientists refer to this period of shifting light as "crepuscular" but my preference is "transitional light." Crepuscular light occurs during any day of the lunar cycle, whereas transitional light takes place on all days of the cycle except around the Full and New Moons. Timing and duration of transitional light differ, depending on the phase of cycle and due to when the moon rises and sets. The moon does not rise at the same time every day. At New Moon, moonrise occurs at about the same time as sunrise, and moonset occurs at about the same time as sunset. In the first half of the lunar cycle from New to Full Moon, the moon rises later each day and sets later each night. At Full Moon, moonrise occurs at sunset and moonset occurs at sunrise. During the second half of the lunar cycle from Full to New Moon, the moon rises later each night and sets later each day [Appendix 2-5]. Due to the timing of the rising and setting of the moon, there are longer transitional light periods during the evenings of the first half of the lunar cycle and the mornings of the second.

These increases in activity during the transitional light periods are physiologically connected with spikes in the synthesis of melatonin from the pineal gland. The function of this hormonal change is to allow the salmonid to shift its fairly rigid retinal structure from day (cone) to night (rod) and back again at dawn in sync with the shifting light. The salmon takes 20 to 25 minutes to become light-adapted while dark adaptation takes almost an hour.[17] The headlights of a car would temporally blind the salmon. In contrast, humans can walk from a dark room into a brightly lit one and adjust in seconds. The salmon's photochemical shift is an advantage, as the mechanism affords this predator the ability to see prey fish during periods of shifting light. The big-eyed prey fish, which require much better visual acuity to pick up tiny slow-moving invertebrates, have lower-intensity melatonin synthesis during transitional light periods. However, they are at an advantage during the afternoons. The result is that during transitional light periods the predators can see the prey first, while during constant light the advantage is reversed.[18]

A hypothesis of the salmon having varying physiological opportunities for feeding that are partly influenced by their reaction to light and darkness can be supported by research from the University of Guelph in Ontario, Canada. Scientists demonstrated that under controlled conditions over the lunar cycle, salmon exhibited patterns of alternating periods of rapid and slow growth in body mass, the peaks of which were significantly different from one another. The alternating growth rate changes were rhythmic in nature, of approximately 15 days in length, with peaks around the first and third quarters of the lunar cycle. The slow-growing periods turned out to be during the New and Full Moons,[19] which have the least amount of transitional light. This suggests that lunar timing in these animals is a consequence of behavior that occurs when certain conditions, such as the timing and degree of light and darkness, and a certain physiological state, are met.

This physiochemical reaction not only helps the salmon to gauge time but also where to be in space. During the day, the salmon will hold where the water is cooler—usually where it is deeper—and they can metabolize their food more efficiently. They migrate up to the surface during the evening transitional light period to feed. As juveniles in the ocean, salmonids primarily eat zooplankton, tiny free-floating crustaceans. Zooplankton feed on phytoplankton, a generic name for algae that floats near the water's surface. Most evenings, the zooplankton and a wide variety of other tiny aquatic animals migrate to the surface to feed on phytoplankton. During the illuminated evenings around the Full Moon, they stay down deep and at the darker New Moon will rise closer to the surface.[20] The position of the food supply also determines its availability. When the salmon graduate to feeding on other fish, the lunar rhythms of the zooplankton will still influence their behavior, as their prey will be entrained to the behavior of these tiny crustaceans.

Such daily rhythms start for the salmon as juveniles in freshwater. These rhythms are partly how out-migrating juveniles become conditioned to migrating during the darker phases of the lunar cycle. These rhythms carry over to the marine environment, influence their timing of arrival to freshwater and continue into the salmon's spawning run.

In-Migration of Adults

If increasing day length in the freshwater environment provides the impetus to begin the smoltification process, we can speculate that a shift in the photoperiod during their ocean sojourn affects the physiology of the salmon, thus stimulating the reverse activity. This would appear to be the case since the spawn timing of salmonids generally occurs after the Summer Solstice, which marks the beginning of the shortening of the days.[21] In further support of this hypothesis, wild Pacific salmon species in Alaska spawn, and often return, in the same order as coastal stocks in more southern latitudes. The order is Chinook, sockeye (*Oncorhynchus nerka*), pink (*O. gorbuscha*), chum (*O. keta*), Coho (*O. kisutch*) and then steelhead trout (*O. mykiss irideus*), as illustrated in Figure 2-3.[22] My suggestion is that the two primary factors determining their

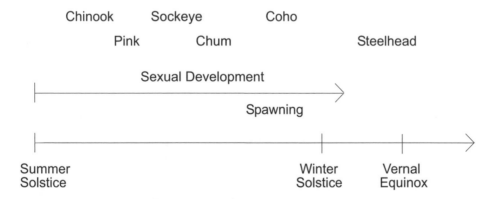

Figure 2-3: There is a linear relationship between sexual development of the Pacific salmonids and their spawning positions in time and space. What separates steelhead trout from other Pacific salmonids is that they spawn during increasing day length. This temporal position may encourage them to return from the salt via the same hormonal processes that stimulate the out-migrating juveniles.

relative position in space-time as adults are (1) the amount of time (years) they need to spend in the saltwater environment to achieve a physiological state to reproduce successfully in their freshwater environment and (2) their relative position to the photoperiod (increasing night length after the Summer Solstice).

Salmonids in the Great Lakes may help us to understand the effect of photoperiod on the timing of migration. Steelhead trout in all New York State tributaries of the Great Lakes are of the Chambers Creek, Washington, strain.[23] In Washington and Oregon where this brood stock has likewise been widely planted, the hatchery-propagated fish return during the latter part of December into the end of January.[24] In contrast, the Chambers Creek stocks in the Great Lakes enter the rivers beginning in late October. Why? We can speculate that when these fish are in the Pacific Ocean they are being drawn back to Washington and Oregon rivers starting at a specific night length occurring on or about the last week in October in upstate New York. However, since the journey of the Pacific Coast-bound fish from the Bering Sea (or other more northern regions) is much farther away from the rivers than their New York cousins (which may be just a few miles away) they arrive months later.

If the length of night, along with a certain physiological condition, induces sexual maturation in the same order as the salmon return to the freshwater as adults, the suggestion can be made that timing is a differentiating characteristic of species [Appendix 2-6]. The timing of reproduction results in the period of egg hatching, and ultimately the experiences during the juvenile stages. For the salmonids, timing is even related to whether the fish will die after spawning. An example of this idea is shown by the steelhead trout, which spawns under decreasing night length after the Winter Solstice (many stocks after the Vernal Equinox).[25] Spawning during decreasing night length drives the fish to the salt afterwards. The ability of the steelhead trout to survive after spawning is due to this solar timing and the nutrition for recovery that another ocean migration affords, continuing to define the difference between species. In contrast, the other Pacific salmon spawn before the Winter Solstice during periods of increasing night length, when there is not this urge. Survival after spawning is the key characteristic cited for the separation of steelhead trout from Pacific salmon. The Atlantic salmon has a time-and-space strategy similar to that of the steelhead trout and can survive after spawning as well.

The rhythms of light and darkness are not the only clocks the salmon become entrained to in the ocean. Lunar tides move these fish and their prey around, creating opportunities to feed and periods to rest. Tides influence the timing of the salmon's in-migration through the mouth of the river as well. This can be observed with the in-migration of adult sockeye salmon from Cook Inlet into the Kenai River, Alaska, where they peak around the Neap Tides [Appendix 2-7]. The Neap Tides are the lowest of the high tides, occurring just after the first and third quarters of the lunar cycle when the sun and moon are at right angles to the earth, as pictured in Figure 2-4. The Spring Tides are the highest of the high tides. These tides follow the New and Full Moons when the sun and moon are in alignment to the earth. The Neap Tides usually have the least impact, in terms of rough oceans, which makes for an easier migration. The Neap Tides probably carry the smolts out to sea as well.

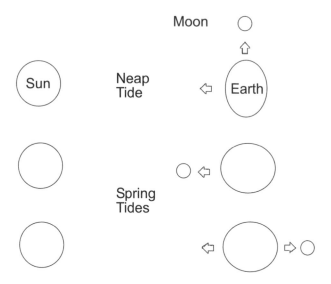

Figure 2-4: The strongest high tides, called "Spring Tides" occur when the earth, moon and sun are in alignment around the New and Full Moons. The lowest of the high tides are called "Neap Tides," when the moon is located at right angles to the earth-sun line. These occur just after the first and third quarter moons. The Neap Tides offer the easiest flow of water for the salmon to transit from the salt to freshwater environments.

To peak at these times, the adult sockeye would need to be staged in the bay around the New and Full Moon phases. This concurs with the timing of the Tulalip Tribe of Washington's First Salmon Ceremony, when they caught the Chinook salmon in the bay at the highest tide during the middle of June. For the Kenai sockeye salmon, the only question is which Neap Tide they will peak on from year to year. We will answer this in a later chapter.

When the salmon enter the freshwater as returning adults, they move in these tidal as well as solar and lunar light/dark rhythms. The slowest periods during migration up the river are around Full Moon, whereas this migratory behavior is more pronounced during the darker phases of the cycle, in a manner similar to when they out-migrated as juveniles. A conversion of data to the lunar cycle for wild winter steelhead trout from a Washington Department of Fish and Wildlife multi-year research project on the Kalama River, Washington, was used to demonstrate this behavior, as described with one year in Figure 2-5 and supported statistically in the appendices [Appendix 2-8]. This finding (and that of Neap Tide migrations) is previously unreported and is valuable to commercial fishermen and recreational anglers. Knowing when the fish are present is half the game. Nevertheless, I cannot take credit for the discovery. The phenomenon was recognized hundreds, if not thousands, of years earlier by the Yurok tribe, who had constructed a fish trap in the Klamath River on a schedule to coincide with the salmon peaking during the darker phases of cycle. Through our own ignorance of the natural world, we misinterpreted their sun and moon observances as worship and indoctrinated them to other, more comfortable beliefs. This philosophy dates to when any place that hadn't been explored before by Western man was marked on our maps with monsters. The remaining Yurok are not familiar with this timing. Stories of the fish dam and the days when salmon were plentiful are all that is left.

Some observers suggest that water flow is the key to the salmon's movement and ultimate timing of reproduction. This idea is a basic premise in the development of conservation strategies for these fish. Nevertheless, the river has to be very low to actually inhibit in-migration. Additionally, these fish certainly cannot predict what the water levels will be in their spawning areas. Thus, their speed of travel (and time of spawning) may be reduced under extremely low, life-threatening water conditions.[27] More importantly, water flow (and temperature) is too variable for the synchronization of important events.[28]

Spawning

One of these time-critical events is spawning. This is the climactic moment when the female drops her eggs and the male fertilizes them with sperm. We often see salmon in the river during their spawning run and refer to them as "spawning," but our observation may be one of the many steps before this event. The first step is for the returning adults to home in to the same area where their parents spawned them. Scientists believe that this is largely based on the scent of the river as well as the particular location. The salmon have an extraordinary sense of taste and smell and have demonstrated the ability to use these senses to choose between different streams.[29, 30] The precise spot where the salmon spawn is a function of suitable habitat, which may change from year to year.[31] Redds are created in areas of the bottom where there is sufficient water flow through the gravel to provide the developing eggs and embryos with oxygen and to remove the waste products of metabolism.

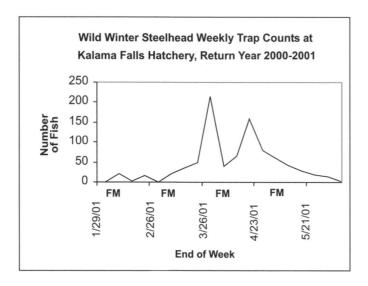

Figure 2-5: The evening illumination around the Full Moon (FM) appears to inhibit the in-migration of adult steelhead trout in rivers much as it did when these fish out-migrated as smolts.[26]

A step following in-migration into the freshwater is for the fish to group. This is a mating ritual of sorts that gets the fish together and primed. The male and female will meet in the river. He sports his dark red flanks and elongated snout or kipe. They exchange pheromones, a chemical signal, to show their intentions and demonstrate that they are at similar stages of sexual development. The male may have to compete for the female with one or more presumptuous males that have been tagging along beside her. There will be biting and pushing among the males and both could become scarred in the process. One will succeed. The male and female will resume their courtship, get into a rhythm with the flow and move in synchrony around the pool. They will become unaware of the world around them. While in this mood, pairs of big Chinook salmon have bumped into my leg. The occurrence was probably startling to the fish as it was to me.

I have observed salmon and steelhead trout exhibiting this behavior during the day under the most illuminated periods around the Full Moon. One such day on the water with Rogue River guide Steve Godshall, we observed about twenty ripe female and aggressive male steelhead trout stacked up in a shallow pool and on the adjoining spawning grounds. Fishing other usually productive pools on a three-mile stretch before this honey hole we found no fish. Salmonids typically hold in deep pools and under cover during the day and come out at dusk and dawn. In order for us to have observed these fish, they must have been day-active. Over the course of fishing the pool, we observed a few instances where two to three males fought over the same female, suggesting that spawning was due to occur within a few days. A conversion of ODF&W data for Coho salmon from a 13-year period in Lobster Creek, a tributary of the Alsea River in Oregon, to the lunar cycle gave credence to our observation. Over these years, the salmon became day-active around the Full Moon, as pictured in Figure 2-6 [Appendix 2-9].

ODF&W biologists who counted Coho salmon on Lobster Creek observed the largest numbers of redds just after the peak counts of fish. They also calculated into the Coho models that the adults will spend seven days on the redds after the peak in live counts. This would suggest spawning (fertilization of the eggs) for these fish occurs just after the Full Moon.[33] Basic rhythms related to timing, the length and degree of illumination, are likely to be how and why they synchronize their events. The most important objective of reproduction is for the males and females to coordinate the act. The salmon cannot think to make a date to spawn. Nor do they release their eggs and sperm at random into the currents to be mixed by chance. The timing has to be synchronized to other cues. In the case of salmon, one cue appears to be lunar light (or lack thereof).

According to Dr. John Palmer from the University of Massachusetts at Amherst, most species, including those with internal fertilization, produce their gametes rhythmically, perhaps at New and Full Moon. He suggests that evolution carries modifications even further by providing each organism with its own means of timing, a biological clock that signals in advance when Full Moon is due. Thus, the organism can complete the physiological preparations for breeding before the important moment. The precise timing of gamete liberation is also critical in external fertilization. This helps to ensure that fertilization will take place and at the same time releases the organism from a life of full-time gamete production.[34] Synchronization of reproduction is critical for the success of a species. Reproduction is the entire point of being alive. Many evolutionary biologists consider the body as merely a protective

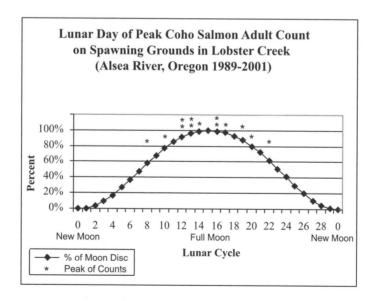

Figure 2-6: The number of live Coho salmon on the spawning grounds is greatest on Lobster Creek during the week around the Full Moon. These fish spawn a few days after the peak.[32]

container for DNA, allowing it to survive long enough to undergo recombination and proliferation.

Why spawn just after the Full Moon? A possible answer is that synchronizing short-term time-critical events to changes in environmental conditions is easier than to continuous conditions. My long-time angling friend and fishing guide, Bill Kremers, demonstrated to me the concept of changing environmental conditions on salmon behavior at the mouth of the Columbia River. One day on the water, he showed me that the ideal times to catch in-migrating salmon are during the daily incoming mid tides (strongest tides halfway between high or low). The salmon can be viewed in the fish finder during other periods, but they are not active and appear to be in a resting mode. Change excites organisms, while constant conditions have just the opposite effect.

This timing to change may be why some anadromous fish migrate at shifting solar light around the Vernal Equinox, as marked by Pisces. Similarly, around the quarter moons we have much greater shifting of light due to the height of the transitions of the moon at the solar dusks and dawns [Appendix 2-8]. In contrast, longer-term events, such as grouping, are better to synchronize to continuous light, such as around the Full Moon.

Period of Day	Light Period (Lunar Days 6-21)	Dark Period (Lunar Days 22-5)
Dawn (morning transitional light period)	Hold and Restless in pools	Migrate
Day	Hold and Restless in pools/ Pre-spawn grouping	Hold in pools
Dusk (evening transitional light period)	Hold and Restless in pools	Migrate/Spawning
Evening	Hold and Restless in pools	Migrate (juveniles) Hold and rest in pools (adults) Spawning

Figure 2-7: The juvenile and adult salmon will have different activity levels and place during each day of the lunar cycle and time of day.

The salmon (or any other organism) cannot have a lunar-timed behavior that isn't preceded by similar cues. Each solar/lunar-timed event leads to another one. For the salmon to spawn just after Full Moon, the fish needed to be on the spawning grounds. Finding a mate precedes the actual spawning event so conditions needed to be present (Full Moon) for the grouping to have taken place. This activity must have been preceded by a dark moon migration through the river. The Yurok's fish weir in the upper Klamath River was timed to the darker phases of the lunar cycle. The harvest timing of the Tulalip's first salmon indicated that the fish are in the bays during the Spring Tides, around the New and Full Moons. Therefore, we should expect migration through the tidal waters about the Half Moons, or Neap Tides. These rhythms can also be monitored by time of day and the day of the lunar cycle, as described in Figure 2-7.

The consecutive nature of these lunar-timed events suggests that these animals have daily lunar rhythms that are actually behaviors associated with light and darkness. The grouping of the juveniles before they out-migrate to the ocean is no different than when the adults pair before spawning. Their position in the solar year (i.e., spring out-migration vs. fall pre-spawn grouping) along with a physiological condition provides them with a different activity to coordinate with that period in the lunar cycle. The argument can similarly be made that all organisms have such solar/lunar-timed behavior, a hypothesis we will explore throughout most of this book.

Summary

Steelhead trout and salmon have internal clocks that are influenced by their environment (light/darkness, temperature, predators and prey). The rhythms of light and darkness aid these fish in determining their proper location and activity throughout each day, over the lunar cycle and solar year. The salmonid becomes entrained to these rhythms as a juvenile. These rhythms help the fish to avoid predators, find their cohorts, feed, etc. These fishes are most active around the transitional light periods when their food is in the drift or moving to and from the surface. The increased illumination around the Full Moon appears to group the fish, while darker phases stimulate movement. These rhythms carry over into their adult stage in the ocean and when they in-migrate to the rivers.

Out-migration appears to be stimulated by three environmental cues, which need to occur in synchrony during a certain physiological condition. These triggers are when waters are warming, nighttime illumination is low and night length is decreasing. In combination, they make the fish less freshwater-tolerant. A reverse shift in light levels (increasing night lengths) while in the ocean may stimulate chemical changes in the salmonid. These changes appear to make the salmon less salt-tolerant, encouraging these fish to migrate back to their home waters to spawn. These light/dark cues also stimulate gonadal development in the fish.

Once reaching the mouth of the river, the Neap Tides allow easy passage through the estuary. In the estuary and/or at some point upstream, the salmonid picks up the scent of its natal spawning grounds and follows this cue to that position. Over their journey upriver, the fish will rest in pools during the day and migrate most heavily during transitional light periods. Each solar/lunar event has a rhythm that leads to others, such that the salmon will also migrate upriver over the darker phases of cycle, group around the Full Moon and spawn shortly afterwards. These time- and place-critical events are most reliably synchronized by changes in illumination, with significant weight on the lunar cycle. Synchrony of events, such as reproduction, is essential to the survival of these species.

Steelhead trout and salmon are unique. They are able to spend their juvenile period in the safety of freshwater environments, dramatically change their bodily processes to live in saltwater and then migrate to the ocean to feed on more abundant food sources that determine their ultimate size and lifespan. They later have the ability to revert their biochemistry so as to be comfortable in freshwater where they spawn and start a new generation. The steelhead trout is most extraordinary as this fish can repeat this grueling series of transformations more than once. The changes in their physiology that make this possible are tied to rhythms of light and darkness.

The preceding also demonstrates that there is a sound scientific basis in support of the traditions of the Yurok and Tualip tribes, which gauged when they would have fishing success based on the relative positions of the sun and moon. The appearance of Pisces in the sky might also have signaled to ancient people the solar period during which fish migrated to and from the saltwater.

CHAPTER 3

Interconnectedness

FOR EVERYTHING THERE IS A SEASON, AND A TIME

FOR EVERY MATTER UNDER HEAVEN.

~ ECCLESIASTES 3:1

In 1280 ADE, the Mongolians conquered the Song Dynasty and ruled the Middle Kingdom for almost a hundred years. Under Mongolian rule, in a period called the Yuan Dynasty, the Chinese people were oppressed and persecuted. The Chinese finally had enough of their foreign overlords and planned a revolution to be kicked off during an August Moon Festival held on the 15th day of the eighth lunar moon. This holiday was an ideal time to stage a takeover, as all Chinese would be grouped together under the Full Moon. A clever scheme was hatched to disseminate the information by sending secret messages in ceremonial moon cakes. The bakers instructed the Chinese families to hold off on biting into the moon cakes until a specific time so as to not encourage anyone to jump the gun. The message inside was to execute all Mongolians. This practice of hiding secret messages has been carried forth to current times with fortune cookies.

The Chinese still congregate outside their homes to look up at the sky during the "Moon Festival." Neither the type of clothes they wear nor their rank and class have any bearing on their standing in this festival. Everyone is the same under the moon. Even the many species of animals and plants unconsciously observe the Full Moon's luminance. The Full Moon is an ideal time to celebrate an evening festival as the glow can assist the revelers in walking home that night without artificial illumination. Celebrations at this time are shared by many cultures on different continents.[1] I celebrated Moon Festival during three of my four years in China. The first year I missed the event while sitting at the front of my classroom waiting to teach students who never showed up. I was infuriated until the next day when I found out what had transpired, and was embarrassed by my lack of cultural knowledge. All of the students had been either staring up at the sky or preparing for parties in celebration. One asked me why Americans didn't look up to the moon for answers. To the Chinese, whose calendar is both solar and lunar, these cycles are both of equal value. The Chinese are correct in their interpretation. The moon, roughly one-quarter the diameter of earth, steadies our motions like the keel on a boat. Without the stabilization of this celestial body, we would wobble chaotically like the moonless planet Mars[2] and have constantly changing global conditions. Antarctica would be desert-like and the Sahara covered with snow. We depend on the moon for more than the light that illuminates our nights and patterns the movements of many organisms; without the moon, life on earth just wouldn't be the same.

Invertebrates

If we accept the Chinese philosophy of a common lunar influence, then the concept should apply to all organisms. In the previous chapter we established that the life history of the salmon is both solar- and lunar-timed. We can carry this finding a step further by suggesting that any animal that preys on the salmon will need to be in tune to this fish's solar and lunar rhythms of behavior in order to be successful. For example, the Alaskan bear that arrives late for the salmon run may not build enough fat stores to cover the animal's winter requirements. Somehow all of the bears arrive at certain stretches of rivers on time from one year to the next. Similarly, the surface feeding bird that hunts when the salmon juveniles are resting at the bottom of a pool isn't going to have fish for dinner. The bird will have much greater success when targeting these fish as they move into shallows during the transitional light periods to forage on actively feeding invertebrates, or when these insects rise to the surface as they emerge into their adult forms. This vein of thought suggests that lunar behavior is not just about when and where the predator will be successful, but is also tied to the time and place the prey will have some advantage in feeding and escaping from predators. To begin to build a foundation for this hypothesis, we need to establish lunar and solar rhythms of insects, zooplankton and other invertebrates at the bottom of the food chain.

In the 1960s, Dr. Norman Anderson and his students from the Entomology Department at Oregon State University discovered the drift (migration movement) of insects was more pronounced during the New Moon (when the insect's predators could not see them) than during Full Moon (when they could be seen) [3] [Appendix 3-1]. Anderson studied the low-illumination behavior of insects moving from one plant or rock to another to scrape and feed on periphyton (algae on the surfaces of plants and rocks). Under strongly illuminated conditions, these insects often hide from predators under rocks or in dense vegetation. Many people walking along a stream have picked up a rock and viewed a mayfly nymph clinging to the bottom. If they picked up the same rock during a dark night and quickly flashed a light on it, the bugs would be seen on the top.

A cleverly devised study demonstrated the validity of this hypothesis by transplanting insects from a troutless stream, where they did not have a strong nocturnal rhythm, to one where this fish was present. The insects were found to have changed their periods of activity to take advantage of the protection of the lower light levels. [4] Such anti-predation behavior will put all of these invertebrate species, and those above them in the food chain, into lunar rhythms as well. [5] The salmon will similarly change its behavior so as to not rely on insects when this food is not present, such as around the Full Moon. But the salmon uses its biological clock to keep the time. Therefore, these rhythms are both exogenous (externally influenced) and endogenous (internally controlled). The rhythms of the insects are a response to predators, which could be fish, birds and other animals. The rhythms will extend above the surface of the water. Bats, another predator of insects, have been shown to have minimum activity at the Full Moons. [6] This stands to reason, as they should not be actively hunting at times when their food is least available.

The establishment of a lunar rhythm for insects has consequences that extend beyond the dynamics of predator-prey relationships. Let's consider that a population of insects is ready to feed on April 1 (during a stage in their development) and the food is available. But this year, the Full Moon falls on that day and they are unable to feed without being consumed by a predator. We could suggest the insects missed a chance that would have been beneficial to them and/or they were negatively affected in the absence of being able to feed. Alternatively, if the New Moon fell on the same day, the insects could capitalize on the food while avoiding their predators. We can take this a step further by suggesting that during the course of the insect's development in one year, the invertebrate might be shifted by the moon in or out of the prime window for the food item. Thereby, the rhythms of the moon provide insects with experiences that ultimately affect their success rates.

One would expect that a healthy aquatic insect population could have a positive influence on salmon juveniles, which rely on these invertebrates for food. In the field, a large population of a pollen-disseminating insect may help to increase the successful fertilization of flowers. A spike in an invertebrate population may have a negative effect on organisms that compete for the same food as the insects, ranging from rabbits to larger mammals, such as elk, and even us. Plagues of locusts and other agriculturally devastating insects have been documented. Periodicities for locusts have also been demonstrated.[7] Might their success at the peak in their cycle be a result of a positive lunar shift? Given this idea, one has to question whether the biblical patriarch Moses and his brother Aaron brought on a plague of locusts and other insects, or did they know how these were timed?[8] Our historical interpretations may have been limited by our own scientific knowledge. We will return to method-ologies that might have been employed by the ancients to predict the peaks and valleys of animal cycles via the sun and moon in Chapter 6. While Dr. Anderson's work did not cover such terrestrial insects, his samples did contain a variety of species. The three dominant taxa were mayflies (*Ephemeroptera*), stoneflies (*Plecoptera*) and black flies (*Simuliidae*). This suggests that lunar migration and shift are not unique to one invertebrate species, although the timing of events (such as reproduction) for each animal may differ.

Zooplankton (microscopic aquatic crustaceans) have behavioral patterns similar to the riverine insects. In both fresh and saltwater environments, zooplankton spend their daytime hours in the cool and dark depths or, in the case of shallow waters, on the sediment where they maintain a low metabolic rate and expend little energy. At dusk, or when the illumination diminishes, they migrate up to the surface to feed.[9] Limnologists refer to this activity as a diel vertical migration, which is also influenced by moonlight. The moon acts like the sun to cue a descent upon moonrise and ascent upon moonset. Since the light intensity of the moon must be sufficient to have this effect, the greatest influence would be at Full Moon. Dr. Gerard Tarling and his associates with The Scottish Association for Marine Science showed that during a lunar eclipse the zooplankton demonstrated vertical migration movements that were closest to the surface during the dark period. During nonlunar eclipse nights, the zooplankton did not rise. The earth coming between the sun and the moon creates a lunar eclipse. Lunar eclipses always happen during the Full Moon phase. Tarling and his associates' work helped me understand the relationship between lunar cycles and animal behavior.

This lunar light effect on zooplankton diel vertical migration will influence the feeding rhythms of small fish that prey on them. Zooplankton feeders generally hunt with their vision and can most efficiently find this food source when there is some illumination. When zooplankton migrate toward the surface, the fish ascend as well to feed on these small animals. The effect of the different degrees of illumination on the food chain has been observed with the feeding depths of Bonneville ciscoes in Bear Lake, Utah [Appendix 3-2]. These freshwater fish (*Prosopium gemmiferum*) are a food source for the large cutthroat trout (*Oncorhynchus clarki utah*). During the New Moon phase (lower light), the fish were found to be holding higher in the water column than during the (more illuminated) Full Moon evening.[10] The findings suggest that the Bonneville ciscoes migrate vertically under lower light intensities to catch the ascending zooplankton and avoid the trout.[11]

It would stand to reason that if animals are entrained on a daily basis to light/dark lunar rhythms over a period of time, then specific stages in their lives might be timed in this manner as well. Research on a subarctic copepod (form of zooplankton), *Neocalanus plumchrus*, by researchers at Fisheries and Oceans Canada may help us to explore this hypothesis.[12] They recorded multi-year data on a specific stage of this animal's adult life. The stage was determined by the amount of an orange pigmentation in the animal and its length and weight. A conversion of the peak dates for this stage of development/event reveals that it occurs just before the New Moon [Appendix 3-3]. For this entrainment to the lunar cycle to be possible, earlier stages must also have been similarly timed. One could conceivably work the stages of the copepod back against the lunar cycle to when they awoke from the depths of the ocean and rose up to near the surface to begin their spring feed. The seasonal arrival of phytoplankton (their food) appears to be the key annual event to which these animals are timed, although they may not always time it right due to the lunar shift against the solar year. Like the insects under Dr. Anderson's study, zooplankton are a primary food source at the lower level of the food chain and what affects them will pass up through the system.

If animals have events that are lunar-timed, then the argument can be reasonably made that the timing somehow provides them with the best chance for success. A documented case of this phenomenon is the lunar synchronization with the emergence of the mayfly (*Povilla adjusta*) on Lake Victoria in Africa. This event only occurs within five days of the Full Moon, with the greatest number of swarms on the second night. The British entomologist Hartland-Rowe, who studied this mayfly, hypothesized that the nighttime illumination synchronizes the emergence of some swarming insects and helps them to find mates,[13] just as we are seeing with the salmonids. The synchronization is especially important for small populations of animals, such as this mayfly, which have fewer potential mates [Appendix 3-4].

Other Fish

The most comprehensive study of lunar timed behavior of fish was done by the Australian scientist Dr. Bob Johannes and presented in his brilliant book, *Words of the Lagoon: Fishing & Marine Lore in the Palau District of Micronesia* (1981).[13] During work in the South Pacific Islands, Johannes examined native fishing practices and learned that the islanders keyed in on periods when fish grouped, just prior to spawning, around the New and Full Moons. Other key times were when the fish migrated through channels to and from the ocean. The Islanders were tuned to the rhythms of the fish and even schoolchildren could tell the researcher the best times and places to find and catch key species. One elderly fisherman could recite the specific lunar spawning cycles of forty-five species. Johannes provided the patterns for over fifty species in his book. To confirm the islanders' claims, he examined the gonads of various species through the lunar month by visiting the sites of reported spawning aggregations, and he found that the information provided was very reliable.

Johannes noted that many of the fish are more docile and approachable when in spawning aggregations, as anglers have also observed with Pacific salmon and steelhead trout. The native Palauans refer to these fish as being "stupid" since they could be more easily netted and speared during this period. Johannes's review of the work of other Oceania scientists on the islands of

Raroia, Tahiti, Hawaii and Palau revealed that those natives had identical lunar fishing patterns. Although the natives could determine the phase, and therefore the day to fish, neither they nor Johannes were able to predict which lunar month in the solar year that the fish would spawn.

The most celebrated case of lunar synchronization of a fish, or any animal, in North America is the spawning of the California grunion (*Leuresthes tenuis*). The grunion is the only known fish to reproduce out of water, which is the main reason that this animal's lunar rhythms have been observed. Grunion always breed on the Spring Tide, the highest of the high tides, which occurs twice a month, three to four nights after both the New and Full Moons. We should recall these are periods of lengthening transitional light (sun and moon) before dusk (following New) and after dawn (following Full) due to the timing of moonrise and set. On the nights the grunion spawn, the female fish bodysurfs toward shore and purposely beaches herself in the wet sand. Once beached, she frantically wiggles her body to dig herself up to her pectoral fins in sand before releasing some 2,000 eggs. A nearby male grunion then discharges milt to fertilize them. The entire process of egg deposition and fertilization takes about 25 seconds. The fish then return to the sea on the ebb of the wave after the one that carried them in. The eggs remain in the sand for two weeks, covered by the cool and damp sand, until the next Spring Tide, which provides a more hospitable environment for the young hatch as they are washed to sea. The runs are so predictable that the California Department of Fish and Game provides the optimal times to the minute on their webpage. The prime spawning areas are popular tourist destinations.

The grunion's Spring Tide spawning is not its only lunar behavior. Their organs must be developed for this event and the animals must be in the right position to catch the waves. There are likely a series of lunar timed experiences that lead back to the previous year's spawning. Why haven't these been previously observed for the grunion? The grunion is more difficult to track than other fish such as the salmon, since a greater amount of its life is spent in the ocean. Monitoring individual fish in this environment is costly and time-consuming. Nevertheless, clues can be found to the behavior of fish in the ocean by looking at their otolith, found in the "inner ear." This organ records the growth of the fish-like rings on a tree and can be used as a surrogate for movement into or out of feeding areas or stages of development. The Polish scientist T. B. Linkowski analyzed the otoliths of four species of Atlantic lantern fish, genus Hygophum (Myctophidae) with an electron microscope. The different otolith structures he observed provided a long-term record of the vertical migratory behavior of these fish. What was most interesting about his find was that they were tied to the phases of the moon.[15] Thereby, lunar events among fish can be monitored, even when we do not see the animal, and such behaviors are not singular occurrences but part of a series of activities.

Birds

Birds that feed almost exclusively on aquatic invertebrates or fish need to be entrained to solar and lunar rhythms in order to survive. They can't think to determine the right times to feed and rest. Such an idea of celestial rhythms among birds is not new. There was a bird of unknown species pictured in the Mesopotamian cylinder seal. We can speculate that the bird was some sort of waterfowl based on its physiology and the locations of their cities on rivers. To evaluate the proposition that the ancients could have timed the behavior of waterfowl (and these birds are entrained to both the sun and moon) we ideally need a population that has been closely monitored over a long period of time. Perhaps one of the most comprehensive studies of waterfowl is with the lesser snow geese (*Anser caerulescens caerulscens*) of La Pérouse Bay in Hudson Bay, Northern Manitoba, Canada. Teams of scientists, coordinated by the Canadian Wildlife Service, have braved the harsh weather of this region since 1968 to better understand the general condition of the bird as well as the relationship between harvesting and survival rates. The researchers documented their findings in a number of scientific papers and the book, *The Snow Geese of La Pérouse Bay* (1995). One of their findings was that there was low repeatability and heritability of egg laying date, suggesting that most of the differences in timing are due to nongenetic factors. The specific reasons for the variability were not known but a possible answer could be to look at the snow geese from the perspective of solar-lunar timing.

The first step to look at these geese from this viewpoint was to transpose their mean hatching dates (which generally occur from the middle of June to early July) to the lunar cycle. The result was that they fall between lunar days 21 and 6 with a tendency to center on the New Moon [Appendix 3-5]. This leads to the conclusion that the young hatch from eggs when there is the least amount of illumination at night. This timing possibly serves as a predator avoidance mechanism for the newborn and defenseless goslings, much like migration under the dark moon does for the salmon. But the geese needed to be entrained to longer-term solar and lunar patterns in order for the timing to consistently have taken place during this period. They must have arrived first, built their nests, copulated and laid the eggs. Therefore, this relationship of hatching around the darkest nights of the lunar cycle likely fits into a series of events.

In one of the few long-term studies of the effect of the moon on birds, ornithologists (scientists who study birds) researching the Moluccan Megapode (*Megapodius wallacei*) noted lunar synchrony when they nested. This bird, which nests on the islands of Haruku and Halmahera, Indonesia, buries its eggs deep in the sand of sun-exposed beaches and abandons them to be incubated by the sun and hatched unattended. Villagers, who harvest the eggs for food, have long asserted that megapode activity varies with the phase of the moon. In support of the islanders' belief, when the researchers followed the harvesters, they found that the number of eggs was greatest between the Full and New Moons.[16] Scientists also observed that more Moluccan megapodes visited the nesting grounds on bright nights than during the New Moon. On moonlit nights, the birds also excavate burrows in communal groups and spend a longer time at the nesting ground digging deeper burrows. The scientists suggested that a benefit of this timing strategy is that the digging adult can see approaching lizards and pythons, neither of which needs light to hunt.

Although the avoidance of predators may be a benefit of the timing for the Moluccan megapodes, the pattern is not unique and fits into the solar-lunar behavior/events of the many animals we have thus far observed as well as other birds. The peak drumming periods of the ruffed grouse (*Bonasa umbellus*), for example, coincides with the Full Moons during the breeding season in April and May. The behavior of this wooded bird is an element of its courtship behavior. The estimated copulation dates coincide with the latter peak in drumming.[17] In contrast, the spotted owl (*Strix occidentalis Xantus*) calls more frequently during the darker nights of the moon than the lighter ones.[18] Therefore, based on these cases, we can reasonably conclude that the lunar cycle synchronizes behavior of these birds, the timing methodology of these events is not particular to shorebirds and events/behavior are a consequence of preceding ones.

In a similar vein of thought, we know that some birds fly south for the winter and then back again in time to breed. But how do they do it at the same time? Surely the thousands of geese in separate flocks cannot follow the lead of one smart bird. The changes in solar light levels are too flat and the weather too variable and unpredictable to coordinate the movements of the many flocks. Is the moon a signal? A lunar migration cue was established in another study on the nocturnal migration of land birds at Southeast Farallon Island, California. Here it was found that decreased moonlight in the fall resulted in an increased percentage of departures and, presumably, caused a larger volume of migration over the region.[19] With more data from other locations we could probably trace the lesser snow geese through generations of solar and lunar light cycles. The geese likely have a biological time mechanism similar to that of the salmon. This would be a logical conclusion. Neither have any ability to reason, yet they both migrate for thousands of miles in synchrony with their kin. There are not many options to achieve this once you take thinking out of the equation.

Based on these examples of birds, the suggestion can be reasonably made that the phase of the moon within a solar window of time is the primary influence in the timing of nesting, hatching and other important events for birds. Moreover, the survival rate of these lesser snow geese is at least affected by their lunar-shift timing to the solar year (and associated weather conditions). In the study of these birds, it was noted that success rates varied based on early and late eggs dropping and hatching. The abundance of predators, ranging from canines and bears to other birds, which will also vary yearly based on their own lunar-to-solar shifts and resulting success rates, will also be important. If the plant food supply down the food chain is also lunar-timed, then this might be a confounding variable as well. We will return to these ideas over the following chapters.

Summary

Any animal that synchronizes daily or seasonal events, such as feeding, migration or reproduction to the lunar cycle, will have time shifts in the solar year. The time and place shift partly determines the experiences of an animal and should result in varying success rates. In this chapter, we have observed the lunar synchronization of invertebrates, fish and birds. Ground birds need to catch insects, but at the same time avoid coyotes, foxes and other predators. All of these animals will hunt when conditions are most efficient to do so and rest when these conditions are not optimal. Thus, the solar and lunar entrainment is not just physiological but also due to environmental conditions, such as predator-prey relationships. All animals will become entrained to solar-lunar conditions, with timing dependent on what they are trying to catch or escape from. Each lunar event will lead to another. If the meteorological conditions, such as heavy cloud cover, prohibit timing gauged to the Full Moon, previous lunar-timed events should keep them on a predetermined pace.

CHAPTER 4

The Harvests We Reap

The *Torah* (meaning "instruction") and *The Holy Qur'an* both convey the story of Joseph (Hebrew "he shall add"), great-grandson of Abraham, who professes to be able to foretell the future through the reading of dreams.[1] This biblical patriarch has since gained even more notoriety among nonreligious people through Andrew Lloyd Weber's musical, *Joseph and the Amazing Technicolor Dreamcoat*. In these great books of wisdom and the theatrical production, the story begins when Joseph is in Canaan where he has two revelations. One tells him that the crops will be under his control and in another, the sun, moon and eleven stars bow down to him. Joseph relates the dreams to 10 of his 11 brothers who see the disclosure more as a nightmare than good fortune and as their brother's veiled desire to rule over them. In anger, they throw Joseph into a pit. He is rescued by Midianite traders, who in turn sell him to Egypt-bound Ishmaelites. Joseph, enslaved in this new country, is released years later to interpret the dreams of Egypt's leader, the pharaoh, assisted by the archangel Gabriel (prince of fire and the spirit who presides over thunder and the ripening of fruits) who teaches him the 70 languages of Babel.[2] The dreams relate to the success of the crops. Joseph predicts there will be seven years of bountiful harvests followed by seven lean years. Through his counsel in agricultural matters, the Egyptians are saved from the crisis. Joseph is highly revered, becomes the Prime Minister and his people are invited to stay in this land.

Another ancient story related to the theme of crop forecasting and the seven years of famine is found in the Mesopotamian *Epic of Gilgamesh*. This story, recounting the adventures of Gilgamesh, king of the ancient Mesopotamian city of Uruk, in his quest for immortality, is recited at the Vernal Equinox New Year's festival. The story was translated from clay tablets dating back to about 2000 BCE and rediscovered in the 19th century. In the first passage, the goddess Ishtar (guardian deity of the city) proposes marriage to Gilgamesh who rejects her advances due to the hideous acts she bestowed on previous suitors. One suitor was a shepherd who was turned into a wolf and chased by his own herd boys; another, a gardener, was changed into a blind mole to roam under the earth. Ishtar is outraged by Gilgamesh, who freely reminds her of these improprieties, and asks her father, Anu, lord of the heavens and father of the gods, for help in seeking revenge. Anu says to Ishtar, "If I do what you desire, there will be seven years of drought through Uruk when corn will be seedless to the husks. Have you saved enough grain for the people and grass for the cattle?"

This story is typical of those where the ancients in Mesopotamia suggested there was a relationship between the deities and nature and that Ishtar (goddess of spring, sexual love and fertility) had power over the crops. Earlier we found Ishtar in the Mesopotamian cylinder seal surrounded by a plant, grain and fruit. Her association with Shamash (the sun god) and Ea (god of omens) at the Vernal Equinox New Year's festival suggests that Mesopotamians thought that timing the harvest of plants to the sun and moon were related and might even be as predictable as we have found with the fish and fowl, and alluded to in the story of Joseph.

The ancient Mesopotamians took the concept of predictability based on the relative positions of the celestial bodies much further than just preparing for lean years. These ancients believed that they could forecast the market price. One clay tablet foretells, "If Mars keeps going around a planet, barley will become expensive."[3] In another, "[If Jupiter in] Sivan [III] approaches and stands where the sun shines forth, barley and sesame will increase, and the equivalent of [only] 1 qa will [have to] be paid for 1 kur." These notions appear to be very exact, and as suggested by the Greek philosopher Pythagoras (582? - 500? BCE), everything that has happened before will recur.

A Scientific Perspective

There is strong evidence to support the notion that the rhythms of plants are affected by light and darkness. This is an age-old idea. In the 4th century BCE, Androsthenes, scribe to Alexander the Great, noted that the leaves of the tamarind tree tended to be up during the day and down at night. Much later in 1729, the French scientist, Jean Jacques D'Ortous de Mairan (1678-1771), found that if some plants were kept in total darkness, they continued to open and close their leaves on schedule for several days. This observation suggested that living things keep time without being directly cued by the light of the sun. Building on the groundwork of de Mairan, Charles Darwin, in his book, *The Power of Movement in Plants* (1881), described the nighttime folded-leaf state of plants as "sleep" and suggested that the mechanism was a way for plants to reduce exposure and thus conserve energy. We can observe similar behavior with the common dandelion (*Taraxacum officinale*) that generously, albeit uninvited, graces our lawns with its yellow flowers. An examination during evening hours will find the petals of the flower folded up while they splay out during the light of day.

In the last century, scientists found that an interruption in the night resting period could be achieved by the introduction of light. A most curious finding in these experiments was that summertime blooming plants (long day/short night) flower more prolifically if interrupted by light during the night.[4] This finding opens up the opportunity for the moon to affect the rhythms of plants. The lunar cycle of light is not just the degree of the disk illuminated, but there is also a daily shift in the time of moonrise and set. Around the last quarter of cycle, the moon rises late in the evening, often after midnight; thus the skies go dark after sunset and then light again when the moon rises.[5] This natural condition for the plants is similar to the experience in the laboratory experiments. This lunar period is also when the Coho salmon on Lobster Creek spawned. Why would a plant and the salmon have the same timing mechanism? One answer is that neither can think and must rely on time-specific environmental cues to synchronize events.

A lunar effect on plants is not a new idea in botanical circles; however, it is one that has not been widely examined. One of the reasons is that many years of observations are required to come up with any statistically significant conclusions in a natural environment. Whereas in a temperature- and light-controlled greenhouse, one can bring plants to a set of circumstances at any time and test one hypothesis with many plants continuously throughout the year just by adjusting the environmental conditions. Nevertheless, there is one published work we can draw from. In 1972, Giovanni Abrami reported from the Botanical Garden of Padova that several species of land-based flowering plants (*Angiosperma*) had slower growth during cold weather and faster growth during warm weather, but there were more positive correlations at New Moon and more negative at Full Moon.[6] The botanist noted that the cycles of growth varied by species (the range under his observation was between 36 to 80 days). Each species also had slight variations on the moon phases that most affected them. His work suggests that lunar cycles of light and darkness are not strictly timers for events among plants but the processes leading up to them as well.

Pollination

A lunar experience with plants set me in motion to study this issue further. During the early part of June 2003, I had my worst allergy attack in recent memory. While driving home one evening a few days later, I noticed my old friend, the Full Moon, was illuminating the road for me. This led me to investigate whether the pollination of plants is on lunar clocks. Pollination is the transfer of pollen grains from the male structure of the plant to the female part to fertilize it. The pollen contains the male reproductive cells. As a start, I contacted Susan Kosisky, a microbiologist with the Allergy Immunology Service at Walter Reed Army Medical Center in Washington D.C., who graciously provided me with her data on pollen counts from trees in the area since 1989. This is a valuable, laboriously compiled dataset. Every morning Kosisky climbs to the roof of her building to retrieve two small plastic rods that have been collecting grains and spores in the air for 24 hours, and takes them to her laboratory where she meticulously identifies and counts each one.

The sycamores, an angiosperm, were a good subject to work with as there were only two species present in the area compared to the beeches/oaks (family: *Juglandaceae*) which have 21. Each species can have its own unique timing, as Abrami found; thus, trying to find a precise singular rhythm with a family of plants containing many species may not be possible. Timing may even be one way to differentiate between species within the same family. The two species of sycamores are the American sycamore (*Platanus occidentalis*) and the London plane tree (*Platanus x acerifolia*). The latter is considered to be a hybrid between the American and the Oriental sycamore (*Platanus orientalis*) and has close, if not the same, timing. The sycamore is fairly common in the eastern United States, providing shade and ornamental value. They attain heights of 170 feet and have trunks measuring to 11 feet in diameter. The London plane tree is commonly planted in urban areas because it resists smoke, gases and dust. The sycamores are monoecious, meaning that both male and female parts grow on one tree. Insects are the primary carriers of pollen to the female organ, although some become airborne and land in Kosisky's trap. Rainfall can also affect disposal of the pollen. As such, when looking at the results we need to watch for generalizations around periods of the lunar cycle and cannot tie the day down to a specific phase.

The data showed that sycamore pollen had one yearly peak for the two species. Peaks in pollen counts shifted each year between the second week in April to the first week in May. When comparing these peaks to the lunar, each peak was closely associated with the first Full Moon that occurs on or after April 7 [Appendix 4-1]. The Full Moon didn't specifically trigger the initiation of the pollination process, as it began slowly two weeks earlier each year, and was probably a result of other solar-lunar timed behavior. Pollination is one step in a continuum whereby behavior leads up to and follows this event. But the peaks were tied to the moon, suggesting that this force might have the effect of synchronizing some segment of the population.

Grapes

We can also look at these continuum and synchronization hypotheses further with grapes, a fruit many of us have some association with, whether with wine, juice, raisins, preserves or just table grapes. There is a great deal of commerce surrounding this fruit. California alone produces about 500 million gallons of wine per year, which is only about 7 percent of worldwide production. We are a grape civilization, with cultivation going back to at least biblical times although wild varieties were surely eaten earlier. Noah planted a vineyard and became drunk from too much wine.[7] Our celestial observer, Joseph, interpreted a dream concerning grapes and wine.[8] Solomon examined the budding of grape vines and blooming of pomegranates.[9] Were his observations designed to determine the timing and success of the crops? If so, how do the stories of Joseph and Solomon fit together?

Several French grape growers believe there to be a celestial connection to grapes, and suggest that at Full Moon there are high maximum energy flows, which they deem to be the best time to pick the fruit. In contrast, they propose that at New Moon the lunar influence is the lowest, providing an opportune period to rack the juice, as the sediment is least perturbed and the fluid clearest. Racking is the process of removing the deposits of sediment before barreling. I have not seen quantifiable evidence supporting the energy flow claims of the French growers. Nevertheless, traditions generally persevere based on success rather than failure, so there may be truth to the timing, regardless of the interpretation.

To consider the hypothesis of the French growers, we need to recognize first that the characteristics (optimum levels of sugar, acid and pH) of the grape mainly determine when the fruit is picked. Some growers also add a more subjective taste analysis. In order for the French growers to harvest around Full Moon, while achieving certain fruit characteristics, the vine must have worked from lunar cues earlier in the year, accumulating up to this celestial period. One key event back in time is at bud break, a term used to describe the unfurling of the grape buds on the vine, and when we found Solomon in the vineyard. Viticulturists consider bud break to be when the clock starts ticking, although there would be events leading up to this one as well, such as bud formation. Growers are generally aware that the date of bud break moves around in about a one-month window of time between years, sometime in March and April in the Northern Hemisphere. The timing is usually considered to be early, late or on time, similar to that of other organisms we reviewed. A substantiated reason to explain this phenomenon has yet to come forth. Most growers credit the yearly shift of bud break in the solar year to the weather.

One method of monitoring the ticking clock is to count the accumulation of the number of days of sunshine and inclement weather, summing up to what are called "degree days." These days are the degrees in Fahrenheit over 60 from May 1 to October 30. A yearly average of the total number of degree-days from bloom can be generally used to predict the timing of the harvest. The wine industry totals them each day to prepare for upcoming events and speculate about the characteristics of the crop, which in turn partly determines whether it will be a good or bad year for the wine. Mature vines and a stable climate should result in the least variation in the harvest. Growers usually start sweating when they hear of an unusual climatic event. The biblical record does not tell us that Solomon counted degree-days or tested for chemical characteristics, so there may be an alternate method for pacing the development of the fruit.

In the tradition of Solomon, a conversion of the date of first bud break for Pinot Noir (*Vitis vinifera* Pinot Noir) grape vines from a vineyard in Salem, Oregon, associated with Chemeketa Community College, revealed that they fell in a one-month solar window but the tendency for them was to gravitate around the darker phases of the lunar cycle. Data on bloom was in a narrow lunar window as well [Appendix 4-2]. Bloom for the grape is the onset of flowering. Fertilization (internal) occurs during the bloom. We can make some suggestions as to the timing to light or darkness since the peaks of each follow by a week or so later. Additionally, the dates of first bloom all fell after the first New Moon succeeding May 24, so we can use this relationship as a tool to predict this event in future years. We unfortunately do not have data to time the harvest from the first bud break, as might have Solomon, or the first bloom at this vineyard since the grapes were picked to the availability of wine-processing equipment, as is common among growers. As a side note, Pinot Noir is considered to be one of the noble red grapes. It is a little on the lighter end of the red spectrum and has wonderful hints of black or red cherry.

Another dataset on the harvest of four varieties of grapes—Chardonnay, Merlot, Pinot Gris and Pinot Noir—dependent on the chemical character-istics of the fruit, primarily the balance between the brix and pH levels (from Dr. Carmo Vasconcelos with the Department of Horticulture at Oregon State University in Corvallis) might help us make the connection between bloom and the harvest. The brix is a measurement used to determine the sugar con-tent of grapes and unfermented grape juice. Measuring pH tells the grower the level of acidity in a wine. The lower the pH, the higher the acid level. The two must be balanced for a good wine. Her data revealed the harvests to be in a tight lunar window concurrent with the dark phases of the lunar cycle [Appendix 4-3]. Since Dr. Vasconcelo's harvest timing is lunar (unbeknownst to the research team), we can reason that the harvest date/development of the grapes is a function of the solar/lunar timing of bud break or bloom.

Although the data from the Salem vineyard and Dr. Vasconcelos are from different years, we can use them to test whether or not the hypothesis presented can be modeled to predict the timing of the harvest. This is what scientists refer to as a "blind test." Suppose the hypothesis is that the first New Moon after May 24 drives the timing of the harvest; then when that phase of the moon falls earlier, one could expect a harvest closer to that calendar day. Alternatively, an occurrence toward the end of June should result in a later harvest. Both premises assume similar climatic conditions from year to year. Indeed, this model held rather strongly when the two datasets were compared, indicating that the grape harvest can be predicted, almost to the day, by the relationship between the sun and moon [Appendix 4-4]. One should note that the weather was fairly even during the four harvest years under study, which might have helped to test this hypothesis.

This is an interesting finding for growers and producers, but does not answer the primary question most wine aficionados are interested in. That is, will the grapes in any given year have a better opportunity to result in a good or bad wine? The buyer can then purchase options for wines in advance at a discounted rate, knowing what the characteristics will be. This is a problem we may be able to tackle as well. We can reasonably argue that an early or late harvest related to a lunar shift of bloom will affect the probability of the fruit experiencing different weather conditions. The temperature profile during the early part of the summer can be different from the later. Similarly, in Oregon where I live the summers are generally dry with heavy rains falling during the later part of September, coinciding with the grape harvest in some years. A rainfall just prior to the picking of the grapes is a sign of disaster, as the water can swell the fruit; this causes cracks, dilutes the flavor factors and allows openings for spoilage microorganisms.[10] Growers sometimes harvest a few days earlier than optimum if they see storm clouds approaching. A lunar shift of bloom to earlier in the year is more likely to move the harvest to before the storms than after them.

This question was posed to Dave Teppola, owner of Laurel Ridge Winery in Carlton, Oregon. Over his 25 years as a grower and winemaker in the Willamette Valley, Teppola's experience has been that producing good Pinot

Noir, and other wines, in the region is done most easily during years when temperatures throughout the summers are even. This stands to reason as the great grape areas in the world, Napa Valley, California; Bordeaux, France; the Italian Peninsula and perhaps the Willamette Valley, Oregon, are close to large bodies of water which serve to moderate temperatures throughout the growing season. In contrast, Teppola noted that the worst years for wine were when heat waves occurred during the latter part of the summer or when there was rainfall just before the grapes were harvested. This can be stated in another manner. We tend to prefer, or have become accustomed to, a type of wine that is produced when the conditions for the grapes are relatively constant. Whereas less desirable wines, which we have not become accustomed to, are produced when conditions are more variable. In the past few years, the weather has been even and overall the wines were good. Therefore, with a technique to pattern the timing of the grape and some past history on what is desirable, it may be possible to better predict the characteristics of wines for upcoming seasons. Ideally, we would want to look at these phenomena over 20, 30 or more years. This is problematic in Oregon as memories past ten years tend to fade and the differences in opinion become wider as time goes by. In a more developed wine region, such as France, where records are kept for hundreds of years and standards for taste established, one should be able to confirm such a trend.

Although the solar and lunar relationship is set, one may be able to employ management techniques to adjust development of the fruit and thus mitigate the effects of being too early or late. Teppola suggests that growers can move the timing of harvest a few days by managing the crop load of the vine. His experience has been that by reducing the amount of grapes on the vine, the remaining ones mature a little faster. Inversely, allowing an increased quantity will result in slightly slower-growing fruit. The vines ideally need to be pruned in January to achieve this. Waiting until after bloom (when you know the plant is early or late) is not very effective, as the energies of the plant have already been directed (and lost) towards all of the fruit. Vintners are very cautious about employing this technique, since the down side of pruning heavily during a good year is that you could lose 25 percent of your yield and subsequent revenue. You might also move your grape harvest earlier and inadvertently have undesirable characteristics in the wine. With an understanding of the solar and lunar relationship to the grape vine, growers can make more reliable decisions about how much to prune in advance of bud break and perhaps move the harvest date closer to the optimal window.

The preceding analyses do not make any assumptions as to the quality of grapes. "Quality," as the term relates to grapes, is difficult to quantify. Winemakers each have their own views of the palatable relationships between grapes, making any study on the matter highly subjective. Similarly, choosing one year over another in a side-by-side taste test is ultimately a matter of personal preference. Nevertheless, based on the preceding analysis, one can make the suggestion that under recurring conditions there will be more commonality of wines. An earlier or later lunar shift under a relatively constant climatic regime should result in recurring personalities of wines. What is, has been . . . and will be again.

This result also gives credence to the French growers' timing of their harvests to the Full Moon, although not for the reasons they suggest. They may be inadvertently applying the biological time hypothesis without a complete understanding of its workings, much like the indigenous peoples mentioned throughout this book. This finding also suggests that, contrary to conventional wisdom, weather is not the sole determinant of the timing of bud break, bloom and harvest, or the resulting characteristics of the wine.

The finding of a solar- and lunar-timed plant has implications that go beyond the wine industry, and even agricultural management. Animals that feed on the leaves or fruit of this and other plants may have more or less success, depending on whether this food source appears earlier or later in the solar year. There are fluctuating numbers of buds each year. Therefore, not only will the timing of food vary but also the amount available. This may have a significant impact on the animals. We will return to this train of thought in Chapter 6.

Blame It on the Weather

The problems associated with fluctuating climatic conditions are not unique to grape growers in Oregon. The historical record dates our struggles with the weather to the first documents of man. Ten famines are recorded in the Bible. About two thousand years before Joseph, an Egyptian pharaoh spoke words that were later inscribed on the famous Famine Stele as follows: [11]

I am mourning on my high throne for the vast misfortune, because the Nile flood in my time has not come for seven years. Light is the grain; there is lack of crops and of all kinds of food. Each man has become a thief of his neighbor. They desire to hasten and cannot walk. The child cries, the youth creeps along, and the old man; their souls are bowed down, their legs are bent together and drag along the ground, and their hands rest in the bosoms. The council of the great ones of the court is but emptiness. Torn open are the chests of provisions, but instead of contents, there is air. Everything is exhausted.

While the Nile appeared to be the immediate source of the pharaoh's problems, this river has tributaries from which the water is derived. One tributary of the Nile is the Blue Nile in Ethiopia, which is fed by streams and rivers that run during the rainy season. Extreme droughts in Ethiopia are considered to be a result of the worldwide El Niño phenomenon. The name El Niño (or "the Child" referring to the Christ child) relates to the period around Christmas when the Andean people notice the currents off their coast starting to warm. This, in turn, affects global weather patterns and the timing and amount of precipitation in the Andes.[12]

Mountain people in Peru and Bolivia look to the skies to predict El Niños so that they can manage their crops according to the rains. One of their most important ceremonies is held during the June Solstice when they climb to the peaks of the highest mountains during the cold winter nights to view the rising of the star cluster Pleiades. They relate that when the 11 main stars in this cluster are observed to be bright in June, abundant rainfalls follow, accompanied by a good harvest.[13] However, when the five dimmest stars are masked, drought follows with a poor harvest. To minimize the impact during dry years, villagers postpone the planting of potatoes by four to six weeks. Being a shallow-rooted plant, the potato is highly susceptible to drought in its early stages. To add credence to this practice, scientists studied the weather patterns in the region and concluded that when high-level cirrus clouds are more prevalent over the Andes, they dim the stars. The clouds are generated by distant thunderstorms, which develop in relation to warming in the eastern Tropical Pacific. This usually results in reduced rainfall during the growing season several months later.[14]

How to predict the weather has been an important issue to man for thousands of years and forecasting via the stars is common among many cultures. Three passages in the Bible mention the Pleiades and Orion together with the weather: In Job we read, "Who alone stretches out the heavens and tramples down the waves of the sea. Who makes the Bear, Orion and the Pleiades . . ."[15] and "Can you bind the chains of the Pleiades, or loose the cords of Orion? Can you lead forth a constellation in its season, and guide the Bear with her satellites? Do you know the ordinances of the heavens, or fix their rule over the earth? Can you lift up your voice to the clouds, so that an abundance of water will cover you?"[16] And in Amos, "He who made the Pleiades and Orion and changes deep darkness into morning, who also darkens day (into night), who calls for the waters of the sea and pours them out on the surface of the earth."[17] A Canaanite Baal myth (the people of Joseph) similarly considered the weather to be heavenly divined.

She scoops up water and washes,
Even dew of heaven, the fatness of earth,
The rain of him who mounts the clouds,
The dew which the skies pour forth,
The rain which is poured forth by the stars.

In the Genesis story of Joseph we heard about his first dream, where the sun, the moon and 11 stars bowed down before him.[18] What were these 11 stars? We do not have direct evidence they were the Pleiades; however, one could imagine the priests looking up to the sky at the same time they read the story of Joseph. They probably approached this star cluster differently than the Incas. After about 1,800 BCE, only six of the brightest seven stars were visible. Joseph was the great-grandson of Abraham, who lived in the period between 2,000 and 1,500 BCE, so he probably didn't see seven stars. How do we account for the other five? They probably included the nearby Hyades cluster of five stars, which share the Taurus zodiacal constellation and appeared on the horizon when Pleiades was high in the sky.

We should recall that Pleiades and Orion were also found on a disk in eastern Germany. The functions of Pleiades on the disk, and perhaps in the story of Joseph, are not definitely known but stars are commonly associated with the weather. Lord Tennyson wrote in his poem "Ulysses" that "Thro' scudding drifts in the rainy Hyades vext the dim sea." In other words, if Hyades were blanketed, wet weather was in the forecast. Similarly, Pleiades and Hyades were called the "sailing stars" for early Greek seamen who would set sail only when they were visible. The connection between Eurasian knowledge of the relationship between Pleiades and Hyades and climatic events is further established with second-century Alexandrian astronomer Ptolemy's listing both star clusters as being tied to weather in his book, *Phases of the Fixed Stars and Collection of Weather Signs.*

Agricultural Management

The ancient Canaanites would have been interested in knowing the weather forecast as well. The seeds of a corn-like plant could only be sown after the first rains of winter softened up the hard, sun-baked earth. If these rains were long delayed, the plant would miss the window of time for development of the ear and the crop would be nothing but straw. Planting seeds with an impending drought would be equally disastrous. Sowing seeds according to the rhythms of the plant and the moods of the rainmakers would have been key to the success of each year's harvest. The knowledge of multi-year weather patterns would have helped the Canaanites gauge when and if to plant, as well as how to manage stores of food for the lean years.

This returns us to the question of whether or not Joseph was able to predict the success rates of crops and perhaps adjust the timing of planting or crop load on the vine for optimal yield. Joseph's lineage and circumstances before his arrival in Egypt may help us find the source of this talent. He originated from Canaan, which encompasses Palestine, Israel and Lebanon in modern times. At the time of Joseph, Canaan was part of Babylon, which stretched into what we refer to as Iraq and, more anciently, Mesopotamia. Joseph would have been familiar with the Mesopotamian principle that the rhythms of nature could be paced through the movements of the sun and moon, and timed by the positions and visibility of the stars, as Mesopotamian myths were much like those of the Canaanites. The names of the characters are different but the stories are almost identical.[19] There was a great deal of cultural interaction in the region, and the various tribes were sure to have absorbed the ideas of others, especially those that helped them to be successful. The early Israelites utilized the same calendar as the Babylonians, as documented in chapter 29 of the Biblical book of Numbers (note that the number of this chapter equals the days in a lunar cycle), positioning the lunar against the solar at an equinox. The reason to have such a calendar is clear. Forecasting the harvest and timing of animals helped these people to plan for the future, rather than just reacting to the circumstances in which they found themselves. This was a crucial understanding for peoples without a sophisticated transportation system and refrigeration. They would perish without such knowledge.

Joseph was an educated youth of noble birth. Until he was seventeen years old, he frequented the Bet ha-Midrash (high school for the study of law and traditions), and became so learned that he could impart the Halakot (religious regulations) to his brethren. Joseph was considered a teacher. His receipt of the famous "dream coat" may have been a symbol that certain knowledge would be passed on to him, either directly or by his self-realization of hidden meanings. Joseph also wrote his dreams in a book, recording all of the circumstances, the day, the hour, and the place. The story tells us that the Holy Spirit cautioned him, "Take heed, these things will surely come to pass."[20] Canaanites are now considered to have been pagans, based on such astronomical beliefs.

Joseph's story also involved his management of agricultural affairs on behalf of the pharaoh. This position may have entailed two roles. The obvious one would have been to store food supplies during bountiful years for the leaner ones. In an agricultural society, you do not need to know the average years. The lows are the most important ones. Preparing for a low year in advance determined success as a people. Picking stocks is much like this. You want to know the projected high and low and put money down before the upswing. Another possibility is that Joseph might have realized if certain crops had timed success rates, then there might be benefits to planting more of these crops (i.e., beans) or varieties in a year when they are expected to do well, and perhaps another (i.e., lettuce) during a year when it has a greater opportunity for success. He might even have known the best periods to plant. Research in the 1920s by the botanist Lily Kolisko demonstrated seeds of various vegetable plants—such as lettuce, tomatoes and beans—sown two days before Full Moon, germinated better, grew larger, had more blossoms and produced a larger harvest than seeds sown two days before New Moon.[21] We rotate crops today to regenerate the soil but not to maximize the success rates of crops based on biological time.

The ability to predict crop output is not only helpful to a farmer but also beneficial to bankers and merchants who have the opportunity to choose where and when to hedge their bets. A poor crop is not a financial woe to the clever investor. The laws of supply and demand dictate that prices should be higher in the lean harvest years. If the merchant knew in advance to buy low in an up year and store product until a projected higher price in a following poor harvest, he would make more money. Such a skilled astrobiologist would have the advantage of the inside trader of stocks, without the legal repercussions, although there might be social consequences. If the forecasting of crops is less risky, bankers will invest in yearly agricultural products (instead of the market), which may eliminate the reliance on crop futures. The collection of debts could also be better gauged if you knew when the economy would be strong again. Joseph used his inside information to the advantage of the pharaoh by first reaping all of the people's money and cattle in exchange for corn and then their land. By the end of the second year of famine, the pharaohs had subjected all of the peasants in the Nile Valley to serfdom.[22]

This hypothesis may also be used for the benefit of mankind. Underdeveloped countries that need more food can plant varieties that are expected to be successful that year, based on their timing. They should also be able to better plan for the years of famine. In developed countries, which do not want more food production, the cost per unit can be reduced, such as by investing in the crop only during expected bountiful years.

There is a great deal of value in knowing the peaks of pollination for nonfruit-bearing plants as well. I can plan to go to another environment, such as the beach, during the Full Moon that occurs around June. Allergists will know when they shouldn't take vacations. General medical practices can better screen patients over the phone. And companies that sell antihistamines can gauge their production and marketing to the trends of each region.

Summary

Were the budded plant and fruit pictured on the Mesopotamian cylinder seal those of the grape? One cannot say either way for sure, but these people did have grape vines. Regardless of what crop was illustrated, all flowering plants should have both solar and lunar rhythms; each with its own time and place. These solar and lunar rhythms guide them in their growth and regeneration patterns. The timing of bud break, bloom and fertilization appear to be synchronized to the phases of the moon in a solar window of time. Lunar patterns carry through over the yearly experiences of plants, thus events that occur early in the year can be used to predict the timing of later ones. Plants are also affected by the weather, and some cultures forecasted the weather based on the appearance of certain stars in order to manage the crops. This solar/lunar relationship is important information for commercial purposes, allowing growers and producers to better schedule their resources. With more analysis, they should be able to better forecast the yield and characteristics of the crops, such as grapes, with a high degree of accuracy. There was knowledge of these rhythms in ancient times as related through stories and rituals.

CHAPTER 5

The Art of Time

THERE IS NO CERTAINTY WHERE ONE CAN NEITHER APPLY ANY OF
THE MATHEMATICAL SCIENCES NOR ANY OF THOSE OF WHICH
ARE BASED ON THE NATURAL SCIENCES.
~ LEONARDO DI VINCI

In southwestern France an underground cave called "Lascaux" has walls and ceilings decorated with approximately 1,500 engravings and 600 paintings of horses, deer, goats, bison and a 2,000 lb. ancestor of the domestic oxen we now refer to as an auroch. The art dates from 15,000 to 9,000 BCE, with most of the work from the earlier part of this period. Some of the styles are quite imaginative, such as using crevices in the rocks to depict flowing water and subtly controlled shading to enhance muscular forms. Upon exiting the gallery, Pablo Picasso was said to have exclaimed, "We have learned nothing."

The cave was re-discovered accidentally in the past century by truant schoolboys and is now considered by some to be one of the world's most significant archeological finds. Only a few fortunate researchers have been able to see the inside of the cave due to the harmful agents we unconsciously import, but each year hundreds of thousands walk through a nearby replica, called Lascaux II, and countless millions, including myself, have seen the images in books and magazines.

On one wall of this gallery the early art consists of a series of markings along the apparent path of a horse, as sketched in Figure 5-1. Thirteen dots are succeeded with a box that reaches up from the center to form the animal's front legs. Another wall has a roaring male red deer (*Cervus elapus*) that walks on a row of 13 large dots followed by a rectangle, as pictured in Figure 5-2.

Markings totaling the number 13 are seen with other animals at Lascaux. One set of 13 lines flanks an engraved 6-½ foot high red deer, called "The Major Stag," and another precedes a herd of seven male Ibexes, or wild goats,[1] as pictured in Figures 5-3 and 5-4, respectively. I have not seen a substantiated hypothesis in print to explain these markings. Most texts suggest the works were a mixture of magic, ceremonial art, rituals and drugged trances. A common belief is that the Ice Age men painted the animals so as to harness the spirit of the beasts and make them more successful hunters. Few published images even picture each complete set of symbols with the corresponding animals. Could the 13 dots signify the number of nights counted from the Crescent Moon to first Full Moon, as Christian calendars use to set Easter? Does the box represent the Full Moon? Could this art be expressing the nature of time?

The first time I viewed these images was in the local public library. I was with my daughter, then a two-year old, and a *National Geographic* feature about the caves perched on a bookshelf.[6] Wanting to see through the intuitive eyes of a child, I asked her to identify the antlered animal in Figure 5-2, to which

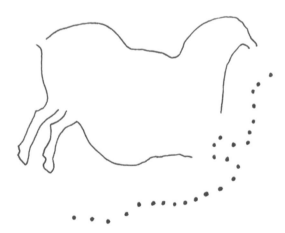

Figure 5-1: This horse in the Lascaux cave rides on a series of painted markings. Thirteen dots are succeeded with a box that reaches up from center to form the animal's front legs. This box likely signifies the beginning of the Full Moon period when animals group and then mate.[2]

Figure 5-2: This Lascaux cave red deer is roaring during the Full Moon period, as signified by the window after the 13 markings (nights from the first Crescent Moon to the Full Moon). The stag (male) roars to call in the hind (female). Animals herd during this period and are much easier to find and harvest at night with primitive equipment. The large and fully developed antlers suggest this is during the Autumn when the animals mate.[3]

Figure 5-3: Thirteen lines flank this engraved 6-½ foot high stag at the Lascaux caves, called "The Major Stag." These markings signify the lead up period of the lunar month from the Crescent Moon to the Full Moon when this large mammal groups.[4]

Figure 5-4: This herd of seven male Ibexes (wild goats), plus one female, is separated by a box (likely representing the Full Moon) and noted to the left by 13 marks. The number 13 in this illustration may be the lead up period from the Crescent Moon to when the males mate with the females.[5]

she replied, "A deer." I then asked what the box in front of the animal might mean. Without hesitation she answered, "A window." What this window might signify was another question that was beyond her comprehension. But, building on her unbiased intuition, I said to myself, "Perhaps the box is a window in time." Indigenous peoples looked at the moon as such a window. The Yurok considered the Full Moon to be the prime lunar period to hunt by land. Perhaps, these Ice Age men also identified this period as an opportune window of time to kill big game. The hunter's moon is, of course, fully illuminated.

My observation has been that elk also group and migrate around the Full Moon, making them easier to find. From experience I know one can hunt through the night without a torch under this moon. I often hike under its luminance into my hunt zone when pursuing the North American elk or wapiti (*Cervus canadensis*) with bow and arrow. Elk, primarily a transitional-light migrating species, are fairly large animals, many weighing over a thousand pounds. They often live in rocky or heavily wooded terrain. My prey is taxonomically the same as the European red deer although the former grows much larger. The wapiti is believed to be a red deer that migrated from the Old World to North America in the Pleistocene epoch.

Elk watchers find that the bull does not bugle without purpose. He uses his deep and throaty voice to summon the cows during the fall mating season.

I listen for his call to find the herd, sometimes miles away, or just to know if they have arrived. One can also imitate the calls of the animals to bring them in closer. Big game author, Gary Lewis, gave me an initiation to his calling style while archery hunting for elk in Central Oregon. Lewis started off with a high-pitched lost-cow call, which he used about every two minutes over a period of ten minutes. This call is intended to bring in straggling females looking for the protection of a herd. If there is no reaction, Lewis then moves into the bugle of the young bull. The idea behind imitating this animal is to suggest to an older herd bull that an unwanted suitor may be intruding into his harem. Both techniques are effective for about half a mile and can bring animals charging in to the caller.

British game manager and professional stalker Richard Price takes the game up a notch with roe deer (*Capreolus capreolus*). To a gentleman, such as Price, the hunt is only considered fair chase if the shooter is within 25 yards of the prey. Roe deer, like elk, do not normally walk up to the stalker. They must be enticed to the hide. Price finds that he is most effective calling in active males during the transitional light periods on days other than the Full Moon.[7] His observations are that the peak of breeding (the rut) occurs for all species of deer during the illuminated evenings around the Full Moon and the animals rest the following morning. Price does not hunt by night due to the laws and traditions of his countrymen. Nevertheless, based on his observations of deer during the glow of the Full Moon, he suggests that this would have been a prime period for the Lascaux hunters to slaughter groups of preoccupied animals.[8] Price knows a great deal about deer behavior. He has presided over the harvest of more than 14,000 animals and monitored countless others as a game manager. He is without question one of the foremost authorities on deer behavior. The Lascaux Ice Age hunters would have known the same and appear to have etched and painted their hunting methodology on the cave walls.

Pacing the Deer and Elk

To explore the biological time of deer and elk, and determine if the Ice Age men could have keyed off of the moon for their hunts, we need to look for major quantifiable events, such as antler shedding, migration past a specific point, dropping of young, etc. Any analysis needs to be based on what happens in the wild where the animals are affected by the solar and lunar rhythms of light and darkness, a natural food supply and predators. Just such a study from back in the late 1950's was conducted in Connecticut. The researchers examined the records of 184 white-tailed deer (*Odocoileus virginianus*) antler sheds on killed animals. Differences in timing of antler shedding were observed between different years, for unknown reasons, though little variation was found among the state's eight counties, suggesting that a universal force affected all.[9] After the differences between years were examined, a pattern became apparent that indicated biological time. During the years when the first Full Moon fell closer to the Winter Solstice, antlers dropped earlier than when this moon phase fell later [Appendix 5-1]. A notation should be made that some antlers were shed a week earlier than the Winter Solstice, so the lighted evenings leading up to the Full Moon (or other solar-lunar condition) may have triggered the events, instead of this specific event. Nevertheless, the Winter Solstice and the Full Moon are good points in time against which to pattern this behavior.[10]

To understand this extraordinary phenomena we need to look at the physiology of the antler and its function. What we view as an antler is actually two structures, the pedicle at the base and the antler that develops from it. The pedicle is a permanent bony outgrowth of the frontal bone of the skull while the antler is replaced every year. Deer and elk are the only mammals with bones that are shed and regenerate. The pedicle grows under the influence of testosterone at the onset of puberty with the increasing light of spring. Researchers have found that the antlers grow when the lengths of day and night have more light in the order of 1.5 to 2 hours.[11] Such a solar light condition would occur in the wild in the Northern Hemisphere after the Vernal Equinox.

The synchrony of the antler shedding appears to be a bilateral disarmament so that one doesn't have an advantage over another. The ultimate use of the antlers is to impress desired females during the rut and keep away competing suitors. Mature males seem to be able to estimate social class and rank through antler size and shape.[12] After the rut, the males leave the females and the heavy antlers no longer have a function so they are dropped. The new set is larger than the previous one so as to keep up with the animal's stature and physical capacity to carry a larger load.

This returns us to the questions of why the Full Moon induces the old antlers to shed or perhaps the new set to grow. One consideration may be that the ratio of the lengths of day and night in the period around the Winter Solstice is not correctly apportioned for antler growth (or to induce shedding). However, when a Full Moon (or light evenings leading up to a Full Moon) occurs before or during this period, the number of light hours increases, thus triggering this change. The light-induced hormonal spike may not actually bring on significant growth of the pedicle (which often coincide), but just enough to shed the old antler. White-tailed deer in Connecticut appear to cast their antlers starting at the end of December, and peaking in January. In Hartford, Connecticut, at the Winter Solstice, the length of day from beginning to end of twilight is around ten hours. But, during a Full Moon period, the length of light is extended. This appears to be a logical hypothesis to explain why the deer shed their antlers shortly after the Full Moons during this solar period.

The hypothesis that antler shed is entrained to the moon can be further supported by an interesting case of a male white-tailed deer that was studied by scientists at the University of Mississippi in the 1980's. Over an eight-year period, the researchers found the dropping of the antlers to range from 368 to 391 days,[13] so the date shifted in the solar year. What the deer was being entrained to was not known. The animal was kept penned outside under natural lighting conditions and near other deer. A translation of the published data to the lunar revealed that the animal had both solar and lunar rhythms. During six of the seven years, the antlers were cast in an 11-day lunar window on the waning half of cycle – the period succeeding Full Moon (see Appendix 5-2). The death of the animal prevented the observation of casting in the eighth year. At the time of his death, the antlers had de-mineralized at their base indicating casting would have occurred in the near future. The lunar day of his death was 18; therefore, we can assume that the day of casting would have fallen in line during the waning half with the other years.[14] What is most interesting about this case is not that the deer was sensing both solar and lunar cues, but that this particular animal accomplished this without the benefit of eyes. The deer was blind from a condition referred to as congenital anophthalmia. Therefore, there must be another mechanism that this animal used to sense the natural rhythms of light and darkness. Might the animal be sensing the changes in light at the cellular level?

What the light rhythms are probably triggering is the secretion of testosterone from the testicles, which coordinates an annual cycle of growth, calcification, cleaning, shedding and regeneration. Each of these events is tied to other important ones. If testosterone is affected by length of day/night, and the Full Moon extends the number of light hours, then all of these events, including the timing of their mating, could be lunar-synchronized as well. The people of Lascaux may not have known the physio-chemical reasons for the light timed behavior of the mammals, but their observation of the animal's behavior, relative to the lunar cycles of light, taught them what was truly important.

Migration & Reproduction

The Lascaux hunters also appeared to be cued into the time and place of red deer migration. On a cave wall, in what is referred to as the Main Gallery, there is a series of antlered red deer heads in frenzied swimming movements, as pictured in 5-5. They ride along a crevice in the rock wall that gives the impression of a flowing river. One trailing red deer stag has what appears to be seven spheres floating among the animal's antlers. We can assume this migration is occuring during the autumn because these stags have fully developed antlers. My interpretation of the image is that the hunters counted the number of Full Moons from a solar point, likely around the Vernal Equinox, to determine when the stags would out-migrate, and used a large moving body of water as a point in space to time the migrations of these animals. The flow of water is probably the Vézère River. The Vézère is a wide river where it passes by the caves. One could assume that red deer do not ford large rivers more than once in a seasonal migration.

The time of migration might affect the timing of reproduction, which should shift from year to year, as the red deer males cannot service the females when not present. I was not able to observe this behavior with red deer, but we can use published studies of other large hoofed mammals to test if the moon shifts these animals in a different space over time. Two we can work with to explore the hypothesis involved spring migrations: one with Roosevelt elk (*Cervus elaphus roosevelti*) near Crater Lake, Oregon and another

Figure 5-5: On the walls of the Lascaux cave there is a herd of male red deer pictured in a head jerking motion as if they are swimming through a river. The stags ride along a crevice in the rock wall (not pictured) that gives the appearance of a river. The seven spheres between the horns of the second from last deer pictured probably signify the number of Full Moons from an event in the spring that the Lascaux hunters used to measure when these animals would leave for their wintering areas after the rut.[15]

with Rocky Mountain elk (*Cervus canadensis*) in the Selway River Drainage in Idaho. The former elk were observed crossing a road and the latter by changes in elevation, as surveyed biweekly from an airplane. After converting the solar calendar dates to the lunar, the data suggests that more migrated around the Full Moon than around the New Moon [Appendices 5-3 and 5-4]. Their timing of migration makes a great deal of sense as the increased illumination around the Full Moon affords them easier passage at night. In the latter study, the migrations over two years were almost the inverse of each other due to the lunar shift against the solar year. These patterns from both populations demonstrate that temperature and precipitation are not the primary inducers of migration.

The ecologist Anthony Sinclair demonstrated lunar synchrony in the mating period of the Serengeti wildebeest, another ungulate (hoofed mammal).[16] Using data on births (actual and calculated) and first appearance dates of calves by a park warden, he worked back 255 days (assumed gestation length) and found a strong lunar relationship to mating, which commenced at the Full Moon. He also found that the calves dropped during the darker phases of cycle, as we have observed with many other animals. Similarly, in the Crater Lake study, migration ceased at day 18 of cycle, presumably for birthing. The biologists suggested that this period coincided with the onset of calving.

Sinclair noted in his paper that to the best of his knowledge the Serengeti wildebeest work was the first case of a strong relationship between conception and lunar cycles in mammals. Sinclair should be noted for his fine work but at the same time we need to recognize the cavemen in France had the lunar and solar timing of large mammals figured out many thousands of years before him.

Price suggests that does (females) ovulate under a Full Moon and that this lunar influence may have some kind of "draw" on their metabolism. These mechanisms seem to combine and bring all of the females of ovulation weight into estrus together which in turn allows for a rut of as short a duration as possible. This serves to shorten the herd's most vulnerable period and allows the spent males, which may lose up to 28 percent of their body weight, to feed up and mend before the onset of winter. Late, or prolonged, rutting activity is very damaging for a herd as it will kill many of the older proven males.

These mammals also benefit from the cover of darkness, since the hind (female red deer) and cow (female elk) leave the herd to give birth. And during the first few days of life, the juvenile is left hidden in the undergrowth while the mother is away feeding. Young animals would have the maximum number of dark evenings to hide from predators if dropped close to the third quarter of cycle, but since the stag (or bull elk) cannot service all of the females in one day, the calving is spread out. Elk ranchers have noted that cows appear to hold off the dropping of the calves by a day or two when there is a great deal of commotion from other nearby animals. They may be holding the young until closer to the dark evenings as well.

Dark evenings offer protection from transitional light nocturnal predators and the timing of the drop (earlier or later in the year) will determine where the deer, elk or wildebeest will be birthed on the migration. Also, the availability of different qualities and quantities of food will vary. As such, the time of dropping will affect their survival. In some environments, earlier conception of the elk is thought to benefit survival of the young as they have more time to gain weight before the onset of their first winter. Larger elk calves have been shown to have higher rates of survival than smaller ones.[17] Very light calves are more likely to die in summer than heavier calves and late-born calves show higher mortality than those born early or within the main birth period.[18] Timing is everything for the survival of these mammals and the moon partly determines where the animal will be in the solar year.

The Mind of a Hunter

There may have been other reasons for Ice Age hunters noting the red deer's migration across the river. They might have considered this an opportune time and place to hunt them. This is a period when the animals' herding mentality works against them. Follow the leader is an excellent strategy to escape most predators, with the exception of the human who can plan ahead and entrap them. My first elk was taken when the animals in a large herd were consecutively crossing a creek. A logger had spooked the animals on a hill across from me and pushed the herd in my direction. A few dozen elk quickly stormed through the brush, single file behind the herd bull. As I ran in the direction of where the animals were crossing my path, one by one, they each saw me, alerting their successor, who had no other choice, but to follow. When I came into a safe 40-yard archery distance, an elk halfway through the herd provided a clear broadside kill shot. Broadside shots provide the largest target and have the best angle to the vital organs in the front area of the chest. The cave men at Lascaux knew which part of the anatomy was a kill shot and would not leave a wounded animal walking for miles. They left us an engraving of a collapsing stag with two spears pointing at the lungs.

With their primitive hand-held, catapult-like spear throwers the Lascaux hunters probably needed to be at closer range and targeted areas where the terrain gave them such an advantage. I had previously, and unsuccessfully, attempted to sneak up on resting herds. The Ice Age hunters surely knew the value of targeting big game when they were active. They appear to have made special note of when the animals were in single file, such as when they were walking up the banks after crossing rivers or traversing through canyons.

The Lascaux hunters required different strategies for each phase of the moon. Their art indicates that they were not only interested in the Full Moon but also the lead up period to this phase. A Full Moon strategy probably included targeting animals in an open area at night where a big herd has plenty of room. This period of time requires the stalker to know precisely where the herd will be. He probably won't stumble into a single animal. The longer transitional light around the two half moons would have required a different hunting strategy. Hunts needed to be timed to dusk and dawn when the animals may not have been in large herds, but moved each day between feeding and resting areas. They might have waited on the edge of a grassy field or outside of an apple tree grove for the animals to walk back to the cool and shaded timber where they spent their days. Harold Blackwolf, the hunter and provider for the Warm Springs Tribe in Central Oregon, related to me similar observed behavior for large mammals and preferred timing of hunting based on the phases of the moon. Modern day deer hunters tend to have their most success during the transitional light hours around these two periods of the lunar cycle, as the animals are scattered and move to and from food/water sources. This period of activity also overlaps when the human hunter can see his prey.

Timing the Year

In addition to knowing under what moon phase to hunt, the Lascaux hunters appear to have been able to calculate which lunar cycle in the solar year the animals would have specific events. Earlier I pointed out the group of seven stags with one carrying seven dots in its antlers. On other walls in the Lascaux cave, there are series of rectangles next to other animals, as described in Figure 5-6. Between two ibexes there are six boxes with a clear mark in the middle of one. A cow has seven, one horse has six and another is accompanied by five markings. The order of the Full Moons was probably read on these four in a clockwise fashion with the marks designating the first lunar month. The greatest number of boxes is seven, thus these Ice Age men may not have measured the time and space between the appearance of the animals, like the Yami fisherman in Chapter 1 who found the flying fish returning in 12 or 13 lunations. However, the Ice Age hunters may have had a better method of figuring this out which ensured they didn't have a false start.

One could suggest that the pictograms at Lascaux are the earliest writing, as well as scientific notation, of man. This would allow the French to lay claim to being the first documented scientists. But why illustrate the Full Moon with squares instead of circles? I have never seen a square Full Moon. My illustrator, Kit Richards, suggested that etching straight lines in rock is much easier than scratching circles. Straight lines can also be used for more than one lunation by positioning them next to and above each other, thus minimizing tiresome strokes. One can test this hypothesis by using rock to scratch against a concrete sidewalk. You will also notice that the coloration of the rock where you just stroked will be different from the surrounding area. When you throw some water on the surface, the loose rock will be washed away. The Lascaux hunters might have used this observation to count lunation, with the groves becoming deeper each year. They were also known to use different colored paints in each box. Perhaps the colors had significance in the countdown as well.

The geometry of these Ice Age symbols is much like Chinese characters. Among the more than 40,000 characters in the Chinese writing system, few, if any, circles are used. Pictograms representing circular objects are also drawn with squares, such at the one for the lunar month - 月. This stands to reason as the oldest discovered Chinese calligraphy, dating to earlier than the 14th Century BCE was on bone (cattle and tortoise) surfaces, presenting a challenge similar to rock. There are few circles among the writings on the

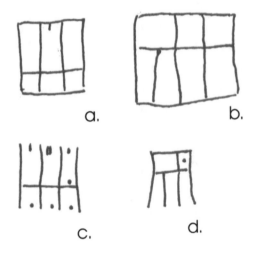

a.   b.

c.   d.

Figure 5-6: Rectangles in the Lascaux caves associated with (a) two ibexes, (b) a leaping cow, (c) a horse, and (d) above a horse. The boxes probably represent Full Moons and the marks other calendar points of reference. The order of the Full Moons was probably read in a clockwise fashion with the marks designating when to begin counting. The first Full Moon marked is probably the one that succeeds the Vernal Equinox. Straight lines are easier to scratch on rock and paint than circles. They also allow the artist to use the same line twice and present the date in an organized fashion.[19]

so-called "oracle-bone" inscriptions, which also include references to the stars and lunar eclipses.

We observed another indigenous people, the Yurok, counting six New Moons from the Winter Solstice to determine when to begin preparing their fish weir to catch migrating steelhead trout at a specific point in the Klamath River. Perhaps the people of Lascaux had a similar methodology. In Oregon, the elk rut in the month of September and migrate to their winter ranges shortly afterwards. If I knew how to determine a specific time around the Vernal Equinox, then added seven Full Moons, I would be able to predict the timing of the post-rut and when the animals would be out-migrating. This is the number that we counted in the antlers of the Lascaux red deer. These hunters didn't need to know the date of the Vernal Equinox. They could have timed the cycle off of another event in the animal (a return migration to Lascaux) or a different creature (like the Tulalip's white pine butterfly) or plant. Interestingly, there are images of animals and plants in the caves that are clearly associated with each other. Alternatively, they might have keyed off the stars. Patterns that have been referred to as "sky maps" appear in the caves.

As a side note, a seven-month lunar calendar indicates that these people were, at the most, nomadic for just a little more than half of the year. The out-migration from Lascaux probably began after the Autumnal Equinox (where their calendar stopped) with a return near the Vernal Equinox (where it began). Their continued existence in one location may infer an early civilization. They could tell time and plan for the future.

I have observed the biological time of the elk while hunting Oregon's Coast Range. In some years, herds of 20 or more animals are grouped in my zone at the start of the season. Other years there are no elk for the first two weeks and then small groups start showing up at the periphery of the rut area, forming a cohesive unit almost all at once. Local residents have also noticed that the timing of their movements varies each year. Conventional wisdom has their migrations being related to climatic conditions and moving to the food. But how would an elk know when food would be present dozens of miles away or at drastically different elevations? To make this idea more impossible, the growth of plants also shifts between years with the moon. I looked back at the appearance of the herds in my area over the last few years and after applying the biological time hypothesis, the seemingly random movements became precisely coordinated patterns.

Modern Applications

The application of the biological time hypothesis to the deer and elk may seem trivial for some, but for others, the notion is serious business. The hundreds of thousands of big game hunters can know when to time their forays and develop techniques for each behavior of the animals. State and provincial wildlife commissions can schedule hunting seasons that encourage success or failure. Wildlife biologists can predict the success rates of animals years in advance and manage the harvests. If they know the narrow windows of time the animals will be present in a specific area, they can conduct more accurate counts. There are other important wildlife management issues to be gleaned from the biological time hypothesis. In wild populations, the behavior of the animals should only be interrupted around the New Moon (other than during the birthing period), when no significant activity appears to take place, so as not to put them out of sync with their natural rhythms. Another area to consider is the lighting in zoos. Artificial night lighting may inhibit animals from synchronizing to natural cycles at the critical periods in the solar year when they would have been most successful. Breeding in captivity is a habitual problem and the lack of natural light cycles may be part of the reason. There are probably many applications of this idea to animal husbandry. For example, when can the rams and bulls be released to the females during the mating period? There are perhaps many other areas to explore with this relationship.

Summary

Deer and elk synchronize their major events such as antler casting, dropping of offspring, migration and the rut to both the solar and lunar cycles. The movements of the moon give reliable cues to aid the population in coordinating these events at the same time. The increase in light around when the Full Moon occurs is beyond the normal solar condition and may be one cue that they time to. Early dropping of calves (elk) and fawns (deer) results in a more successful year class of animals. If the moon is driving the time shift in the solar year, then the lunar cycle partly determines the survival rates of the young.

Ice-Age men appear to have known how the animals were timed and used this information to develop productive hunting strategies. They left the methodology on the walls of the cave at Lascaux in France. This may be the first form of writing and scientific notation. Some modern day game managers and ecologists have recorded this information as well.

CHAPTER 6

Patterning Plants and Animals

IN ALL CHAOS THERE IS A COSMOS, IN ALL DISORDER A SECRET ORDER.
~ CARL JUNG

A few years ago, I had the privilege of animal tracking with Jon Young, a well-known master of native ways, protégé of the legendary Tom Brown and founder of the Wilderness Awareness School in Duvall, Washington. The hunt started by picking up fox tracks in the damp morning sand of a riverbank. On all fours, noses to the ground, we crawled along the beach measuring the animal's pace, a calculation based on the distance between the paw prints. Young further demonstrated that the movements of the canine could be predicted by laying down a stick broken to the same length as the gait of the animal. The technique required some manipulation as the tracks changed with the interest of the fox. The trick to decipher the animal's changing moods was to study the positions of its paws. If the front paws landed first, the fox was assumed to be sniffing along. When the hind paws preceded the front paws, the animal was on the run, like a racing horse. If both the hind and front paws on each side fell into each other, then the fox was casually walking. One can test this methodology by observing the tracks of a dog on the beach.

At one point we came to a rocky area and lost sight of the fox's prints. Young was not deterred by the apparent loss of sign. He continued to measure the pace by walking the stick through the area. On the other side, where the sand resumed, the animal's tracks were found to be an inch or so off from where the measuring stick plotted them to be. Young explained that indigenous Americans used this technique when there was little sign in order to track people and animals.

The tracks also told a story of what had transpired long before our arrival on the beach. For example, we observed the prints of the fox apparently chasing a small rodent. We were not able to determine if the canine had actually caught its prey. The sand also revealed splayed markings from a walking bird that were heading in the direction of the fox but turned sharply away. Perhaps the bird didn't want to be part of the chase. Recreating a window of time in the animal's life by studying misplaced grains of sand was fascinating and told stories that humans could not easily view firsthand. By understanding the pace, we could piece together events in the fox's life without ever having seen the animal. We didn't know the age, sex or even what species of fox we were observing. This practice probably dates back to early man. We earlier observed Ice Age man's notations of the deer's pace on the walls at Lascaux. The ancients in Mesopotamia had similarly computed the paces of animals, both wild and domesticated, by using the appearance of the sun, moon and other celestial bodies as reference points. They probably knew little of what we refer to as biology, but enough about the natural rhythms of organisms to pattern the movements. The patterns told them what was truly important, such as when animals would arrive or plants would be ready for harvest, how bountiful the numbers of fish or crops would be and what they needed to do in order to survive.

Timing the Run

In the previous chapters, we built a foundation of knowledge with the salmon that can be developed further to pattern these animals. The data is not as complete as we would like, largely because we lose them at sea. Nevertheless, we can pick up the salmon's pace during their spawning run years later, as Young did with his measuring stick across the rocks. One stock with which to continue our inquiry is the sockeye salmon that migrate up the Kenai River, Alaska. Most anglers who fish the Kenai River for sockeye time their trips to a multi-year average that does not account for the yearly lunar shift. Some years they are lucky and hit the runs right, while others are said to be either "early" or "late." The usual explanations are climatic changes, a greedy commercial fishery, or an anomaly. Regardless of these claims, we earlier found that the timing of the run is very precise, and only on a different calendar than most modern Kenai anglers utilize. The peak dates range over 13 solar days and are closely tied to lunar tide patterns [Appendix 6-1]. One pattern has a first peak around lunar day 27 and the second pattern has a first peak close to day 12. These lunar numbers follow the Neap Tides. The count is on the lower river so the difference between the Neap Tides and these peaks is probably the passage time through tidewater. The all-important question for the Kenai angler is which one the salmon will come in on.

Indigenous people probably didn't know much about the biology of these fish. They might not have known the fish were moving through the inlet. Fishermen located miles upstream would not be able to monitor the tides. A simple technique was required to time the runs. The tribe's shaman probably stood on the banks of the Kenai River during the night of the Vernal Equinox, in the same year the fish would return as adults, and looked up at the night sky. If a phase related to lunar days 20 through 2 of cycle (post Full Moon going into New Moon) were sighted, then the shaman would have predicted a 27 pattern. If a phase relating to days 4 through 17 were observed (post New Moon going into Full Moon), he would say the 12 pattern would occur [Appendix 6-1]. He would then have counted from either the Vernal Equinox (115 days) or the Summer Solstice (23 days) to work out the specific Neap Tide to target. The solar position utilized was probably determined by how much time the people would need to travel to the river or prepare for the harvest. The anthropological research on the Yurok and Tulalips suggests the indigenous people near the Kenai River might have also utilized such techniques. This finding also demonstrates that the Yurok and Tulalips methodologies of timing the salmon based on the sun and moon was scientifically valid. This window of time would have been a prime opportunity for a tribe on the Kenai to net, spear or trap the large number of sockeye salmon migrating in the lower river.

Modern man can use the timing of Easter, falling early or later per the lunar shift, in a similar manner. The Kenai River sockeye data demonstrated that when Easter fell from March 30 to April 4 and from April 19 to April 23, the 12 pattern occurs. Whereas when Easter occurred between April 7 to April 16, the sockeye migrate in the 27 pattern. There is no magic in this practice. Both events are solar- and lunar-timed. Early Christians might have used this religious day in a similar manner to time a fish or other animal. The Mesopotamian cylinder seal, which also keyed off the Vernal

Equinox, was likely direction on how to time the sbour and other animals as well as plants.

Predicting the Future

A shaman might have been able to take solar-lunar forecasting one step further by predicting the return rates of the fish and thereby know how much food his people would have. In the early part of the last century, a pair of enterprising statisticians similarly set out to determine if anglers had a better chance of catching Atlantic salmon during some years than others.[1] They were not studying the solar/lunar timing of the fish, but their findings are nonetheless valuable in our path of discovery.

What probably stimulated their interest in the project was the well-known cyclic activity of this salmonid's abundance. Extreme highs and lows in the numbers of fish are common. In modern times, the returns have been lean during the high and low years in cycle and Atlantic salmon anglers (called "sports") sometimes count into the thousands of casts between hook-ups. Guides at the finer camps cast for the sports, who recline with a good book until the magic moment. Atlantic salmon anglers celebrate their misery over the lean years by boasting about how much time has elapsed since their last catch. The one who has endured the most wins by reason that the odds are now in his favor. To compare fishing success when there is little, anglers resort to counting the salmon that came up to look at their fly and then turned away. This measurement is, of course, highly speculative. A few years ago, I had the opportunity to fish the Restigouche River in New Brunswick, Canada, for Atlantic salmon. My visit was during a low year in the cycle. Over the course of a week, one angler in the camp hooked into a salmon, which was subsequently brought to the net. He counted the fish as the second in his angling career. The sport's first had turned on his fly years earlier.

The statisticians only counted fish brought to the net and further supported their conclusions with findings from research on the juvenile stages of this animal. They looked at a number of rivers in eastern Canada, but primarily studied records from the Ristigouche Salmon Club, named after the river where it is located and the very water from which I didn't catch my first Atlantic salmon. The Ristigouche Salmon Club, founded in 1880, is a highbrow establishment frequented by old-blood names and is said to have a proper dinner dress code. Membership is by invitation only. The club has many other traditions, including the careful recording of all particulars about each landed fish.

The researchers used data from its founding until 1930 (50 years) to form two sets of conclusions about the Atlantic salmon. The first find related to catches of fish. They demonstrated in a rigorous quantitative manner that some years are indeed better than others for Atlantic salmon fishing. There also appeared to be a 10-year cycle of fish abundance unrelated to any possible generational span of the fish. The second part of their discussion focused on the probable causes of these fluctuations and cycles. The statisticians noticed that cohorts (from the same smolt year class) returning over multiple years exhibited similar relative return rates. A good year of return of two ocean fish was followed by a good return of three ocean fish. They also found that there was no correlation between the numbers of breeding fish in the river during any one year and the numbers of offspring returning as adults. They reasoned that something at the smolt stage, yet to be discovered, was driving the survival of the fish. The authors compared the figures against those from other camps on the Restigouche and other rivers in the region and found similar results.

My suggestion is that early or late migration of juveniles to the ocean, per the solar-lunar shift in the solar year, and their subsequent experiences, primarily determine their success rates. As mentioned earlier, the Atlantic salmon juveniles migrate down river in solar-lunar rhythms. The food web in the marine environment is also tied to the rhythms of the sun and moon which might make early migrations, for instance, good, but some more profitable than others. We have seen evidence of the zooplankton (food for salmon juveniles in the marine environment) moving in the solar year with the rhythms of the moon. Perhaps the salmon have the greatest success when all of the positives are in alignment. This hypothesis, however, needs more investigation before a definitive conclusion can be drawn.

Regardless of what forms the base of these cycles, we can pattern them to the relative positions of the sun and moon. One approach is to look at the moon phase that fell on the Winter Solstice. A review of the data from the Restigouche River study indicated that when the first Full Moon occurred on this solar day, the returns one or two years later were at the peak in cycle, as described in Figure 6-1 [Appendix 6-1]. Indigenous peoples who understood this relationship could have used this information to time the highs and lows in the cycle and prepare for bountiful or lean years. The Full Moon at the Winter Solstice would have signaled that the best times were about to arrive and soon to pass. This year would have been when they had the means to trade with inland tribes, excess salmon to fertilize their fields and perhaps a good one to be born in. By combining this finding with those we have learned about from the other salmonids, the skilled astrobiologist can also predict when the fish will arrive over the solar year, the peak day in the lunar cycle and the time of day the fish are moving. This would certainly have provided a shaman with power and ensured the success of his people. I would have planned my trip to the Restigouche differently with this knowledge and perhaps scored an Atlantic salmon.

The Lynx and the Hare

The hypothesis of using the lunar shift to pattern success rates can be further explored with a terrestrial animal—the Canada lynx (*Lynx canadenis*). This big cat, along with its cousins in other Northern Hemisphere countries, is

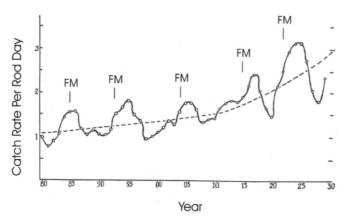

Figure 6-1: The Atlantic salmon fishery for the Restigouche River, New Brunswick, peaks in years just after the first Full Moon (waxing) occurs on the Winter Solstice. One could position other lunar phases against the Winter Solstice to predict the low years or upward and downward slopes. Indigenous peoples who charted the paths of the sun and moon could have observed these patterns and used this information to prepare for bountiful and lean years. The graph covers the years 1880 to 1930 and consists of a three-year moving average.[2]

ideal to continue this investigation due to the wealth of data available from trading companies dating back to the 1800s. In trying to explain the cycles of the lynx, ecologists also study those of the snowshoe hare (*Lepus americanus*), a major prey item of this carnivore. What is most interesting about the lynx and hare is that they both have recurring peaks of about 10 years. The cycle of the lynx is pictured in Figure 6-2. Arguments to explain the rhythmic patterns of the lynx focus on the availability of the hare, but the data doesn't support such a conclusion. In one Russian study, researchers found that the lynx pattern lagged one to two years behind the hare cycle. Populations of the hares rose with those of the lynx, but the number of cats increased even after those of the hares had crashed. How is this possible if they are exclusively tied to each other? Even if a predator-prey relationship could be established, it cannot be used to explain the precise timing over the years. The most compelling argument against this circular relationship is the existence of similarly timed cycles with Atlantic salmon and other animals. Surely this fish does not control the zooplankton populations in the ocean and create the relationship proposed for the lynx and hares. Thorough statistical analyses suggest that an exclusive circular cause-and-effect explanation between lynxes and hares is rather weak.[3]

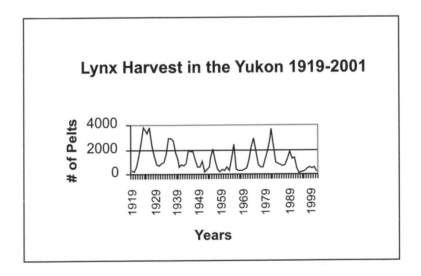

Figure 6-2: Lynx populations have a recurring pattern of about 10 years. The peaks, valleys and changes for each year can be timed by the lunar cycle.[4]

There may be another approach to this riddle. We previously observed the budding and blooming of the grape vine shifting with the moon against the solar year. The timing will provide food for an animal that feeds on it earlier in some years and later in others. Earlier or later budding will also affect overall growth of the leaves and fruit. The up years of hares may be partly tied to those of such a food supply, as well as to the animal's own lunar shifts. In regions such as the Arctic, with limited vegetation (food for the hare), the effect of the lunar shift should be more extreme than those in areas with a greater variety of food items. Other lunar shifts for the lynx, such as how early or late in the solar year the kittens are born, will offer this animal the opportunity to be more or less successful in the solar year. The time and place of this event will determine the opportunities for survival at the earliest stages. Another factor might be the health of the female cat during gestation. This could determine the fitness and possibly the number of kittens. There might be other critical events as well.

Whatever analysis is used to explore this matter, it must be confined to the smallest geographical area possible. Temperature and light varies by latitude and will have an effect on the food supply from the bottom up. The area of the northern provinces of Canada is much too broad; instead, I chose the smaller Yukon Territory. Data on the number of pelts harvested for the species is available from the Canadian government back to 1918. Data is not available on the specific timing per year for events, such as birthing of kittens or the food supply for the hares, but we can look at the behavioral patterns and pace them in the absence of this information.

Suppose we pattern the success of the lynx based on the lunar day that fell on the Vernal Equinox of each year. This tells us when conditions of light and darkness, and those organisms entrained to them, will recur. Using this methodology, the data of lynx abundance revealed that the peaks in the 10-year pattern generally occurred during the same lunar sequences of numbers [Appendix 6-2]. Similarly, if certain numbers occurred, the population would be increasing or decreasing from the previous year. In other words, the lynx, like the Atlantic salmon, were successful under the same (recurring) solar and lunar conditions. The recurring nature of the lynx pelt harvest and the frequency of the numbers strongly supports the application of the biological-time hypothesis, even if we cannot pinpoint the direct relationship between the lynx, the hares and the hares' food supply each year. The pace of the lynx can be patterned with the movements of the sun and moon, just as we have done with other plants and animals.

An obstacle in drawing a definitive conclusion with the lynx data is that it is based on numbers of pelts harvested. These figures are only an indirect indicator of the size of the population. Economic issues may sway the willingness of the trappers to harvest. In order to build a stronger case, we need a dataset based on actual counts of animals designed to estimate the population. One study where researchers counted collared lemmings (*Dicrostonyx groenlandicus*) in Greenland's high-Arctic tundra over a 15-year period may help us to better substantiate the biological-time hypothesis as being the base of long-term cycles in animals.[5] The duration of this study helps us to form conclusions that cannot be made in short-term fieldwork. An analysis of the data, whereby a lunar day that fell on the Vernal Equinox was tabulated (in the same manner as the lynx), demonstrated that there is a clear pattern for the changes in the population relative to the previous year [Appendix 6-4]. One could argue that these patterns are a result of a number of timed variables. The lemming primarily feeds on vegetation, thus the timing, quantity and quality of plants in its environment will be important. The numbers of predators of this lemming (arctic fox, stoat, snowy owl and long-tailed skua) will also be a factor, but they too will have their own fluctuations based on the lunar shift.

In the absence of a detailed multi-year study of all the organisms in the lemmings' environment, one can precisely time the fluctuations in the lemming population to the rhythms of the moon and sun. These patterns are likely present with all terrestrial animals. The recurring amplitude of the population, as it relates to the lunar cycle, strongly suggests that the role of meteorological conditions are minor in the timing and success rates of these animals.

Fruits and Nuts

If we can find predictive patterns between the sun and moon and animals that migrate, the pollination of the sycamore tree and the harvest of grapes, then why not with fruits and nuts from trees? I considered this question with hazelnuts (*Corylus avellona*), regionally called "filberts" in my home state of Oregon, which produces over 99 percent of the national production. Hazelnuts are commonly found in bowls of holiday mixed nuts, chocolate-covered and in breads and coffee. I am hardly a nut baron with an 18-acre orchard that has ended up serving as a well-groomed backyard and source of holiday gifts in some years. There are no fortunes to be made with such a small orchard, and with a coming blight the prospects do not look good for the long term.

One of the reasons for the low return on investment is that we have yearly shifts in the harvest levels, much like the runs of salmon in our rivers. Sometimes we have a big harvest, followed by a small one and then a good one again. Other times we may have three mediocre harvests in a row. Harvest levels are in proportion to other orchards in the state, suggesting that what affects our trees is common to all. The question that has puzzled hazelnut growers, and those of apples, plums, etc., is what controls these patterns.[6] To know how they were timed would give one the advantage of preparing for the harvest, both in managing the trees and the nuts after they fall. Conventional wisdom suggests that the fluctuations in the harvest are related to each other in a growth/regeneration cycle and that the trees have an internal mechanism to achieve this. Under this hypothesis, these trees would be categorized as "biennial." The up-and-down cycle is not regular in degree, thus I do not ascribe to this opinion. Others propose there is also a relationship to the weather, although no one has been able to support this idea in a statistical manner. The region has a mild climate due to its proximity to the Pacific Ocean, partly explaining why hazelnut trees were planted here.

What causes these patterns is difficult to say without yearly data for the events, such as the pollination of these trees. But we can make some reasonable guesses based on what we know about this plant and have learned from the sycamore and grapes. Hazelnut trees are monoecious, like the sycamore; however, they are rather unique in that the stamen (flower with male reproductive structure) and pistil (flower with female reproductive structures) are borne separately on the same plant. The stamens are encased in a part called the "catkin." The pistils are located next to the stigmas (pollen-receiving surfaces) that are only visible during the flowering season. For the majority of varieties, pollen shedding occurs over a period of one month or more, beginning at about the Western New Year. The pistils begin their blooming at the same time and typically last for over two months.

In some years, the pollen is so plentiful that the sky turns yellow during high winds, making an allergy sufferer like me miserable. Although millions of pollen grains are produced from each catkin, only a few pollen grains make their way to the female flower. Additionally, stigmatic surface receptivity reaches its optimum, on average, 15 days after the opening of the flower bud,[7] so a spike in pollen at that time or later, but perhaps not otherwise, results in a good set. Nut growers relate that a strong pollen count and set toward the end of January results in a good harvest. A review of hazelnut harvests indicated that they also peaked in years when the New Moon fell from January 15 to February 2. Inversely, the data demonstrate that the lowest harvest years were when the New Moon occurred from January 3 to January 14. This is a pattern indigenous and ancient people with solar and lunar calendars might have noticed.

Following pollination (the deposit of pollen on the stigma of the flower to begin fertilization), the pollen tube grows to the base of the style and remains there while the ovary matures. The ovary develops into what we call the meat of the nut, which is encased in the shell. In Oregon, the nuts generally fall during the month of October and are swept up by machines, dried and then packaged.[8]

The synchronization of the male and female parts for this tree alone does not determine the yield. Whether the tree directs its energies towards the development of the nuts or limbs during the year before the harvest is also important. The hazelnut tree pistils and stamens only flower on new growth. In spring, the maximum rate of shoot (limb) growth occurs at the same time as the development of the female ovule and in May with male flower induction. All of the tree's energies cannot be directed equally to each of these processes. In years with less nut development, there is greater growth of the branches, which in turn have the opportunity to produce more flowers the following year. High-yield years of nuts are generally associated with a following year of increased limb growth and lower nut production. If we were to combine the growth/regeneration and solar/lunar cycles of this plant, the rules to predict the harvests would be as follows:

1. There is an up/down cycle that periodically changes direction.

2. The optimal windows are when the first New Moon day of the harvest year occurs from January 15-February 2.
3. There is a peak in the optimal windows when the first New Moon day of the harvest year occurs from January 21-26.
4. The poor window is when the first New Moon day of the harvest year occurs January 3-14.

A more rigorous statistical analysis of the data revealed that during up years and when the New Moon was in the peak of the optimal window, the harvests were almost 15 percent better than when an up year coincided with a poor window. Similarly, when a down year in the cycle concurred with the optimal window, the harvests were about 15 percent better than when a down year coincided with a poor window [Appendix 6-5]. Can farmers pattern the yield of a tree based on the relative positions of the sun and moon? The answer is yes.

Self-Regulation

If salmon, geese, invertebrates, deer, elk, lynx, lemmings, grapes and hazelnut trees travel in a different time and space each year per the lunar shift against the solar year, thereby experiencing different environments, we should expect varying success rates and abundance. One could suggest that this is a form of self-regulation, since the mechanisms within each organism, conscious or not, respond to light or darkness. The moon does not reach out and physically move the animal, with the exception of lunar tides. Such a suggestion would challenge the "survival of the fittest" theory, as suggested by Charles Darwin, who partly premised his hypothesis on the proposition that without checks the number of species would instantly increase to any amount. The naturalist admitted in *The Origin of Species* (1859) that the checks for each species were obscure in any single instant, although he looked to climatic fluctuations (i.e., extreme hot or cold) as the primary cause of population control.

Changes in population are easy to substantiate with yearly climatic fluctuations, as these forces are difficult to measure and have wide latitude for interpretation. Was the snow pack heavier this year than last? Was it deeper everywhere or just where the elk migrate, causing a delay or death? No one can say for sure. Meteorologists even have different opinions on what has occurred. The cycles of the Atlantic salmon and lynx are too exact to be attributed to the weather. Most of the yearly variations for the timing of events and behavior demonstrated with the lunar cycle in this book were previously in print as being attributed to weather. For example, salmon runs are erroneously considered to be early or late each year due to fluctuations in river flow and temperature. In all cases, there was no mention of the moon in the papers or in correspondence from the agencies that provided the data. Based on the preceding analyses, climate did not appear to significantly influence the timing of migration and other major events for the plants and animals presented in this book. The lunar shift in timing, to early or later in the solar year, has a more consistent, predictable and greater influence on organisms than yearly fluctuations in the weather.

Summary

The relative successes and abundance of plants and animals appear to be partly based on specific alignments in their environment, as timed by the positions of the sun and moon. I refer to this phenomenon as "self-regulation", since the mechanisms within each organism respond to light or darkness. The sun and the moon do not have the capability to physically move terrestrial animals and plants. Self-regulation of species, as patterned by the lunar shift against the solar year, appears to be one explanation for the fluctuations in the numbers of individuals in populations.

Indigenous and ancient peoples could have compared the phases of the moon on a specific solar day, such as the Vernal Equinox or Winter Solstice, to pattern the timing and success of species. We have more information available to us than primitive man and the ancients in Mesopotamia, enabling us to not only see the patterns, but also to find natural and quantifiable reasons why they occur. We need not rely on superstitious rituals or the generosity of celestial deities to solve the riddles of time. The answers are in the rhythms of light and darkness above and around us. We just need to look more closely to see them.

CHAPTER 7

The Times of Our Lives

THE FATE OF THE SONS OF MEN AND THE FATE OF BEASTS IS THE SAME.
AS ONE DIES SO DIES THE OTHER; INDEED, THEY ALL HAVE THE SAME BREATH
AND THERE IS NO ADVANTAGE FOR MAN OVER BEAST, FOR ALL IS VANITY.
~ ECCLESIASTES 3:19

We start our journey through life being indoctrinated about how all life forms under the heavens are different. At the outset, one babbled sound is equated to mother and another to father. We are later told there are distinctions between plants and animals and learn of our special status above them. The dissimilarities between cats and dogs and the names of individual breeds are taught to us. We become adept at distinguishing by the variations. A German shepherd dog's ears are up while a Basset hound's flop down. The former has long legs and the latter short. There are volumes of books on the shelves of libraries about breeds of dog. Close inspection of each gives the impression that they are more different than horses and cows. The commonalities are rarely presented.

Small emotional rewards, such as a smile or clap, are given for our recognition of the difference between these life forms. Our vocabularies expand as we progress through the educational system. We become more knowledgeable about the smallest nuances between species of the same genus and how they may have changed through time. To demonstrate the validity of our hypotheses, we focus on one aspect of a plant or animal and attempt to separate our subjects from the many influences that control them. The highest degrees are awarded to those who have learned the most about one aspect of an organism under restricted conditions. At this stage in life, we have come a long way from the infant who made no distinctions.

Some scientists have turned full circle in their efforts by studying the influences of natural rhythms of light and darkness on life. Others inadvertently consider one measurement of light when they compare their data against a solar calendar. Although these researchers work with different organisms, there are common questions being asked and similar approaches applied across a wide range of fields. A limnologist may investigate the migrations of zooplankton to the darkness and from the light in a lake, while an aquatic entomologist might explore similar influences on the movements of insects in a stream. Yet despite all of the differences we learn about the creatures that inhabit this planet, we return to a single common denominator that controls all life. This force is the direct light that emanates from the stars, especially our closest one, and indirectly from the moon, and the darkness in their absence. All life forms share them and are commonly affected. This should be no surprise since we are all made from the same stardust.

The Rhythms of the Night

Based on the range of species given as examples in the preceding chapters, one can reasonably argue that the rhythms of all organisms, from the smallest invertebrates to the majestic elk, are primarily governed by natural cycles of light and darkness. These rhythms are the most basic conditions that all organisms encounter. We do not have endogenous (internally driven) lunar rhythms, but biological clocks that are reset, primarily by cycles of light and darkness, are in our design, just as they are with plants and other animals.

The question about actual synchronization to the moon for humans has been considered in studies of women in post-industrialized societies. The results vary, suggesting that if such rhythms exist they are not endogenous.[1] Similarly, a salmon in an aquarium may not appear to have lunar rhythms, but in this environment the fish does not experience the range of natural illumination nor does it require certain lighting conditions to feed or escape from predators. The salmon are fed, much like when we pull a packaged meal from the refrigerator or sit down in a restaurant. Perhaps our rhythms are a matter of conditioning, currently tied to artificial light and dark cycles via electric lighting.

This is not to say we cannot or have not experienced lunar rhythms. The South Pacific islanders that Johannes studied posted a tide table to a wall in the hospital room to predict when women would deliver. Johannes curiously followed up on this practice by checking two years of birth records from the hospital and learned that there was no relationship between the daily tides and birthrate, but that 25 percent more births occurred during Neap Tides than Spring Tides. The statistical likelihood of this happening by chance is one in twenty. Is this a general human condition or does the phenomenon occur because the islanders synchronized their lives to those of the fish, that were in turn entrained to a lunar clock via their own predator-prey relationships? I suggest the latter. If a normal pregnancy lasts 280 days, then the day of birth can be worked backward to have the conception timed close to a specific day, or at least period of cycle. We know that the islanders were targeting the grouping and migrating fish during certain phases of the moon, and were traditionally given to dancing and revelry on nights around the Full Moon. Therefore, their opportunities for copulation would have been more opportune during some days of the lunar cycle than others.

Johannes noted in his book that these women typically carried out their daily garden and house routines in groups, so synchronization of their cycles was likely. There is a wealth of research to support the hypothesis that animals secrete chemical cues, commonly called "pheromones", which can help to synchronize behavior within the same species. When I lived in China, a young co-ed related to me that all of the eight ladies in her cramped dorm room had the same emotional highs and lows. I took this to mean, in a veiled manner, that their menstrual cycles were in sync. The idea was difficult for me to believe at the time, but later studies with human females confirmed that a group could synchronize their menstrual cycles based on the pheromones of one person.[2] The female deer under Richard Price's observation probably had such pheromone synchronization as well. Thus, the female islanders were not internally in tune with the rhythms of the moon. The environment in which they lived and their lifestyle conditioned them to this cycle of light. We might be better entrained to the light of the moon if we were more exposed to the natural environment and/or dependent on harvesting wild fish and game for survival.

The effect of light and darkness during the nights is not unique to the human primate. Apes have been found to be very active for the whole night at Full Moon, while at New Moon their activity is at a minimum, restricted to dusk and dawn.[3] Why might this be so? Continuous light affects organisms differently than during a light/dark sequence. Such differences help to time certain behavior. Examples include the pre-spawn grouping of Coho salmon and the herding of deer and elk under the continuous light of the Full Moon.

The light of a Full Moon night has an eerie comfortable feeling that keep us awake while camping in the bush. Scores of songs have been written about the power of these evenings. There is magic in the air when the afterglow of day bridges into the rising moon in all its brilliance, as if the sun never sets and continues through the night. Countless lyricists have set this mood with tunes. One music group, King Harvest, expressed the feeling in their song: *Dancing in the Moonlight.*

We get it on most every night
When that old moon gets so big and bright
It's a supernatural delight

Everybody was dancin' in the moonlight
Everybody here is out of sight
They don't bark, and they don't bite
They keep things loose, they keep things light
Everybody was dancin' in the moonlight

Dancin' in the moonlight
Everybody's feelin' warm and right
It's such a fine and natural sight
Everybody's dancin' in the moonlight

This human connection to the moon might have been more functional than just when to dance. A woman's menstrual cycle, at an average of 29.5 days, is perfectly timed to the moon. This is probably not accidental. But the how and why of this design are unanswered questions. Some peoples such as the aboriginal New Zealanders, the Maori, call menstruation "mata marama" which means moon sickness, and in many countries the words moon and menstruation are the same. The Seneca people in the northeastern region of the United States refer to the moon as "grandmother." Through her changing cycles, she tells women when their bodies are fertile and when they experience their moon times, or menstrual flows.[4] The capability to be entrained to moon light is inherently within us.

Early man may have similarly associated the phases of the moon to the cycles of people. Found at the Lascaux cave was an extraordinary 1-foot-6-inch stone carving called "Venus of Laussel," as pictured in Figure 7-1, of an apparently pregnant woman with her left hand on her womb and what I would suggest is a Crescent Moon in her right hand. Others have suggested the object is just a horn with incidental marks. But, note that there are 13 notches. If the Crescent Moon is day one and 13 are added, then we enter into the Full Moon period, just as these Ice Age men likely counted the phases to determine the behavior of red deer and other animals. Is this a relationship to the female's menstrual cycle and when she is most able to conceive or give birth? If the Ice Age hunters were not available for copulation during certain lunar phases, as were the islanders under Johannes's study, then there would

Figure 7-1: This stone-carved image called "Venus of Laussel" appears on an outcropping outside the Lascaux cave. The apparently pregnant woman holds a Crescent Moon-shaped horn with 13 markings. The markings on the horn are likely leading to the Full Moon, and probably have relevance to the timing of childbirth and/or menstrual cycles.[5]

have been a tendency for childbirth to occur under certain moon phases. The relationship would have been even stronger if the menstrual cycles of the women in the tribe were synchronized.

Message in a Tumor

No one can definitively say what Venus of Laussel, real or mythical, was telling us. The artist is no longer here to confirm her message. One interpretation might be that time is an integral part of us. We can neither avoid its passing nor should we disrupt its natural rhythms. This is a concept modern man has yet to come to terms with. We muse that birth, death and taxes are the only sure stops on our journey through life, but each minute of the day and night are purposely designed. Yet, in spite of our limited mortal capacities, we distort time and our physiology when we artificially control light to lengthen our days, as if attempting to make the sun stand still. This feat enables us to do more of the pleasurable things in life. We might also add overtime to our paychecks, appease the boss and find employment when others are less willing to work. Some of us push our bodies even further when we travel to other time zones and unnaturally experience a great deal more hours of direct sunlight. As such, we shorten our nights and miss the vital physiochemical changes that go along with this important period of rest. One consequence of this behavior appears to be an increased risk of breast cancer.

Breast cancer is a malignant tumor in the glandular tissues of the breast. It falls in the category of carcinomas, which form when the processes that control normal cell growth break down, enabling an abnormal cell to multiply rapidly. The cancer tends to destroy an increasing portion of normal breast tissue over time and may spread to other parts of the body. It is the second most common cancer in women, next to skin cancer, and the second leading cause of cancer death in women, after lung cancer. The American Cancer Society estimates that about 220,300 new cases are diagnosed every year in the United Sates and 39,800 women will die from the disease. Breast cancer can affect males, but the disease strikes women about 100 times more often than men. The American Cancer Society has identified people with greater risks of afflicting breast cancer such as heavy smokers and drinkers, those overweight, and people on hormone pills. A close blood relative with breast cancer also increases the odds. Risk is higher in urban than rural areas[6] and women in less developed/agricultural countries have a lower incidence of breast cancer than those in developed countries.

Breast cancer is also an occupational hazard. Increased risk has been documented for flight attendants[7] and night-shift workers.[8] One study with flight attendants in California found that the proportion of females diagnosed with all types of cancers combined was no different than that of the general population. However, female flight attendants on domestic routes had a greater frequency of contracting breast cancer than the general population and those on international schedules had an even higher chance than the domestic ones. Researchers studying Nordic cabin crews came to similar conclusions.[9] The flight attendants and the night-shift workers were exposed to more light hours (less darkness) than women who work in the home or a nine-to-five office day. The extra light is both unnatural under the artificial luminance in the cabin and natural through the cracks in their shades while sleeping during the day. These conditions do not suit our physiology. We are designed to have active and resting components in our daily cycle. The latter allows for regeneration.

There is research that strongly supports the conclusion that mammary cancer is tied to the length and timing of light or darkness received. Studies have also shown that there is a low incidence of breast tumors among blind women, who transmit signals indicating the presence of less light to their pineal body,[10] as well as an inverse relationship between breast cancer incidence and the degree of visual impairment (increasing amount of light received escalates the chance of breast cancer).[11] When animals are given chemically induced mammary tumors, the general conclusion is that experimental manipulation, activating the pineal gland, or the administration of melatonin lengthens the latency and reduces the incidence and growth rate of such tumors.[12] When the pineal gland is removed and the animal cannot synthesize melatonin, the opposite effect occurs.[13] Prolonged oral melatonin treatment in mice significantly reduces the development of mammary tumors.[14] Therefore, we can reasonably conclude that more rest at night, resulting in greater amounts of melatonin, in some manner reduces the incidence of some tumors.

Melatonin production occurs at night and makes us sleepy. It is tied to another chemical—estrogen—that is circumstantially related to breast cancer and used in the treatment of some forms. The synthesis of melatonin is believed to be nature's way of resting the human body. In contrast, the absence of this chemical might not allow the regeneration cycle to fully take place. Studies on the rhythms of women further support the hypothesis that breast cancer is related to biorhythms. A noncancerous breast has a 24-hour rhythm, whereas a breast with malignancies has 20-, 40- and 80-hour periodicities.[15] In other words, the temperature pattern of a breast cancer containing a cancerous tumor is different from a breast with no cancer. This is a fairly important discovery, as it ties an abnormal condition to the rhythms of the body.[16]

The understanding that there is a relationship between biorhythms and breast cancer dates in modern scientific literature to the late 1970s.[17] This may have also been understood in practice by ancient peoples. However, the concept is recently gaining more recognition. A company has developed a device to measure the temperature of a woman's breast over a two-day period to determine if a tumor is present. This device is an early warning system. Thus far, no one has found a cure for breast cancer. Is this because the only cure is prevention through adhering to our natural rhythms? We can hope for a magic pill but the prospects do not look good.

Remnants From Our Past

Breast cancer is not a Euro-American, post-industrialized or ethnic condition. The development of the tumor appears to be a consequence of our abuse of time. Physical and psychological conditions that are influenced by light are similar among people. Around the Winter Solstice we can feel the death of night and become depressed, as we are commonly affected by the reduction in natural light. Through this dark period, we need an alarm clock to wake us in the morning and may still feel groggy until that first dose of caffeine. My family doctor relates that he has many more patients suffering from depression during the two months that straddle the Winter Solstice than the rest of the year combined. There is even a clinical term for winter depression—Seasonal Affective Disorder (SAD). The prescribed treatment is to sit in front of a very bright light for 20 to 40 minutes a day in the morning during the fall and winter months. A week on a Florida beach or ski trip to Utah where the bright sun gleams off the snow can also help us feel better. Ancient peoples did not have these luxuries. The shroud of long nights would have been more profound.

The shift to days of longer lengths after the Vernal Equinox changes us. Daybreak beats our alarm clocks to the punch and we wake in better spirits. We feel new. The birds visit our windowsill, the buds of plants break and "spring fever" is in the air for the young. If Ice Age man and the ancients in Mesopotamia had survived to this time of the year, they would have cheated the death of winter and had another chance at life. This is the biology of time. It controls us and the creatures and plants in our world.

We still possess remnants of these concepts. They are found in religious themes that are common across ancient and modern cultures. The Winter Solstice is tied to death and birth—the Vernal Equinox with rebirth, the Summer Solstice with fertility and the Autumnal Equinox with thanksgiving. As mentioned earlier, Catholics and Protestants time Easter, a day of rebirth, to the Vernal Equinox and Full Moon. The word <u>E</u>aster comes from *Eastre*, the Anglo-Saxon name of a prehistoric German dawn goddess of spring and fertility, whose festival was celebrated at the Vernal Equinox. This name may also be associated with the Babylonian god <u>Ea</u> who also rose in the <u>ea</u>st on the same solar day. Oddly enough, when the words solstice and equinox are brought up, we usually think of pagan festivals. "Pagan" is a term commonly used to describe any number of non-Christian belief systems, but the actual meaning is different. The term's origin is from the Latin word *paganus* meaning "country dweller." What we fail to realize is that these celestial observances were what ensured the survival of the people in a less industrialized age.

The words are sometimes different but the themes remain the same. The Greeks use the word "Pascha" for Easter. It is the eternal "pass over" from death to life and from earth to heaven. One Greek legend tells of the return of Persephone, daughter of Demeter, goddess of the earth, from the underworld to the light of day. Her return symbolized to the ancient Greeks the resurrection of life in the spring after the desolation of winter. Other ancient peoples shared similar beliefs. The Phrygians believed that their omnipotent deity went to sleep at the time of the Winter Solstice. At the Vernal Equinox, they performed ceremonies with music and dancing to awaken him. If we look back even further, the Mesopotamian New Year on the first Crescent Moon after the Vernal Equinox was celebrated with the awakening of the god Marduk from the dark underworld, and represented the creation of world order. This ceremony also meant renewal, a common theme of religious celebrations held at this time.

In Greece, the Winter Solstice ritual was called *Lenaea*, the Festival of the Wild Women. In very ancient times, a man representing the harvest god Dionysus was torn to pieces and eaten by a gang of women on this day. Later in the ritual, Dionysus would be reborn as a baby—birth again being celebrated as well as ritually eating the deity. This story probably originated from ancient Egypt where the god-man/savior Osiris died and was entombed on December 21. At his moment of death, the priests brought out a baby, indicating his immediate rebirth.

The Roman emperor Aurelian (270 to 275 BCE) blended a number of solstice celebrations of such god-men/saviors as Apollo, Attis, Baal, Dionysus, Helios, Hercules, Horus, Mithra, Osiris, Perseus, and Theseus into a single festival called the "Birthday of the Unconquered Sun" on December 25. The date Christians celebrate the birth of Jesus Christ is closely aligned to the Winter Solstice, and the birth of St. John the Baptist is celebrated around the Summer Solstice or the flipside of solar time.

Western civilization is not alone in using celestial movements to find meaning in life. At the Winter Solstice, the Eskimos held a festival to rejoice over the return of the sun and the coming good hunting conditions. Such a festival would have been warranted in the long arctic winter. In a more moderate climate, the Incas held their great festival of the sun in December, regulated by both the sun and moon. Many indigenous peoples in North American held festivals that were closely tied to the solstices and equinoxes.

The Chinese, and other Asian cultures, celebrate the beginning of their New Year (literal translation as "Spring Festival") on the second New Moon after the Winter Solstice. Family reunions, the forgiving of grievances and paying of debts take place during the 15-day holiday period, beginning on the New Moon and ending on the Full Moon. During the celebrations, the Chinese set off fireworks to scare away the evil spirit "nian." The word "nian" is the same as the one used for year. The Chinese also celebrate a death-and-rebirth theme on Chun Fen (meaning "Spring Equinox"), and another 15 days after the Vernal Equinox (called "Chen Ming," meaning "pure brightness") by cleaning the overgrown grass from the graveyards of their ancestors and bringing them food. The Chinese are not newcomers to the study of time.

They had started to compute time from 2696 BCE, during the reign of the Yellow Emperor, Huang Ti, when his prime minister devised a system of 60-year cycles. In the twenty-third century BCE, the Emperor Yao commanded his astronomers to observe the solstice and fix the dates of the four seasons so that farmers might know when to plant their seeds and harvest their crops.

Summary

People who have greater contact with natural environments over a 24-hour period and those who live by hunting of game and harvesting fish with primitive techniques may have exogenous solar and lunar rhythms. The rhythms are a reaction to the outside world, both by design and behaviorally initiated. Their entrainment to these rhythms is a requirement for success, much like those of the other life forms we have seen. Some of these people who live and work in close quarters may be synchronizing their cycles among the group, making the lunar effect a part of their daily, monthly and seasonal tribal lives.

One of the peculiarities of our species is that we distort our natural rhythms, via the harnessing of light, in order to achieve nonbiologically constructive economic and social goals. But, in the course of cheating nature, we appear to bring upon ourselves afflictions such as breast cancer. The distorted rhythms of female flight attendants and night-shift workers are just extremes of the unnatural conditions we all experience in our modern world and that we were not designed to accommodate without dire consequences.

We now place our faith in a mixture of religion and physical cycles to understand the nature of our existence and find order in our everyday lives. Some observances of equinoxes and solstices and the movements of the moon to mark time and express seasonal experiences that were common across hunter-gatherer and ancient agricultural societies are still celebrated today.

CHAPTER 8

Losing Our Place in Time

These were the words scribed in chalk on the Caltech classroom black-board of the Noble Laureate physicist at the time of his death in 1988. Feynman considered himself to be a Babylonian thinker, such that his reasoning was based on observation and interpretation of the physical process and not entirely driven by mathematics. He patterned behavior and then went back to find explanations that could be quantified. His intellectual process was likely acquired from his father who walked him through the woods as a youth, examining and reasoning through the wonders of nature. Feynman's nemesis in the world of theoretical physics was his fellow Noble Laureate Murray Gell-Mann (who hypothesized the concept of quarks). In contrast to Feynman, his adversary was a Greek thinker who, in the spirit of the great mathematicians—Pythagoras, Thales and Euclid—needed to have everything precisely planned and measured. To Gell-Mann, there had to be a hypothesis, then a proof and not vice versa.[1]

Feynman's statement can also be considered a criticism of the practice by which we use complex statistics in an attempt to recreate the environment of an organism both numerically and in a laboratory environment before considering how it survives through each day. More specifically, we need to know how the life form is timed. The key questions to begin the study of any organism are how and when events are timed and synchronized with others in its community. From there we can go on to study place and then seek to understand the processes behind the patterns. This nonlinear approach may seem backwards, but alternative methods are sometimes the only way to solve difficult problems, as demonstrated by Feynman through his infamous career. A more prevalent approach today is that of the Greeks, as typified by Gell-Mann, where we seek statistically validated answers to our hypotheses regardless of whether they have any relevance to what actually occurs. We utilize these numbers in an attempt to control the natural world with little knowledge of how plants and animals really tick. Feynman's train of thought speaks the truth to many of our bungles with endangered species and, in particular, to the plight of the Pacific salmon.

Timing is Everything

An example of how our lack of knowledge about the salmon has negatively affected them can be demonstrated with our handling of these fish on the Columbia River. Barging the juvenile salmonids downstream to the lower Columbia has been one of the strategies to help the fish avoid the human-created gauntlet in the main river. Although shipping the juveniles downstream has increased the returns of adults an entirely new problem emerged.[2] Avian predators, especially the Caspian terns (*Sterna caspia*) in the Lower Columbia River estuary have capitalized on the inexperienced hatchery juveniles. Over 85 percent of the diet of the Caspian tern is composed of salmonids.[3] The terns are not the only avian predators. Two other notable birds are the double-crested cormorants (*Phalacrocorax auritus*) and the glaucous-winged western gulls (*Larus glaucescens X L. occidentalis*). In 1998, the estimated total consumption of juvenile salmonids by all fish-eating colonial water birds in the Columbia River estuary was 16.7 million smolts or 18 percent of those that reached the estuary. The terns, however, have drawn a great deal of attention. Rice Island, a dredge material disposal island in the estuary, supports the largest known Caspian tern colony in North America (about 8,000 breeding pairs) and the only known breeding colony of this species in coastal Oregon and Washington. The population has grown by over 600 percent since the island was discovered in 1986.

Why did the terns become so effective in their foraging? The answer is simple. Fish hatcheries do not take into account the amount of light or the absence of this force during the release of smolts. The juveniles are also conditioned to be day-active surface feeders in the hatcheries, on schedules that are more hospitable to humans. Caspian terns are day-active, low-tide, surface-feeding predators. As a result, the hatcheries are conditioning the smolts to look for food when they are most vulnerable.[4]

Moreover, barging, as presently operated, sometimes considers the night, but not the lunar cycle of light. Salmon smolts released from barges around the Full Moon will stay put, whereas a darker-moon release of the juveniles will stimulate seaward migration. Thus, the smolts are being laid out on a table to be easily consumed by avian predators. In contrast, under natural circumstances, the smolts would not be migrating during the periods when the birds could most easily prey on them. It is a wonder that any juveniles from the hatcheries in the Columbia River system survive to adulthood and that the mistimed wild smolts are not decimated.

State and federal fisheries communities are interested in programs that will lessen predation on the salmonid juveniles, which would also involve reducing the tern population. But other groups, such as the National Audubon Society, American Bird Conservancy and the Defenders of Wildlife filed a lawsuit against any action until data is obtained to form a more scientifically sound conclusion. According to Gerald Winegrad from the American Bird Conservancy, "Caspian terns were made into convenient scapegoats for the decline of Columbia River salmon, simply because they eat juvenile salmonids, over 90 percent of which are hatchery-reared."[5] The birders have a point. The terns are doing nothing out of the ordinary. Due to our lack of understanding of the animals, man has created an environment that is helping them to feed more effectively during their nesting period.

Lost in Space

Our interaction with the Columbia River salmon is typical of our practice of attempting to manage species without understanding them, as Feynman chalked on the board.

How did we lose our place in time? Usually old beliefs are replaced by new theories, but this is not the case with the ancient Mesopotamian concepts of time. They were never formally refuted or discredited, but there were competing ideas—some bolstered by the political sway of new and conquering faiths. Any scientific truth that contradicts a religious doctrine is in for opposition. People quickly learn it is expedient to adopt the beliefs of the victors. Inquisitions among a number of religions in the old and new worlds ensured abiding followers.

The transition in thought cannot be entirely attributed to the persuasion of new religions. Man had also reconsidered his position in the cosmos. He determined that there were no answers to be found by observation of the celestial bodies. The seasonal deities of more ancient times and nature worship of indigenous peoples symbolized our having gone astray and when our thoughts were simpler, less complete. A relationship between man and his maker was all that was required for order and balance. An early supporter of this idea was the Greek philosopher, Aristotle (around 370 BCE), who argued that time was man's province alone. This is a concept the hunter-gatherers who lived in concert with the rhythms of plants and animals would have had legitimate cause to doubt. Time is for all organisms in all places. Aristotle's views were corroborated by the Greek astronomer, Claudius Ptolemy of Alexandria (approx. 87-150 ADE), who calculated, although incorrectly so, that the earth was at the center of the universe. Their geo-centrist philosophies became doctrine in Western and Middle Eastern societies, despite the tens of thousands of years of contrary practical knowledge.

There was not a serious detractor to this new dogma until fourteen centuries after Ptolemy when the Polish astronomer Nicolaus Copernicus (1473-1543) argued in his book, *The Revolution of the Heavenly Orbs* (1543), that the earth rotates around the sun and motion should be measured against this fixed point. Copernicus's work was a leap forward in astronomy and physics. But at the same time, the discovery drew attention away from everything else, and the association of plants and animals to the celestial bodies appeared to be forever lost from Western thought. This new Copernican astronomy was strictly a physical science, without any biological association.

Closely following the lead of Copernicus was the Italian astronomer and physicist Galileo Galilei (1564-1642), who looked through a self-made telescope and observed that the moons of Jupiter revolved around that planet. He made calculations that suggested the Earth was also in motion, and that the stars had movements independent of the sun, a concept the ancients in Mesopotamia had documented some years earlier. Therefore, neither the earth nor the sun could be the center of the universe. They are relative to each other; just as time is relative to the object it is measured against. Modern philosophers suggest the undertone in Galileo's argument was that man couldn't be at the center of all things. This is only one perspective. Another would have been that the celestial bodies did indeed control mankind. This notion may be why discussion of the moon's cycles in certain religious circles, prior to Galileo, was taboo. The worry would have been for naught, as this inquisitive astronomer did not appear to make the connection between celestial cycles and the rhythms of plants and animals, as did indigenous peoples and those in the Persian Gulf region a thousand years before him. His colleague and fellow astronomer, Johannes Kepler, argued against the notion.[6] Both Galileo and Kepler looked for the answers to nature in physics.

The Lunar Problem

We sometimes forget our own ancestral beliefs about the cosmos and the importance of the moon. In Genisis we read, "God made the two great lights, the greater light to dominate the day and the lesser light to dominate the night."[7] To Westerners outside the worlds of astronomy, physics and oceanography, the word "moon" brings to mind a connection other than the timing of organisms—lunacy. Westerners often associate the Full Moon with the mythical story of the werewolf, romantic serenades and what they consider Asian and Middle Eastern mysticism. This is a common perception in our solar calendar-entrained society where we are not accustomed to serious thoughts of the moon except for space exploration. The subject of lunar influence on organisms has not been sufficiently considered in the scientific literature. Only recently was there a comprehensive inventory of the work on this subject organized by Drs. Klaus-Peter Endres and Wolfgang Schad from the University of Witten-Herdecke in Germany in their 1997 book, *Moon Rhythms in Nature: How Lunar Cycles Affect Living Organisms*. So much is dependent on moon phase, yet one could leaf through years of biological journals without mention of the word. A great deal of the lunar information we have on animals was derived from the practices of indigenous peoples and later noticed by enterprising scientists. Other information on lunar relationships was found by chance. Many naturalists and biological scientists, who noted lunar phases in their work, found a relationship between behavior, such as mating or migration, and the New or Full Moon. But plants and animals do not have "lunar events". Each day in the cycle has a different exposure to light and darkness. The combination of the sun, moon and physiological condition of the organism are what time the behavior, resulting in the event. To my knowledge, this book is the first to capture and explain the solar and lunar rhythms of plants and animals through their lives. The anadromous salmon made research on the lunar influence possible due to the tremendous amount of data we have on their migratory behavior. These fish are not always in the same portion of the river or ocean; each aspect of their lives is in a different time and place. Solar and lunar patterns are more difficult to find with nonmigrating animals, such as trout, that spend most of their life in a small stretch of river, lake or hatchery. The lack of data throughout the life of an animal does not preclude that animal from having lunar rhythms. We can put together the pieces of the puzzle with one or two experiences.

The Consolidation of Knowledge

The scientific exploration of physics and religious pressures do not fully explain how the knowledge was lost to us. There must be other reasons. The suggestion has been made that the ancients in Mesopotamia had the ability to forecast the success of plants and animals, based on the position of the moon to the sun. The understandings of mathematical processes to perform these feats were probably not widespread throughout any population. The fishermen surely knew to cast their nets and the shepherds to await the dropping of lambs during evenings when the moon was dark, but which lunation in the solar year and the success rate were calculations only a privileged few could have made. The chosen would have been priestly castes who listened to the celestial guardians of time and related their will to the people. This closely held knowledge enabled the Mesopotamian priests to control the kings who were re-sanctified each year at the Vernal Equinox New Year's ceremony. Certification by these wise men was of utmost importance and ensured that prosperous times would follow. They had no hereditary rule. Any Mesopotamian king would have been pleased with this arrangement, as the practice gave him the ability to prepare for lean years and subside unrest among the populace. All that was required of him was to give respect to the priests and follow their prophecies. Meanwhile, the populace in neighboring nations would have lived hand-to-mouth. Expected famine in other lands might even have translated into future campaigns against them. Such campaigns could have been precisely timed and defenses built to withstand them.

The process of keeping this information from the common man might have given the priests a reason to build towers, such as the famous one in Babylon. They didn't need formal observatories to chart the movements of the sun, moon, planets and stars as these celestial bodies can be viewed just as clearly from the ground. Some scholars suggest that the Mesopotamian towers were referencing the positions against distant ones. The towers in the Mesopotamian cylinder seal where the sun god Shamash rises through appear to be of masonry rather than geologic origin. They were more likely using mortared openings at the top of their towers as we find in Middle Age castles. Such architecture remains near Persepolis in ancient Persia and is believed to have been in the working area of the high priests.

Scholars similarly suggest that the cave at Lascaux would have been frequented by a limited number of people, perhaps just the shaman who guided the clan. The tight spaces in the cave did not facilitate large audiences. The construction of the Yurok fish dam on the Kalama River was performed under the direction of one lead man, the shaman, and his assistant. The shaman might not have been the greatest warrior, hunter or even leader, but he had the power to see the future, an important skill that brought success to his people. The towers in Mesopotamia probably had a similar secrecy value. Few would have been allowed access to the viewing areas and an even smaller number would have known how to decipher the code. Only a few priests would have known that the ceremonies were a ruse for the simpler astrobiology and they would not have benefited by disclosing that truth.

This may also be why Joseph said the knowledge came from dreams. Clearly there was no benefit to this patriarch in revealing the solar-lunar mechanism to his sun-oriented Egyptian captors, who were apparently unaware of the cycles and weather-forecasting techniques. He definitely would not have benefited from letting the pharaoh in on his knowledge (he should have learned a lesson after revealing the insight to his own flesh and blood) and thus sharing the credit. The Mesopotamian priests also involved the king in their omen-seeking. The technique was probably not widely disseminated among Joseph's people, let alone offered to their enemies. Only the learned ones were educated to a level that enabled them to read the sacred works, and few in such a class would have the code revealed to them. These ideas may explain why the knowledge was lost as we marched through time.

The Joseph Hypothesis

We have found many common threads of understanding about biological time among prehistoric, ancient and indigenous peoples. They include (1) positioning the movements of the moon against the sun to determine an organism's success rate and timing of events, (2) forecasting weather with the Pleiades star cluster and constellation Orion, and resetting the time to plant crops in response, (3) knowing multi-year patterns of plants and animals, (4) controlling critical astrobiological information by priestly castes, (5) starting each month at the Crescent Moon and (6) the observation of universal religious themes at the equinoxes and/or solstices and around certain phases of the moon. These issues that the cavemen, Incas, Mesopotamians, and indigenous peoples held dear are timeless.

The widespread use of this information begs the question of how diverse peoples, separated geographically and by millennia, came by this knowledge. Technology, such as understanding the biology of time, is learned and passed on. The knowledge is not an innate ability that is genetically with us. Could all of these peoples have independently figured out the same thing? I do not see such a hypothesis as likely. My thought is that there was a man who first came to the realization that there was order in the cosmos. Perhaps an appropriate name for him would be Joseph. This Joseph had some control over his circumstances instead of reacting to them. His discovery led to the precise timing for harvesting fish and game, developing crop management practices for lean and bountiful years, mating domesticated animals most effectively and predicting pestilence. This man's contribution was as significant as the first tool chiseled from stone or the ignition of a flame. Joseph was not the original shaman or priest, but he was the original prophet as he could legitimately tell his people what was to come. When he looked to the skies, the voices from the cosmos gave him answers that were true and valuable to his people.

The concept of a single person being the root of this knowledge is based on the premise that no one in the so-called "advanced civilizations" over the last thousand or more years appears to have fully decoded the biology of time, or at least recorded the hypothesis in a convincing manner for posterity. The clues have been available for all to see. How many millions have read Genesis or heard the story of the Canaanite Joseph and believed that he forecasted the crops through dreams? The *Bible* is the mostly widely distributed book in human history with close to 100 million new copies sold each year. Few would argue against the *Bible* being the most closely examined book of all time as well. Many cultures still use lunar-solar calendars, yet they do not seem to have made the far-ranging connections between the physical rhythms above our heads and the biological ones around us. This suggests that such an understanding is not easily found.

A case could be made that the Yami, Tulalip and Yurok knew of these secrets, but these were actually practices tied to traditions within the tribes. There is no evidence that they were consciously aware of the biological basis for the traditions. Otherwise, they would have made connections to a wide range of organisms. Moreover, in interviews with tribal biologists, connections between the stories from their clans and academic work were not made. The traditions may have been in their tribes for millennia. In any case, if the hypothesis were so easy to figure out, then the common man wouldn't have needed a tribal shaman.

Being in periodic contact with nature (as gardeners, birders, anglers, hunters or even ecologists) does not necessarily result in enlightenment either. Tens of millions of people who fall into these categories have walked with the rhythms of plants and animals without realizing there was a pace. The scientific literature is full of excellent work on biological clocks, although the moon is mentioned in only a small number of them. Even among biological papers with lunar observances, the positioning of a moon phase against the sun seems to have been overlooked. There have been a few instances in the last century where scientists appeared to have been on the trail of this discovery, but for some reason they did not follow through on the work from a broader perspective. Despite these oversights, one must also leave open room for the possibility that some people had come upon this knowledge but kept it secret.

The knowledge of my hypothesized Joseph would not have been as complete, or rituals as colorful, as those of the Inca or ancients in Mesopotamia. He probably knew how to count the phases of the moon and position by this body against a solar reference point (possibly a plant or animal). This early scientist may even have read weather patterns by the stars, although the discovery could have been made by one of his descendants. All of the pieces of this puzzle were not put together in one starry night. There was a wide range of understanding among different peoples. Thus we can reason that cultures developed aspects of the practice to suit their unique needs, applying the basic principles as they went along. Some knew that Pleiades, Orion and Hyades could be used for weather forecasting, as these stars were important to them, while others had no need to keep that tradition. Knowledge among fishermen varied, suggesting adaptation to local circumstances. The Yami are interested in marine fish, the Tulalip focus on the first salmon in the bays, while the Mesopotamians and Yurok were concerned with the runs of fish in the upper reaches of their rivers. Each species of fish and harvest location required a slightly different variation to the calendar.

Where and when did this Joseph realize nature had a grander scheme? Ishango man in Africa deciphered the lunar cycle about 8,500 years ago. But the technology of the cavemen at Lascaux was clearly more advanced, dating to about 8,000 years earlier. Marshack worked out the lunar calendar on bones from southern European sites, believed to date back to roughly 34,000 years ago. In his book, *Guns, Germs, and Steel* (1999), Jared Diamond refers to this period as "The Great Leap Forward." This window in history is when man was believed to have begun stabilizing into the one generalized species *Homo sapiens*. Diamond and others have not been able to explain this transition period. Joseph's realization may have made this revolution in mankind possible.

What have been some consequences of our blindness? Domesticated crops and animals could have been more stably and cost effectively provided. We could have managed our harvest of animals in the wild better or at least not inhibited them during their critical periods. We certainly would have come up with different interpretations about archeological finds and stories from the ancients. More importantly, there might have been a greater appreciation of the advances made by men who walked this earth long before written history. And by better understanding our origins, we could have looked for what commonly binds everything together rather than what tears us apart.

Summary

The Ice Age men who painted animals on the walls of the cave at Lascaux saw the relationship between light and animals and had an understanding of the nature of cyclic time, which gave them the ability to predict the future. Earlier man would have lived in the rhythms of the sun and moon, although he would have just reacted to them and been at the whims of the environment. He could now prepare for the harvests and hunts months or years in advance instead of reacting to the plants and animals, as an insect, hare or deer do today. Perhaps this ability to foretell the future is what gave us the edge over our competitors.

Although the unique relationship between the thinkers, leaders and hunters may have allowed our distant ancestors to succeed over their human competitors, the consolidation of knowledge did not ultimately benefit mankind, the other animals or plants in the long term. Others may have stumbled onto pieces of the puzzle in more recent times but did not know enough to put them together into a workable theory. Physicists lead the revolution in our concepts of time and space, but notions of how the heavenly orbs affect the lifecycles of the plants and animals and us have made little progress.

Appendixes

[Appendix 1-1]

The amount of light received on the water from the moon is not only a function of the earth's position to the sun, but also varies each day based on place, the phase of the moon, cloud cover and terrain. The figure "Maximum Illumination During Each Phase of the Moon" shows the maximum intensity of illumination on the water's surface for each day over the lunar cycle. It assumes a clear day and level terrain. The degree of illumination from the moon on the surface is based both

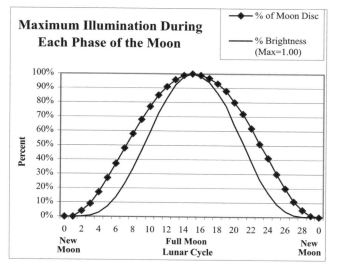

The maximum degree of illumination from the moon is dependent on the percentage of the disk illuminated and its angle to the earth, and changes over each day of the lunar cycle. The top line shows the amount of light reflected from the moon's disk and the bottom adjusts it for the angle to the earth's surface during the month of July. Note that the degree of illumination during the early and latter phases of cycle is almost the same and can be characterized as darkness. The "% of the Disk Illuminated" was drawn from data provided on the US Naval Observatory web page (www.usno.navy.mil).

on the percentage of the disk illuminated and the angle of the moon to the earth. When the moon is low on the horizon, such as in the early and final days of the lunar cycle, very little light penetrates below the surface of the water. This is the difference between the "% of Moon Disk" and the "% Brightness." These figures are calculated with the Full Moon being at 100 percent. The Full Moon provides a luminance of about .267 lux. Starlight during the New Moon provides about .0002 lux. Although the moons at the first and third quarters appear to have half the illumination of the Full Moon, these phases are at 90-degree angles to the earth and only provide us 8 percent of the illumination from the Full Moon. To put lux into a working perspective, adequate illumination for humans to read steadily is about 100 lux and close machine work requires about 400 lux. Full sunlight with zenith sun produces an illuminance of the order of 100,000 lux on a horizontal surface. On most days, 20 lux occurs about the same time as dusk.

[Appendix 1-2]

Timeline in Ancient Mesopotamia

Sumerians	3000 BCE - 2300 BCE
Akkadians	2300 BCE - 2150 BCE
Neo-Sumerians	2150 BCE - 2000 BCE
Babylonians	2000 BCE - 1600 BCE
Assyrians	1300 BCE - 612 BCE
Neo-Babylonians	626 BCE - 539 BCE

[**Appendix 2-1**]

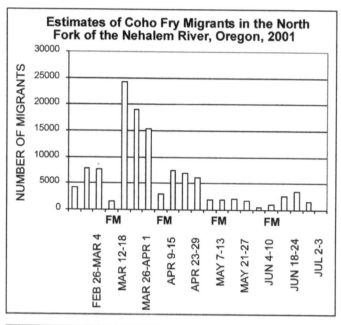

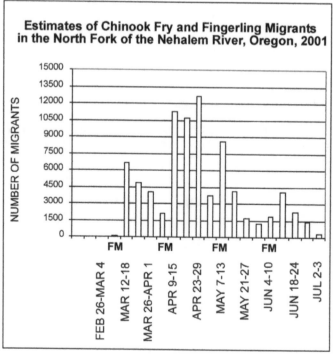

The Coho fry and Chinook fry and fingerlings on the North Fork of the Nehalem River migrate during the darkest evenings with lows around the Full Moon. These fish included fry emerging directly from the gravel in the early part of the run and larger juveniles at the later period. (Source: Data from the Oregon Department of Fish and Wildlife. Lunar phases added by author.)

[Appendix 2-2]

Although all salmonids have strong juvenile out-migration patterns tied to light, or the absence of it, they migrate to the marine environment at different stages of their lives, depending on species. For example, pinks and chums migrate out as newly emerged fry, showing a preference for saline water over fresh water, which may facilitate a seaward migration (Baggerman, B., 1960). Fall Chinook salmon, on the other hand, leave the river throughout the spring and summer as sub-yearling fry and fingerlings, holding in estuaries until they become smolts and are strong enough to survive in the coastal areas.

Species	Years in Freshwater	Years in Saltwater	Life Span (Years)	Typical Size Range (lbs.)
Chinook Salmon	0 to 1	1 to 5	2 to 6	10 to 25
Chum Salmon	0	3 to 5	3 to 5	6.5 to 12.5
Coho Salmon	1	1 to 3	2 to 4	6 to 9.5
Pink Salmon	0	2	2	3 to 5.5
Sockeye Salmon	1 to 2	2 to 3	4 to 6	4 to 15
Steelhead trout	1 to 3	1 to 3	2 to 7	2.5 to 18

The life history strategies among salmonids in North America vary widely by geography. In northern climates, salmonids tend to grow slower as juveniles and spend more time in the rivers before heading out to sea.

Stream Residency (years)	Age Frequency (Percent)				
	Alaska	British Columbia	Washington	Oregon	California
1		.8	6.3	3.8	25.1
2	13.1	39.5	85.7	77.5	66.6
3	69.1	54.2	.8	17.6	8.3
4	17.8	5.5		1.1	

In southern climates, salmon juveniles grow quickly and spend less time in the freshwater than those in northern climates. Migration to the ocean occurs sooner from south to north. This table is for anadromous rainbow trout (steelhead trout) stocks from California to Alaska. (Source: Pascual, M., Bentzen, P., Rossi, C. R., Mackey, G., Kinnison, M. T., and Walker, R., 2002, First documented case of anadromy in a population of introduced rainbow trout in Patagonia, Argentina, *Transactions of the American Fisheries Society* 130 (1): 53-67.)

Even those of the same species do not all migrate on the same lunar and solar days, These cues trigger them at different times over their lives. For instance, inland spring Chinook stocks, found mostly in the Columbia and Sacramento River systems, depart as yearling smolts. Coho salmon also migrate down river as sub-yearling fry and fingerlings, as well as yearlings, but generally do not head out to sea until they are yearling smolts. Steelhead trout and sockeye salmon will remain in the freshwater environment for between one to three years, depending on the latitude, when they out-migrate as smolts.

In general, salmonids in northern climates tend to grow slower as juveniles and spend more time in the rivers before heading out to sea. The steelhead trout and coho fry live in streams behind rocks and fallen trees that break the flow. Protection and restoration programs usually focus on adding such structural components to streams to improve the survival of fry and other juvenile stages. Sockeye salmon fry always migrate to a nursery lake.

When steelhead trout and sockeye salmon get older (1+ years), they are called "parr." Parr are larger than fry or finglering stages and often have colorful markings. The colorful markings present on the fingerlings and parr are a direct consequence of their habitat: The dark stripes (referred to as "parr marks") down the sides tend to break up the pattern of the body shape, making it difficult to spot them in the lake or river environment. As parr, salmon tend to be antisocial and territorial, and the solitary individuals need to reduce their visibility. Such marks are rarely observed on pink or chum salmon, which have very short freshwater residence periods. The steelhead trout parr will live in pools feeding on aquatic and terrestrial insects that get carried into this zone by the current. Dominant individuals in the population who have taken better feeding positions will grow faster and thus have greater survival. This is a particularly vulnerable stage for them. They are at the mercy of diving birds, otters and, for the slower growing ones, other salmonids. These fish are very territorial at this stage and seem to bite at anything. Anglers often catch salmon parr while fishing for the adults, and confuse them with small trout. On the Oregon Coast, trout fishing is closed during the months of peak out-migration so as to not have recreational anglers take these juvenile salmonids by mistaking them for the nonanadromous form. As smoltification proceeds, hormones induce changes in body shape (anticipatory for dramatically increased swimming capacity for downstream and ocean migration) and behaviour: The fish become less territorial and begin to school. Changes in coloration (silvering, loss of "parr marks") are also influenced by melatonin, prolactin and thyroid hormones. The silvery sides/tops of smolts help reduce top/down visibility (as with most surface swimming fish). Thus predation by birds is made more difficult during both downstream migration and early ocean residence. The lighter undersides help reduce bottom/up visibility, reducing predation by fishes and other predators deeper in the marine water column. Predators approaching the schools get confused by the flashes of scattering fish. This theory applies to a wide number of schooling fish. The salmon's body form also becomes torpedo-shaped to allow them to swim faster in the ocean to catch prey. These characteristics will help them to elude predators during their out-migration as well as in the ocean.

[Appendix 2-3]

The phenomenon of orientation during terrestrial and oceanic migration of animals can partly be explained by magnetism. The earth's geomagnetic field gives a geophysical signal, like an enormous magnet, with constant information about position and direction at virtually all times and in all environments. The earth's magnetic field is always changing, albeit slowly. In some cases, it can make radical changes in the life of an animal. Many animals have magnetic receivers, composed of the ferrimagnetic mineral Magnetite. Ferrimagnetic material is a subclass of ferromagnetic materials. Magnetite occurs across the biologic spectrum from bacteria to dolphins. One organism, magnetotactic bacteria, has been shown to use this material in orientation. It swims to the magnetic north in the Northern Hemisphere, to the magnetic south in the Southern Hemisphere and when introduced into ponds on the geomagnetic equator they go both ways. Studies have shown that salamanders and bees can also detect and orient with magnetic fields (Walker and Bitterman, 1989), and fin whales possess a magnetic sense that they use to guide their migration through the oceans (Walker, et al., 1992). Homing pigeons can usually tell longitudinal and latitudinal direction. However, researchers have found that when the homing pigeon was released near an anomaly in the earth's magnetic field, their orientation is deflected away from their home direction, even on clear days when they can see (Walcott, 1978). The pigeon experiments, including the use of coils giving varying magnetic fields around their heads, shows that though they often set off in the wrong direction, they are still able to get home; it just takes a little longer. This clearly indicates than they have more than the magnetic field in their navigation arsenals.

Sockeye salmon contain magnetite crystals in their skull, while Atlantic salmon have them on their lateral line, and rainbow trout in their ethmoid region (nose) and connecting to the optic nerve (Walker, et al., 1997). The crystals for all of these fish have characteristics similar to those of magnetotactic bacteria (Safarik and Safarikova, 2002). There are many navigational forces that help the salmon. Magnetism is probably the primary navigational force for salmon and steelhead trout to find their way back from the ocean to their home river. The fish may use it to log a position at some point in their migration, much like a GPS, and refer back to that point to navigate their return and/or use it to navigate during their entire journey, as in the fin whale. My suggestion is that the former is more likely, as navigation over the course needs to be learned, while the latter need not be. The concept of salmon migrating based on a magnetic signal can be supported in part by research from the University of Washington in Seattle. The researchers demonstrated that sockeye salmon smolts caught at the outlet of Babine Lake, British Columbia, oriented (within a tank) towards the outlet (destination) when given visual cues or when covered (Quinn, 1984).

Dr. David Stone from the Geophysical Institute at the University of Alaska-Fairbanks, suggests that the big problem in using the magnetic field as a primary navigation device for fish is in determining longitude. In the Gulf of Alaska, the variations of magnetic north from true north are fairly systematic. So if the fish could determine true north from the sun, then when true and magnetic north match one another, they are in position to cross the Aleutians, etc. The problem with this as a technique is that 100 years ago this would not have been true, and 100 years from now it will be different again. For North Atlantic salmon, this system would not work at all at the present time, since the variations in magnetic north are small and not systematic. Human navigators had to wait until chronometers were invented before they could determine longitude with certainty, and even then they needed clear shots of the sky. For fish migrating across the Gulf of Alaska, and probably swimming several meters down, this would present a real problem. This is especially true since they appear to swim along straight-line tracks in spite of crossing the Gulf of Alaska. Stone's thoughts are that they probably have some other sort of primary navigation (a beacon of some sort), and the compass is used to dead-reckon at times when the beacon is not working.

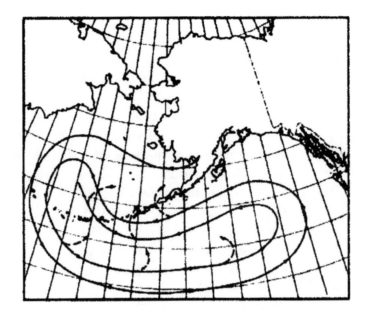

After entering the Alaska Gyre from the west Bering Sea, sockeye salmon will make one or possibly several circumnavigations before abruptly breaking off and returning directly to their spawning groups by passing through the Aleutians (broken lines). It is likely that the adult salmon are using a magnetic compass to find their way to their home river (Source: Geophysical Institute).

[Appendix 2-4]

Michelle Workman, a fisheries biologist with the East Bay Municipal Utility District, in Lodi, California, observed this behavior while monitoring Chinook salmon passage on the Lower Mokelumne River in the Central Valley of California [Appendix 3-2]. She noted that the migration of the fish spiked during the transitional light periods and little migration occurred at night. She also hypothesized that those salmon migrating early in the day were those that had actually begun their migration during the dawn hours and were able to continue to migrate up under the cover of darkness that the ladder provides. The peak days of migration for these Chinook salmon also occurred under the dark phases of the moon. This timing could be the difference between when a fish is on or off the bite. I have observed fresh coastal salmon and steelhead trout go on the move at dawn and dusk and take my offering more readily at that time than during the daylight hours.

Fall-Run Chinook Salmon Passage Recorded from Video Monitoring at the Woodbridge Irrigation, 2000-2001

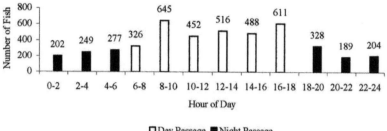

☐ Day Passage ■ Night Passage

The passage of salmon through the fish ladder demonstrates the activity level spikes during the morning and evening transitional light periods. Other fish that move in during the morning will continue up into the dark ladder bays as the day goes by. (Source: East Bay Municipal Utility District.)

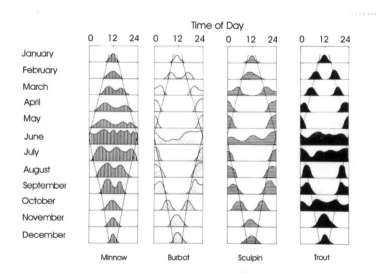

The summer months (May, June and July) in the Arctic (River Kaltisjokk) have continuous light during the nights and days, while the remaining months have clear separations of day and night. The rhythms of fish closely follow these patterns. They are tied to dusk and dawn when present (as represented by the diagonal lines), such as during the months from August to April. In contrast, during the continuous light of the summer period the fish become arrhythmic. (Redrawn from Thorpe, J. E., 1978, *Rhythmic Activity of Fishes*, Academic Press.)

The dusk/dawn hypothesis was similarly demonstrated by Karl Muller on the River Kaltisjokk in the Arctic Circle, where he established that during the winter, spring and fall, fish exhibited peaks in activity with transitional light at the dusks and dawns. In contrast, over the summer months, under the continuous 24-hour glow of the arctic light, they became arrhythmic. Similarly, laboratory studies have shown that the pineal gland releases intermediate amounts of melatonin under dim light conditions in a Light/Dim/Light sequence (Gern, W. A., et al., 1992). The absence of a rhythm under conditions of constant high-intensity light or light/dim light (really constant light) is a basic characteristic of all circadian rhythms in plants and animals. Rhythms are frequently not expressed under conditions of constant high-intensity light or constant low temperature. Arrhythmia is frequently observed in these situations.

[Appendix 2-5]

At New Moon, moonrise occurs at about the same time as sunrise, and moonset occurs at about the same time as sunset. In the first half of the lunar cycle from New to Full Moon, the moon rises later each day and sets later each night, At Full Moon, moonrise occurs at sunset and moonset occurs at sunrise. During the second half of the lunar cycle from Full to New Moon, the moon rises later each night and sets later each day, When the sun sets and it starts to get dark before the moon rises, there isn't a smooth evening transition in illumination from light to dark. On day 21, until the end of the cycle, the sun may set at around 8:00 pm, when it becomes dark.

Date	Moon Phase	Sunset	Moonrise	Sunrise	Moonset
July 10	New Moon (Day 0)	8:33 p.m.	6:00 a.m.	5:56 a.m.	9:18 p.m.
July 18-19	Days 8-9	8:29 p.m.	3:20 p.m.	6:02 a.m.	1:58 a.m.
July 24-25	Full Moon (Days 14-15)	8:25 p.m.	9:10 p.m.	6:06 a.m.	7:13 a.m.
August 1	Day 22	8:18 p.m.	12:22 p.m.	6:13 a.m.	2:02 p.m.

The time of day that the moon rises, relative to sunrise and sunset, partly determines how much light there is in the environment and the amount of hours each day. This table is for July and August of 2002 in the Kamloops region of Canada. (Dates and times from *The Old Farmer's Almanac 2002, United States Edition*.)

[Appendix 2-6]

In most cases extremely large salmonids, such as the Skeena, Dean and Babine steelhead trout of British Columbia, are produced by late entrance into the saltwater as smolts and more years in the ocean before they return to spawn. In general, the average size of steelhead trout entering streams to spawn increases in more northern areas, as shown in the table below. Northern fish also spend a greater amount of time in the ocean before sexual maturation. The extended length of time can partly explain the differences in average size. While at sea, steelhead trout grow quickly with an abundance of large food items. As mentioned earlier, this is a critical period, as they need to grow fast and large enough to avoid predators. In northern climates, there are widespread food events so these fish grow slowly as a result. Due to their slow growth, the northern fish also tend to live longer. The steelhead trout on Russia's Kamchatka Penninsula, such as the Utkholok, Kvachina, Snotalvayam and Sopochnaya and Saichic Rivers, demonstrate this. Anglers can access these Russian Rivers through the Wild Salmon Center, headquartered in Portland, Oregon.

In most hatchery runs on the lower Pacific Coast, anglers harvest the fish so that they do not escape and spawn with the wild fish. A four-year-old (two salt year) returning wild steelhead trout on an Oregon river usually weighs about 9 pounds. If the steelhead trout stays another year at sea, it would return at about 15 pounds. British Columbia steelhead trout on average grow larger than do those stocks in the Great Lakes and southern Pacific coast. However, the extremely fast-growing Great Lakes steelhead trout are generally larger than those found in Washington, Oregon or California.

Ocean age at first spawning (years)	Age Frequency (Percent)				
	Alaska	British Columbia	Washington	Oregon	California
0			.3		
1	.3	1.8	2	7.5	59.9
2	65.8	61.5	65	75.6	36.9
3	31.3	36.0	32	15.3	3.2
4		1.0	1	2	

Frequency of age group of steelhead trout at first spawning for five Pacific Coast locations of North America. Note that fish from more northerly rivers tend to spend more time in the ocean prior to returning to spawn than those from southerly rivers. (Source: Pascual, M., Bentzen, P., Rossi, C. R., Mackey, G., Kinnison, M. T., and Walker, R., 2002, First documented case of anadromy in a population of introduced rainbow trout in Patagonia, Argentina, *Transactions of the American Fisheries Society* 130 (1): 53-67.)

[Appendix 2-7]

The apparent movement of the moon around the earth takes 24 hours and 51 minutes. This leads to high tides every 12.4 hours. Particularly large tides are experienced in the earth's oceans when the sun and moon line up with the earth at New and Full Moon phases. These are called "spring tides" though they have no association with the season of spring. The amount of enhancement in earth's tides is about the same whether the sun and moon are lined up on opposite sides of the earth (Full Moon) or on the same side (New Moon). When the moon is at first quarter or last quarter phase (meaning that it is located at right angles to the earth-sun line), the sun and moon interfere with each other in producing tidal bulges and tides are generally weaker. We refer to these as "neap tides." Superimposed on the lunar tides are smaller solar tides. The sun is much farther away from the earth than the moon is, thereby reducing its effect. The cycle of changes in water level at a coastal site will be determined by an interaction between these two rhythms, with the most extreme tides occurring when the two cycles are in synchrony. The actual change in water level and timing of the tides will also be determined by local geography and geologic conditions. For example, if the flow of water needs to travel around islands it will be altered from the celestial events. This is particularly true for Cook Inlet. Cook Inlet is almost like an organ pipe tuned to the Pacific Ocean tides. The tides in this system produce some huge current velocities up and down the inlet that would no doubt be very important to a migrating fish.

First Peak of Count Lunar Days for Sockeye
Salmon in the Lower Kenai River Relative to
High Tides, 1990 - 2001

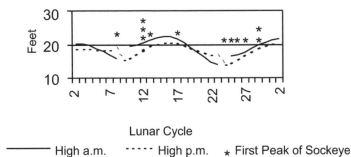

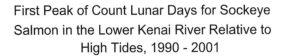

The first peak (as represented by the asterisks) of sockeye salmon in the Lower Kenai River, Alaska, occurs just after the Neap Tides (lowest of the high tides), occurring around the 1st and 3rd quarters of cycle (lunar days 12 and 27). The counting device is located in the lower river so the movement of fish through the inlet would have occurred a few days earlier.

Pattern	First Adult Peak in River	Lunar Day	Second Adult Peak in River	Lunar Day	Spawning Year
1	Jul-18	25	Jul-25	3	1990
2	Jul-20	8	Jul-28	16	1991
2	Jul-13	12	Jul-25	24	1992
1	Jul-14	24	Jul-27	8	1993
2	Jul-25	17	Aug-2	25	1994
1	Jul-25	27	Aug-4	8	1995
1	Jul-15	29	Jul-25	9	1996
2	Jul-18	13	Jul-24	19	1997
1	Jul-23	29	Aug-2	9	1998
2	Jul-25	12	Aug-7	25	1999
2	Jul-14	12	Jul-24	22	2000
1	Jul-17	26	Jul-26	5	2001

Adult sockeye salmon peaks of in-migration in the Lower Kenai River, Alaska. (Source: Data from Alaska Department of Fish and Game. Lunar days added by author.)

Statistical analysis:

The estimated relationship between the first peak day (days are expressed on the lunar calendar) for adult sockeye salmon and ocean tides (High a.m. tide in feet) is observed and summarized in the display below. The peak day is defined as the one with the greatest movement of fish past the sonar. Two different patterns are observed in the data.

Pattern 1

Within the boundaries of the data, there is an estimated average increase of 1.16 days for each 1-foot increase in the tide (95% confidence interval: 0.87 days to 1.45 days). Out of interest, it is estimated that the mean lunar phase day given the estimated mean tide is equal to day 27.2 (95% confidence interval: day 26.8 to day 27.6).

It is noteworthy that 98.2% of the variation in lunar days for Pattern 1 was explained by the linear regression on high a.m. tides (Multiple R-Squared = 0.982).

Pattern 2

In keeping within the boundaries of the data for Pattern 2, there is an estimated average increase of 1.15 days for each 1-foot increase in the tide (95% confidence interval: 0.16 days to 2.14 days). The estimated mean lunar phase day given the estimated mean tide is equal to day 12.3 (95% confidence interval: day 10.4 to day 14.2). Arrows in the display below also indicate this confidence interval.

Of the variation in lunar days for Pattern 2, 72.4% was explained by the linear regression on high a.m. tides (Multiple R-Squared = 0.724).

There is also convincing evidence that the arrival of sockeye salmon based on lunar phase day was observed to be strongly associated with high a.m. tides (in feet), even after accounting for Pattern 1 and Pattern 2 (*p*-value < .00001 from an extra sum of squares F-test). There is overwhelming evidence that Pattern 1 is observed to occur later on the lunar phase day calendar than Pattern 2 by an average of 17.1 days (95% confidence interval equals 15.2 days later to 19.0 days later; two-sided *p*-value < .00001 from a *t*-test on the regression coefficient indicating pattern type).

The display below shows the fit of a multiple linear regression model that specifies parallel regression lines for the arrival of sockeye salmon based on the lunar phase day as a function of high a.m. tides in feet.

Residuals:

Min	1Q	Median	3Q	Max
-0.8719	-0.8336	-0.04667	0.2233	2.858

Coefficients:

	Value	Std. Error	t value	Pr(>|t|)

(Intercept)	6.1942	3.9203	1.5800	0.1528
high.am1	1.1542	0.2134	5.4096	0.0006
PATTERN	-17.0981	0.8383	-20.3954	0.0000

Residual standard error: 1.205 on 8 degrees of freedom
Multiple R-Squared: 0.9823
F-statistic: 222.1 on 2 and 8 degrees of freedom. the *p*-value is 9.796e-008

[Appendix 2-8]

1996-1997			1997-1998			1998-1999			1999-2000		
Week End Date	Fish Count	Full Moon Date	Week End Date	Fish Count	Full Moon Date	Week End Date	Fish Count	Full Moon Date	Week End Date	Fish Count	Full Moon Date
11/8	0		11/7	0		11/6	0	11/4	11/5	0	
11/15	4		11/14	0		11/13	0		11/12	0	
11/22	0		11/21	0		11/20	1		11/19	1	
11/29	0		11/28	0		11/27	0		11/26	0	11/22
12/6	0		12/5	5		12/4	0	12/4	12/3	0	
12/13	0		12/12	1		12/11	0		12/10	0	
12/20	1		12/19	3	12/14	12/18	3		12/17	2	
12/27	0	12/24	12/26	1		12/25	0		12/24	8	12/23
1/3	0		1/2	8		1/1	0	1/1	12/31	2	
1/10	10		1/9	0		1/8	1		1/7	2	
1/17	0		1/16	2	1/13	1/15	6		1/14	2	
1/24	15	1/23	1/23	15		1/22	8		1/21	0	1/20
1/31	8		1/30	16		1/29	2		1/28	3	
2/7	3		2/6	8		2/5	0	2/1	2/4	1	
2/14	1		2/13	2	2/11	2/12	4		2/11	6	
2/21	0		2/20	6		2/19	0		2/18	12	2/19
2/28	8	2/22	2/27	4		2/26	3		2/25	0	
3/7	15		3/6	5		3/5	10	3/2	3/3	15	

Table continues on next page

Table continued from previous page

1996-1997			1997-1998			1998-1999			1999-2000		
Week End Date	Fish Count	Full Moon Date	Week End Date	Fish Count	Full Moon Date	Week End Date	Fish Count	Full Moon Date	Week End Date	Fish Count	Full Moon Date
3/14	16		3/13	34	3/13	3/12	0		3/10	13	
3/21	27		3/20	24		3/19	22		3/17	17	
3/28	74	3/23	3/27	39		3/26	39		3/24	25	3/19
4/4	10		4/3	15		4/2	20	4/1	3/31	49	
4/11	16		4/10	15	4/11	4/9	7		4/7	92	
4/18	77		4/17	28		4/16	25		4/14	242	
4/25	79	4/21	4/24	112		4/23	116		4/21	65	4/18
5/2	33		5/1	39		4/30	52	4/30	4/28	111	
5/9	35		5/8	0		5/7	24		5/5	60	
5/16	35		5/15	11	5/10	5/14	44		5/12	37	
5/23	15	5/21	5/22	14		5/21	48		5/19	60	5/17
5/30	8		5/29	8		5/28	50		5/26	20	
6/6	5		6/5	4		6/4	2	5/30	6/2	5	
6/13	2		6/12	3	6/10	6/11	11		6/9	1	
6/20	7	6/19	6/19	0		6/18	0		6/16	1	6/16
6/27	0		6/26	0		6/25	0		6/23	0	

Kalama Wild Winter Steelhead Trout Weekly Trap Counts at Kalama Falls Hatchery. 1996-1997 Through 1999-2000 Return Years. (Source: Unpublished data from the Washington Department of Fish and Wildlife. Lunar days added by author.)

Statistical analysis:

Four additional years of migration data for wild winter steelhead trout on the Kalama River, WA, also demonstrated the lowest number of fish migrated around the Full Moon. If the fish counts at Kalama Hatchery are unrelated to the lunar cycle, the number of fish that appear in a week ought to be independent of the week's position relative to the Full Moon. Under such conditions, the probability of obtaining the distribution observed is less than 1%.

	1st Week After Full Moon	2nd Week After Full Moon	3rd Week After Full Moon	Full Moon	
Total Count	624	1069	828	693	3214
Sample	42	47	41	40	170
Average	14.85714	22.74468	20.19512	17.325	

Avg. per week: 18.90588

Chi-squared

Week	Observed	Expected
1	624	794.0471
2	1069	888.5765
3	828	775.1412
Full Moon	693	756.2353
	Chi-squared = 81.94	

Our calculated statistic of 81.94 greatly exceeds the critical value for a Chi-squared distribution with 3 degrees of freedom (even at the .005 significance level). We can conclude with over 99% confidence that the fish counts at Kalama Falls are not independent of the lunar cycle.

[Appendix 2-9]

Spawning Year	Adult Peak #	Adult Peak Date	Lunar Day
1989	39	16-Jan-90	19
1990	9	29-Jan-91	13
1991	11	13-Jan-92	8
1992	48	13-Jan-93	20
1993	8	28-Dec-93	14
1994	4	20-Dec-94	17
1995	4	03-Jan-96	12
1996	14	27-Nov-96	16
1997	11	09-Jan-98	10
1998	4	04-Jan-99	16
1999	8	19-Jan-00	12
2000	51	18-Dec-00	22
2001	24	28-Dec-01	13

Source: Unpublished data from the Oregon Department of Fish and Wildlife. Adult counts taken weekly cover a 1.3-mile stretch of river. Lunar days added by author.

Statistical Analysis:

There is overwhelming evidence the peak day (observed counts) for adult coho salmon is observed to be dependent or associated with the lunar phase calendar (p-value = 0.0043 from a Chi-Square goodness-of-fit test).

Chi-Square Statistic with 2 degrees of freedom = 10.8747
p-value = 0.0043

Expected Calculations
Note: expected calculations are based on 29.5 lunar days.

Group	Observed	Expected
0 to 9	1	(10/29.5)*13 = 4.40678
10 to 19	10	(10/29.5)*13 = 4.40678
20 to 29	2	(9.5/29.5)*13 = 4.186441

[Appendix 3-1]

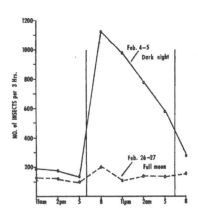

Aquatic insects have greater drift during dark evenings than illuminated evenings such as the Full Moon period. Some scientists believe that these insects are more active during darker periods to avoid predation by fish. Such anti-predation behavior can put the insects into lunar rhythms similar to those of the salmon. (Graph courtesy of Dr. Norman Anderson, Entomology Department, Oregon State University.)

[Appendix 3-2]

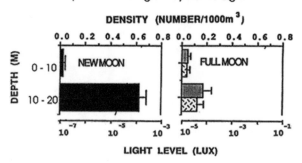

Bonneville Ciscoes in Bear Lake, Utah, migrate vertically to reach their prey (zooplankton) and avoid the big Bonneville cutthroat trout (Bear Lake stock). This chart illustrates that the Bonneville Ciscoes shy away from the illuminated areas (during the evenings) where the trout can more easily see and capture them. Chart courtesy of Dr. Chris Luecke and Dr. Wayne Wurtsbaugh from the Department of Fisheries and Wildlife, Ecology Center, Utah State University.

[Appendix 3-3]

Year	Julian Date	Peak Stage Date	Lunar Day
1971	194	July 13	20
1973	178	June 27	26
1980	162	June 11	27
1984	160	June 9	9
1987	145	May 25	27
1988	164	June 13	28
1993	154	June 3	12
1994	130	May 10	29
1996	134	May 14	26

Stage composition dates of the subarctic copepod, *Neocalanus plumchrus* (from interpolated dates at which half of the population in the upper 150m were C5, half are earlier stages). (Source: Data from Dr. David Mackas, Institute of Ocean Sciences, Canada. Data previously published in a graph format in Mackas, D. L., Goldblatt, R., and Lewis, A. G., 1998, Interdecadal variation in developmental timing of *Neocalanus plumchrus* populations at Ocean Station P in the subarctic North Pacific, *Canadian Journal of Fisheries and Aquatic Science* 55: 1874-93. Lunar days added by author.)

Lunar Day	Observed	Expected
0 – 9	1	3.050847 (10/29.5)*9
10 – 19	1	3.050847 (10/29.5)*9
20 – 29	7	2.898305 (10/29.5)*9

Chi-Square Statistic with 2 degrees of freedom = 8.561988 p-value = 0.0138.

[Appendix 3-4]

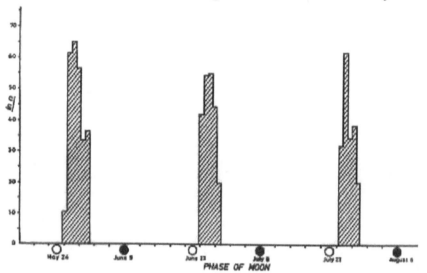

Synchronous Emergence in Povilla Adjusta

The peak of the emergence of the mayfly (*Povilla adjusta*) occurs on the fifth day after the Full Moon. The degree and timing of illumination synchronizes the behavior within the population and leads to a positive environmental condition for the emergence of the entire population. (Source: Hartland-Rowe, R. 1983. The adaptive value of synchronous emergence in the tropical mayfly *Povilla Adjusta*: A preliminary investigation. In Landa, Vladimir; Soldan, Tomas; and Tonner, Martin (eds.), *Proceedings of the Fourth International Conference on Emphemeroptera*, Bechyne, September 4-10, 1983, Institute of Entomology, Czechoslovak Academy of Sciences.

[Appendix 3-5]

Year	Mean Date of Hatching	Lunar Day of Hatching	Dark or Light Lunar Day (1 = light/ 2=dark)	Year	Mean Date of Hatching	Lunar Day of Hatching	Dark or Light Lunar Day (1 = light/ 2=dark)
1973	June 24.3	23	2	1983	July 6.8	25	2
1974	June 26.5	6	2	1984	June 25.4	25	2
1975	June 22.2	12	1	1985	June 19.8	0	2
1976	June 19.2	21	2	1986	June 20.3	12	1
1977	June 15.0	28	2	1987	June 26.0	0	2
1978	July 1.3	25	2	1988	June 25.7	10	1
1979	June 26.8	1	2	1989	June 27.8	23	2
1980	June 14.2	1	2	1990	June 23.6	0	2
1981	June 24.1	21	2	1991	June 19.5	6	2
1982	June 18.0	26	2	1992	June 29.1	28	2

Lesser snow geese have a strong propensity to hatch under the dark nights of the lunar cycle between lunar days 21 to 6.   These hatching days are likely cued by earlier solar and lunar timed behavior and events. (Source: Data from Cooke, Fred, Rockwell, Robert F., and Lank, David B, 1995, *The Snow Geese of La Pérouse Bay*, Oxford University Press. Lunar Days added by author.)

Statistical Analysis:

If we can assume that under random conditions all of the days under the lunar phase are equally possible for hatching, then the probability that the mean lunar days of this event ranging from the dark period (21 to 6) was a random choice is .0172 or 1.72 percent.

[Appendix 4-1]

Site A

Year	Week of Highest Average Concentrations	Beginning Date of Period	Lunar Day	End Date of Period	Lunar Day	Highest Weekly Average Concentrations (grains/cubic meter)	First Full Moon on/after April 7th
1989	4th Week in April	4/25	19	4/30	24	14.8	April 21st
1990	1st Week in May	5/1	6	5/8	13	118.8	May 9th
1991	4th Week in April	4/25	10	4/30	15	84	April 28th
1992	3rd Week in April	4/17	14	4/24	21	32	April 17th
1993	4th Week in April	4/25	3	4/30	8	30.9	May 6th
1994	3rd Week in April	4/17	6	4/24	13	131.7	April 25th

Site B

Year	Week of Highest Average Concentrations	Beginning Date of Period	Lunar Day	End Date of Period	Lunar Day	Highest Weekly Average Concentrations (grains/cubic meter)	First Full Moon on/after April 7th
1998	2nd Week in April	4/9	12	4/16	19	45.52	April 11th
1999	4th Week in April	4/25	9	4/30	14	29.75	April 30th
2000	3rd Week in April	4/17	12	4/24	19	26.98	April 18th
2001	3rd Week in April	4/17	23	4/24	0	77.82	April 7th
2002	3rd Week in April	4/17	4	4/24	11	133.28	April 27th
2003	2nd Week in April	4/10	8	4/16	14	72.28	April 16th

The highest weekly average concentrations of pollen for the American sycamore (*Platanus occidentalis*) and London plane tree (*Platanus x acerifolia*) in the Washington, D.C., area occur after April 10 and peak close to the following Full Moon. (Data: Allergy Immunology Service at Walter Reed Army Medical Center. Lunar days added by author.)

The hypothesis of a Full Moon entrained peak in pollen counts was tested with a calculation of a 95% confidence interval for the average lunar date of the Wednesday of the peak week. The peak week was the one with the highest occurring number. For the twelve years, x-bar=13.5 with standard deviation=5.977. The alpha = .05 two-sided t-value for a distribution with 11 degrees of freedom is 2.201. This yields a 95% confidence interval of 9.7 < true mean < 17.3.

[Appendix 4-2]

Year	Date of First Bud Break	Lunar Day	Date of First Bloom	Lunar Day
1989	4/12	6	6/6	2
1990	4/1	5	6/20	26
1991	4/14	28	7/7	24
1992	3/19	14	5/17	14
1993	4/16	23	6/18	27
1994	4/6	24	6/11	1
1995	4/3	3	6/9	10
1996	4/8	19	6/20	4
1997	4/21	13	6/4	28
1998	4/21	24	6/15	20
1999	4/22	6	6/24	10

The day of first bud break for Pinot Noir grapes falls in a lunar pattern between days 23 to 6 (8 of 11). The day of first bloom falls in a lunar pattern between days 24 to 4 (7 of 11). (Source: Unpublished data from Alan McDonald, Chemeketa Community College. Lunar days added by author.)

BUD BREAKS

Observed

IN	OUT
8	3

Expected

IN	OUT
4.66	6.34

Chi-Square Goodness-of-Fit Test
Chi-Square, df (1) = 4.153
p-value = .0415

BLOOMS

Observed

IN	OUT
7	4

Expected

IN	OUT
3.54	7.46

Chi-Square Goodness-of-Fit Test
Chi-Square, df (1) = 4.987
p-value = .0255

ODDS

	IN	OUT
Bud Breaks	8	3
Blooms	7	4

Odds for Bud Breaks = 2.67 to 1 in Favor of the Window

Odds for Blooms   = 1.75 to 1 in Favor of the Window

[Appendix 4-3]

Variety	Merlot			Chardonnay			Pinot Gris			Pinot Noir		
Year	Date	Lunar Day	RI	Date	Lunar Day	RI	Date	Lunar Day	RI	Date	Lunar Day	RI
2000	9/29	1	242	9/26	27	262	9/22	23	217	10/3	5	233
2001	10/16	28	263	10/5	17	227	10/3	15	226	10/15	27	203
2002	10/8	1	246	10/4	27	235	10/2	25	241	10/5	28	196
2003	10/2	6	268	9/25	28	256	9/23	26	253	9/27	1	230

Date and lunar date grapes harvested at an Oregon State University research vineyard, Corvallis, Oregon. The primary criterion to pick the fruit was a target Ripening Index above 200. The Ripening Index (RI) is calculated as Brix x pH/2. The timing of harvest based on this qualification coincided with the dark period of the lunar cycle. Of 16 observations, 14 fell in a lunar window between days 23 to 6 and 11 fell in a lunar window between days 25 to 1. (Source: Unpublished data from Dr. Carmo Vasconcelos, Dept. of Horticulture, Oregon State University. Lunar days added by author.)

[Appendix 4-4]

Bloom Model			Pinot Noir		Merlot		Chardonnay		Pinot Gris	
Year	1st New Moon After 5/24	Expected Order	Harvest Date	Actual Order	Harvest Date	Actual Order	Harvest Date	Actual Order	Harvest Date	Actual Order
2000	2-Jun	2	3-Oct	2	29-Sep	1	26-Sep	2	22-Sep	1
2001	21-Jun	4	15-Oct	4	16-Oct	4	5-Oct	4	3-Oct	4
2002	10-Jun	3	5-Oct	3	8-Oct	3	4-Oct	3	2-Oct	3
2003	31-May	1	27-Sep	1	2-Oct	2	25-Sep	1	23-Sep	2

By modeling the timing of first bloom to the solar and lunar cycles, we can predict the order of the harvest. Over four years, with four varieties of grapes, earlier and later harvest timing was associated with the predicted order of first bloom. This data is the same as Appendix 4-3.

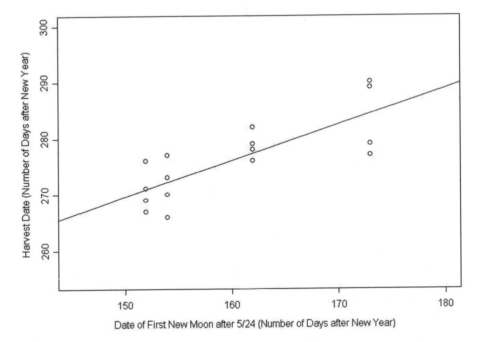

Date of First New Moon after 5/24 (Number of Days after New Year)

A second method of looking at the data is with a regression analysis. The grapes in this graph are modeled as an aggregate cluster (all the different types of grapes are considered essentially the same). This analysis shows an overwhelming relationship between the date of the first New Moon after 5/24 and the date of harvest.

Residuals:

Min	1Q	Median	3Q	Max
-7.371	-2.605	0.3985	4.644	5.629

Coefficients:

	Value	Std. Error	t value	Pr(>|t|)
(Intercept)	173.3323	21.5305	8.0505	0.0000
First Moon	0.6418	0.1342	4.7835	0.0003

Residual standard error: 4.432 on 14 degrees of freedom
Multiple R-Squared: 0.6204
F-statistic: 22.88 on 1 and 14 degrees of freedom, the *p*-value is 0.0002915

[Appendix 5-1]

Percentage of Antler Sheds Within Each Period

Year	First Full Moon After 12/21	Relative Shift in Antler Shed	12/16 - 12/31	1/1 – 1/16	1/17 - 1/31
1955-56	12/28	Earlier	18%	27%	100%
1956-57	1/15	Later	0	18%	82%
1957-58	1/5	Earlier	26%	33%	77%
1958-59	12/26	Earlier	38%	50%	71%
1959-60	1/13	Later	0	20%	50%

Between 1955-56 and 1959-60, when the Full Moon fell closest to the Winter Solstice the white-tailed deer in Connecticut shed their antlers earlier than when it occurred later. (Source: Behrend, D.F. and McDowell, R.D. 1967. Antler shedding among white-tailed deer in Connecticut. *Journal of Wildlife Management* 31 (3): 588-90. Lunar days added by author.)

The below graph is a representation of the data shown in the table. Each line shows the change in the proportion of deer taken with antlers shed as we move from period 1 (Dec 16-31) to period 3 (Jan 17-31) for one particular year (note year 55 means Dec 1955 – Jan 1956). Lines 2 and 5 represent the years when the relative lunar shift was later and lines 1,3, and 4 are for earlier shifts. The lines stay fairly parallel through periods 1 and 2, but become jumbled in period 3. We can see, especially in the first two periods the pronounced difference in the average proportions for the two shifts. Lines 1,3, and 4 are all higher (early shift) compared to lines 2 and 5 (later shift). The shift of the lunar phase has a high probability of being important (the probability that it is not is .0183 or 1.8%).

Together, the period of time the data was collected and whether the lunar shift was earlier or later account for 80.7% of the variability in the observed proportions.

Proportion of deer with antlers shed for each period

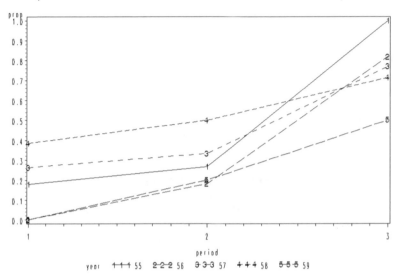

Source	DF	Sum of Squares	Mean Square	F Value	Pr > F
Model	2	1.03822760	0.51911380	25.12	<.0001
Error	12	0.24798373	0.02066531		
Corrected Total	14	1.28621133			

R-Square	Coeff Var	Root MSE	prop Mean
0.807198	35.29157	0.143754	0.407333

Source	DF	Type III SS	Mean Square	F Value	Pr > F
shift	1	0.15376000	0.15376000	7.44	0.0183
period	1	0.88446760	0.88446760	42.80	<.0001

[Appendix 5-2]

Year	Antler Shed	Lunar Day
1983	April 9th	25
1984	April 20th	18
1985	May 16th	26
1986	May 19th	10
1987	April 20th	21
1988	May 5th	18
1989	May 5th	29

This blind white-tailed deer with congenital anophthalmia followed a pattern of dropping its antlers in an 11-day lunar window that fell in the waning half of cycle, after the Full Moon. (Source: Jacobson, H.A. and Waldhalm, S.J. 1992. Antler cycles of a white-tailed deer with congenital anophthalmia. In *The Biology of Deer*, R. D. Brown. Springer-Verlag. Lunar days added by author.)

With the null hypothesis that the antler shed is independent of the lunar day, we can assume the probability of the shed date falling on any particular lunar day is equal. Thus, the probability of the shed occurring between lunar day 18 and 29 in any one year is 12.29, and is independent from one year to year. We can use the binomial distribution to test the hypothesis of randomness. Assuming random conditions, the probability of having six or more out of the seven antler sheds fall in the period from lunar days 18 to 20 is .023, or 2.3%.

[Appendix 5-3]

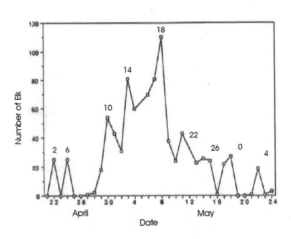

The peak of migration for these Roosevelt elk (*Cervus elaphus roosevelti*) occurred during the Full Moon period between days 14 and 18 of cycle, as marked above the number of elk. The elk were observed between 0530-0700 hours along an 8 mile road transect through open pasture in the Upper Klamath Basin, 22 April – 24 May, 1985. (Source: Jenkins, K., Cooper, K., Starkey. 1988. *Ecology of elk inhabiting Crater Lake National Park and vicinity.* National Park Service Report. Lunar days added by author.)

[Appendix 5-4]

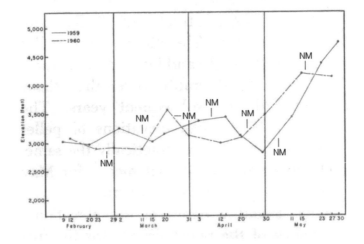

Rocky Mountain elk (*Cervus canadensis*) migrate most heavily during the Full Moon periods and slow down around the New Moons. Each year is the inverse of the previous due to the lunar shift against the sun. These elevational movements of the elk were during the late winter and early spring in the Selway River Drainage, Idaho, during 1959 and 1960. (Source: Dalke, P.D., Beeman, R.D., Kindel, F.J., Robel, R.J. and Williams, T.R. 1965. Seasonal movements of elk in the Selway River Drainage, Idaho. *Journal of Wildlife Management* 29 (2): pp. 333-38. Lunar phases added by author.).

[Appendix 6-1]

Pattern	Return Year	Vernal Equinox Lunar Day	Easter Day	First Adult Peak in River	Lunar Day	Second Adult Peak in River	Lunar Day
1	1990	24	Apr-15	July-18	25	July-25	3
2	1991	6	Mar-31	July-20	8	July-28	16
2	1992	17	Apr-19	July-13	12	July-25	24
1	1993	28	Apr-11	Jul-14	24	Jul-27	8
2	1994	9	Apr-3	Jul-25	17	Aug-2	25
1	1995	20	Apr-16	Jul-25	27	Aug-4	8
1	1996	2	Apr-7	Jul-15	29	Jul-25	9
2	1997	12	Mar-30	Jul-18	13	Jul-24	19
1	1998	23	Apr-12	Jul-23	29	Aug-2	9
2	1999	4	Apr-4	Jul-25	12	Aug-7	25
2	2000	15	Apr-23	Jul-14	12	Jul-24	22
1	2001	26	Apr-15	Jul-17	26	Jul-26	5

This table shows the relationship between the timing of sockeye salmon smolt out-migration to the peaks in the Lower Kenai River, Alaska. It demonstrates that one can time the arrival based on a lunar day against a fixed solar day in the year of in-migration. If lunar days 20 through 2 of the cycle (Full Moon going into New Moon) fall on the Vernal Equinox, a lunar day 27 pattern will occur. If a phase relating to days 4 through 17 were observed (New Moon going into Full Moon), the 12 pattern would occur. One can further time these runs to the Easter holiday. The Vernal Equinox day used in this analysis is March 21. The days of the equinoxes and solstices may vary as per the table "Universal Time" below (Data source: Alaska Department of Fish and Game. Lunar days added by author.)

Year	Event	D	H	M	D	H	M
2004	Equinoxes	Mar 20	06	49	Sept 22	16	30
	Solstices	June 21	00	57	Dec 21	12	42
2005	Equinoxes	Mar 20	12	33	Sept 22	22	23
	Solstices	June 21	06	46	Dec 21	18	35
2006	Equinoxes	Mar 20	18	26	Sept 23	04	03
	Solstices	June 21	12	26	Dec 22	00	22
2007	Equinoxes	Mar 21	00	07	Sept 23	09	51
	Solstices	June 21	18	06	Dec 22	06	08
2008	Equinoxes	Mar 20	05	48	Sept 22	15	44
	Solstices	June 20	23	59	Dec 21	12	04
2009	Equinoxes	Mar 20	11	44	Sept 22	21	18
	Solstices	June 21	05	45	Dec 21	17	47
2010	Equinoxes	Mar 20	17	32	Sept 23	03	09
	Solstices	June 21	11	28	Dec 21	23	38
2011	Equinoxes	Mar 20	23	21	Sept 23	09	04
	Solstices	June 21	17	16	Dec 22	05	30
2012	Equinoxes	Mar 20	05	14	Sept 22	14	49
	Solstices	June 20	23	09	Dec 21	11	11

Solstices and Equinoxes at Universal Time (Greenwich Mean Time), 2004-2012 (Source: United States Naval Observatory)

[Appendix 6-2]

Year	Winter Solstice Lunar Day	% of the Disk Illuminated	Waxing or Waning	Year	Winter Solstice Lunar Day	% of the Disk Illuminated	Waxing or Waning
1880	17	.83	Waning	1906	5	.35	Waxing
1881	0	.00		1907	15	.98	Waning
1882	12	.86	Waxing	1908	27	.06	Waning
1883	23	.51	Waning	1909	8	.63	Waxing
1884	4	.12	Waxing	1910	19	.72	Waning
1885	**14**	**.99 (FM)**	**Waxing**	1911	0	.00	
1886	25	.19	Waning	1912	12	.89	Waxing
1887	6	.40	Waxing	1913	23	.44	Waning
1888	17	.93	Waning	1914	4	.20	Waxing
1889	28	.03	Waning	**1915**	**14**	**1.00 (FM)**	**Waxing**
1890	13	.75	Waxing	1916	25	.17	Waning
1891	21	.69	Waning	1917	6	.50	Waxing
1892	2	.04	Waxing	1918	17	.86	Waning
1893	**13**	**.94 (FM)**	**Waxing**	1919	28	.01	Waning
1894	24	.32	Waning	1920	13	.76	Waxing
1895	5	.23	Waxing	1921	21	.57	Waning
1896	16	.99	Waning	1922	2	.08	Waxing
1897	26	.10	Waning	**1923**	**13**	**.96 (FM)**	**Waxing**
1898	9	.61	Waxing	1924	24	.31	Waning
1899	20	.84	Waning	1925	5	.36	Waxing
1900	1	.01	Waning	1926	16	.96	Waning
1901	12	.75	Waxing	1927	26	.08	Waning
1902	23	.57	Waning	1928	9	.61	Waxing
1903	4	.05	Waxing	1929	20	.71	Waning
1904	**14**	**.97 (FM)**	**Waxing**	1930	1	.02	Waxing
1905	24	.31	Waning				

The highlighted Full Moons (FM) are the first (waxing) phase that reaches near 1.00 of the disc illuminated. The % of the disc illuminated was calculated on the U.S. Naval Observatory webpage based on midnight of December 21 for each year. This model therefore works for that Gregorian calendar date. The Winter Solstice calendar date varies slightly between years between December 21 and 22. Indigenous peoples could have come to similar conclusions by timing off of the Winter Solstice.

[Appendix 6-3]

Biological Year	Lynx Fur Yukon	Vernal Equinox Lunar Day	Change Relative to Previous Year	Biological Year	Lynx Fur Yukon	Vernal Equinox Lunar Day	Change Relative to Previous Year
1919	334	18		1960	302	23	Down
1920	182	0	Down	1961	618	4	Up
1921	626	11	Up	1962	266	14	Down
1922	1433	22	Up	1963	1305	25	Up
1923	2526	3	Up	1964	2395	7	Up
1924	3757	15	Up	1965	408	17	Down
1925	3508	26	Down	1966	290	28	Down
1926	3357	7	Down	1967	247	10	Down
1927	3786	17	Up	1968	334	22	Up
1928	2372	28	Down	1969	395	3	Up
1929	1436	9	Down	1970	443	13	Up
1930	785	20	Down	1971	1122	23	Up
1931	699	1	Down	1972	2264	5	Up
1932	915	13	Up	1973	2950	16	Up
1933	1024	24	Up	1974	1812	27	Down
1934	1693	5	Up	1975	737	8	Down
1935	2943	16	Up	1976	539	20	Down
1936	2964	27	Up	1977	623	1	Up
1937	2752	8	Down	1978	1252	12	Up
1938	1763	19	Down	1979	1982	22	Up
1939	1191	0	Down	1980	2849	4	Up
1940	607	12	Down	1981	3740	14	Up
1941	745	23	Up	1982	2320	25	Down
1942	676	4	Down	1983	961	6	Down
1943	891	14	Up	1984	925	18	Down
1944	1999	26	Up	1985	805	29	Down
1945	1815	7	Down	1986	668	10	Down
1946	1887	17	Up	1987	799	21	Up
1947	1190	28	Down	1988	1235	3	Up
1948	552	10	Down	1989	1875	13	Up
1949	631	21	Up	1990	1256	23	Down
1950	1030	2	Up	1991	1403	4	Up

Table continues on next page

APPENDIXES *Chapter 6* 151

Table continued from previous page

Biological Year	Lynx Fur Yukon	Vernal Equinox Lunar Day	Change Relative to Previous Year	Biological Year	Lynx Fur Yukon	Vernal Equinox Lunar Day	Change Relative to Previous Year
1951	166	13	Down	1992	529	16	Down
1952	408	24	Up	1993	100	27	Down
1953	554	5	Up	1994	187	8	Up
1954	1378	16	Up	1995	152	19	Down
1955	2029	26	Up	1996	310	1	Up
1956	1069	8	Down	1997	442	12	Up
1957	406	19	Down	1998	592	22	Up
1958	153	0	Down	1999	459	3	Down
1959	353	11	Up	2000	603	15	Up
1960	302	23	Down	2001	214	25	Down

Vernal Equinox Lunar Day	Change from Previous Year		Vernal Equinox Lunar Day	Change from Previous Year	
	Up	Down		Up	Down
2	1	1	17	2	1
3	3	1	18		1
4	3	1	19		3
5	3		20		2
6		1	21	2	
7	1	2	22	4	
8	1	3	23	2	2
9		1	24	2	
10		3	25	1	2
11	2		26	2	1
12	2	1	27	1	2
13	3	1	28		3
14	2	1	29		1
15	2		0	1	3
16	3	1	1	1	3

There is suggestive evidence (*p*-value = .0964 from a Chi-Square Goodness-Of-Fit test) the observed year-to-year change ("UP" represents positive change and "DOWN" represents negative change) in the number of lynx furs captured in the Yukon from 1919 to 2001 is dependent on which lunar phase day falls on the Vernal Equinox. The actual day used is March 21. The Vernal Equinox can also be March 20. This may partly account for the grouping of lunar day numbers.

Lunar Day	Up	Down	Expected Up	Expected Down
1	1	1	1.0352941	0.9647059
2	3	1	2.0705882	1.9294118
3	3	1	2.0705882	1.9294118
4	3	0	1.5529412	1.4470588
5	0	1	0.5176471	0.4823529
6	1	2	1.5529412	1.4470588
7	1	3	2.0705882	1.9294118
8	0	1	0.5176471	0.4823529
9	0	3	1.5529412	1.4470588
10	2	0	1.0352941	0.9647059
11	2	1	1.5529412	1.4470588
12	3	1	2.0705882	1.9294118
13	2	1	1.5529412	1.4470588
14	2	0	1.0352941	0.9647059
15	3	1	2.0705882	1.9294118
16	2	1	1.5529412	1.4470588
17	0	1	0.5176471	0.4823529
18	0	3	1.5529412	1.4470588
19	0	2	1.0352941	0.9647059
20	2	0	1.0352941	0.9647059
21	4	0	2.0705882	1.9294118
22	2	2	2.0705882	1.9294118
23	2	0	1.0352941	0.9647059
24	1	2	1.5529412	1.4470588
25	2	1	1.5529412	1.4470588
26	1	2	1.5529412	1.4470588
27	0	3	1.5529412	1.4470588
28	0	1	0.5176471	0.4823529
29	1	3	2.0705882	1.9294118
30	1	3	2.0705882	1.9294118

[Appendix 6-4]

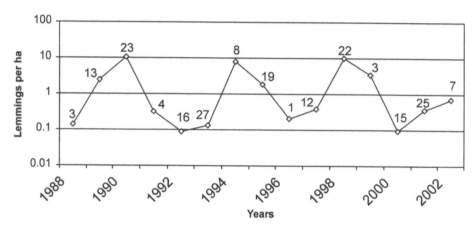

Time series of the estimated density of lemming nests per ha for the period 1988-2002. The numbers above each data point are the lunar day at the Vernal Equinox of that year. The lunar numbers form a pattern (Down = 1 to 4 and 15 to 19 and Up = 7 to 13 and 22 to 25) that can be used to time the number of lemmings. We cannot form a statistical conclusion with the number of years available but the trend is expected to continue on in the same manner as the lynx. The actual day used is March 21. The Vernal Equinox can also be March 20. This may partly account for the grouping of lunar day numbers. (Data source: Gilg, Oliver et al., 2003, Cycle dynamics in a simple vertebrate predator-prey community, *Science* 302: 866-68. Lunar days added by author.)

Lunar Day on the Vernal Equinox	Frequency	Relative to Previous Year
1	1	Down
3	2	Down
4	1	Down
7	1	Up
8	1	Up
12	1	Up
13	1	Up
15	1	Down
16	1	Down
19	1	Down
22	1	Up
23	1	Up
25	1	Up
27	1	Up

[Appendix 6-5]

Harvest Year	Oregon (a) Total Hazelnut Production tons	First New Moon day of Solar Year	Winter Solstice Lunar Day (previous year)	Pattern	Pattern Description	Bearing Acreage
1963	6,960	Jan-25	24		Optimal Window	
1964	8,090	Jan-14	5	B-1	Up – Poor Window	
1965	7,740	Feb-2	17	B-2	Down – Optimal Window	16,800
1966	12,220	Jan-21	28	A-1	Up – Optimal Window	
1967	7,540	Jan-10	9	C	Down – Poor Window	
1968	7,600	Jan-29	19	A-2	Up – Optimal Window	
1969	7,400	Jan-18	1	B-2	Down – Optimal Window	
1970	9,260	Jan-7	11	B-1	Up – Poor Window	16,300
1971	11,370	Jan-26	22	A-1	Up – Optimal Window	
1972	10,150	Jan-16	3	B-2	Down – Optimal Window	
1973	12,250	Jan-4	15	B-1	Up - Poor Window	
1974	7,200 (b)	Jan-22	26	B-2	Down – Optimal Window	
1975	12,120	Jan-12	7	B-1	Up - Poor Window	17,800
1976	7,170	Jan-31	18	B-2	Down – Optimal Window	
1977	11,750	Jan-19	0	A-2	Up – Optimal Window	
1978	14,050	Jan-8	10	B-1	Up - Poor Window	
1979	13,000	Jan-28	20	B-2	Down – Optimal Window	
1980	15,400	Jan-17	1	A-2	Up – Optimal Window	22,000
1981	14,700	Jan-6	13	C	Down - Poor Window	22,000
1982	18,800	Jan-24	24	A-1	Up – Optimal Window	22,000
1983	8,200	Jan-14	5	C	Down - Poor Window	21,300
1984	13,400	Jan-3	16	B-1	Up - Poor Window	22,000
1985	24,600	Jan-21	28	A-1	Up – Optimal Window	23,300
1986	15,100	Jan-10	9	C	Down - Poor Window	24,900
1987	21,800	Jan-29	19	A-2	Up – Optimal Window	24,800
1988	16,500	Jan-19	0	B-2	Down - Optimal Window	26,500

Table continues on next page

Table continued from previous page

Harvest Year	Oregon (a) Total Hazelnut Production tons	First New Moon day of Solar Year	Winter Solstice Lunar Day (previous year)	Pattern	Pattern Description	Bearing Acreage
1989	13,000	Jan-7	12	C	Down - Poor Window	27,100
1990	21,700	Jan-26	22	A-1	Up – Optimal Window	27,300
1991	25,500	Jan-15	4	A-2	Up – Optimal Window	27,470
1992	27,700	Jan-4	15	B-1 (A-2)	Up – Poor Window	27,030
1993	41,000	Jan-22	26	A-1	Up – Optimal Window	26,930
1994	21,100	Jan-11	7	C	Down - Poor Window	27,400
1995	39,000	Jan-30	18	A-2	Up – Optimal Window	26,800
1996	18,500	Jan-20	28	B-2	Down - Optimal Window	28,350
1997	47,000	Jan-9	10	B-1	Up – Poor Window	28,475
1998	16,500	Jan-28	21	B-2	Down – Optimal Window	29,530
1999	40,000	Jan-17	2	A-2	Up – Optimal Window	29,200
2000	22,500	Jan-6	13	C	Down – Poor Window	28,350
2001	49,500	Jan-24	25	A-1	Up - Optimal Window	28,100
2002	19,500	Jan-13	6	C	Down - Poor Window	27,800

(Source: Hazelnut Marketing Board)
a. 1976 to 1986 includes Washington. Washington is less than 1%. / Production = Orchard run
b. Yearly reports state 1974 crop as either 6,700 or 7,200

A-1 = Up year corresponding with the peak in the optimal solar window (New Moon from January 21-26)
A-2 = Up year corresponding with the optimal solar window (New Moon from January 15-20 and January 27-February 2)
B-1 = Up year corresponding with the poor solar window (New Moon from January 3-14)
B-2 = Down year corresponding with the optimal solar window (New Moon from January 15-February 2)
C = Down year corresponding with the poor solar window (New Moon from January 3-14)

The below figure shows the estimated means for the five patterns A-1, A-2, B-1, B-2, and C. There is convincing evidence that some patterns are observed to yield a greater change in tons per acre than others (p-value < .0001 from a one-way ANOVA). Pattern "A-1" is observed to have the largest increase in tons per acre; pattern "C" is observed to have the largest decrease in tons per acre. Pair-wise statistical differences can be seen in the figure below via Tukey multiple comparisons.

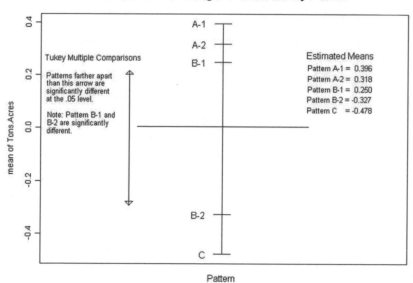

Results for the Change in Tons/Acre by Pattern

Note: Data points are calculated from observed and previous-to-observed years (i.e., the observed year's tons per acre minus the previous year's tons per acre). The data points are then assigned to their respective patterns. The patterns are based on the observed year and they occur nonsystematically over time.

One-way ANOVA Table

	Df	Sum of Sq	Mean Sq	F Value	p-value
Pattern	4	5.0902	1.2725	11.55	.0000049798
Residuals	34	3.7459	0.1102		

95 % simultaneous confidence intervals for specified
linear combinations, by the Tukey method
critical point: 2.8795
response variable: Tons.Acres
intervals excluding 0 are flagged by "****"

	Estimate	Std.Error	Lower Bound	Upper Bound
A-1-A-2	0.0786	0.177	-0.432	0.589
A-1-B-1	0.1460	0.172	-0.348	0.641
A-1-B-2	0.7230	0.167	0.241	1.200 ****
A-1-C	0.8740	0.172	0.379	1.370 ****
A-2-B-1	0.0677	0.172	-0.427	0.562
A-2-B-2	0.6440	0.167	0.162	1.130 ****
A-2-C	0.7960	0.172	0.301	1.290 ****
B-1-B-2	0.5760	0.161	0.112	1.040 ****
B-1-C	0.7280	0.166	0.250	1.210 ****
B-2-C	0.1510	0.161	-0.313	0.616

Endnotes

Chapter 1 Thinking in Space and Time

1. Leach, E. R., 1950, Primitive calendars, *Oceans* 20 (4): 245-62.

2. Smith, Douglas C., 1998, *The Yami of Lan-yu Island: Portrait of a culture in transition* (Phi Delta Kappa Educational Foundation).

3. Tsuchida, Shigeru; Yamada, Yukihiro; and Moriguchi, Tsunekazu, 1987, *Lists of Selected Words of Batanic Languages* (University of Tokyo).

4. Waterman, T. T., and Kroeber, A. L., 1938, *The Kepel Fish Dam* (University of California Press).

5. The statement that Easter Day is the first Sunday after the full moon that occurs after the Vernal Equinox is not a precise statement of the actual ecclesiastical rules. The full moon involved is not the astronomical Full Moon but an ecclesiastical moon (determined from tables) that keeps, more or less, in step with the astronomical Moon. The ecclesiastical rules are: (1) Easter falls on the first Sunday following the first ecclesiastical full moon that occurs on or after the day of the vernal equinox; (2) this particular ecclesiastical full moon is the 14th day of a tabular lunation (new moon); and (3) the vernal equinox is fixed as March 21. This results in Easter never occurring before March 22 or later than April 25. The Gregorian dates for the ecclesiastical full moon come from the Gregorian tables. Therefore, the civil date of Easter depends upon which tables--Gregorian or pre-Gregorian--are used. The western (Roman Catholic and Protestant) Christian churches use the Gregorian tables; many eastern (Orthodox) Christian churches use the older tables based on the Julian calendar.

6. This seasonal shift results from the 23-1/2 degree tilt of the earth's axis. The earth's axis always points the same direction in space; thus, as the earth revolves around the sun, its axis points more towards the sun in summer, more away from the sun in winter, and along earth's orbit at the equinoxes.

7. We can also partly equate light to meteorology and temperature. The heat that we are concerned about comes from the sun and its relative position to the earth. The position determines the amount of light received and temperature generated.

The story is a little more complicated. While the solstices are the extremes of light, temperature depends not only on the amount of heat that the atmosphere receives, but also on the amount of heat that the atmosphere loses through absorption by water and ground or through reflection. The ocean temperatures change much more slowly than the atmosphere temperature because water is much denser than air, and therefore takes longer to heat up or cool down. Although the atmosphere warms up quickly in the spring and summer, the atmosphere still loses much of its heat to the cooler water of the oceans. Eventually, the oceans absorb enough heat to reach equilibrium with the temperature of the atmosphere. Solid ground has a similar, but lesser effect on temperature. For several weeks after the Summer Solstice, the atmosphere of the hemisphere experiencing summer receives less heat than it did at the solstice, but also loses less heat to absorption and reflection. As a result, the average temperature continues to increase. When the loss of heat to the oceans and ground equals the gain from the sun's radiation, the temperature reaches a maximum. In the Northern Hemisphere this effect occurs in August; in the southern hemisphere, in February. The oceans and the ground stay warm and release heat into the atmosphere as the atmosphere begins to cool off during the fall or winter, so the coldest days of winter do not occur until well after the Winter Solstice. But in general, after the Winter Solstice (closer to the Vernal Equinox) temperatures gradually increase and after the Summer Solstice (closer to the Autumnal Equinox) they decrease.

The relationship between the sun and temperature can become complicated by other environmental factors. The changes in temperature and in the length of daylight that accompany the seasons differ greatly at different latitudes. At the poles, summer is three months of daylight and winter is three months of darkness. Near the equator, however, days and nights remain about 12 hours long throughout the year. The Arctic and Antarctic circles, at latitude 66°30' north and 66°30' south, respectively, mark the farthest points from the poles at which there can be 24 hours of daylight or 24 hours of darkness. Midway between the poles and the equator, the length of daylight varies from about 8 hours in winter to about 16 hours in summer. Therefore, the photoperiod and climatic condition in Oregon will not be the same as those in Alaska at the same time of year.

8. In Miller, Harald, 2004, Star search, *National Geographic* 205 (1): 76-87, the authors argue that pieces added to the disk after the stars were placed can be used to time the Winter and Summer Solstices.

9. The bronze piece to the far left is probably the handle. This would have enabled the user to point to the sky with his right hand and make his calculations against the disk.

10. See Huntington, Ellsworth, 1931, The Matamek conference on biological cycles, *Science* 74 (1914): 229-35, and Keith, Lloyd B., 1963, *Wildlife's Ten-Yevar Cycle* (University of Wisconsin Press).

11. Genesis 11:9.

12. The phrase below was translated in Berlinski, David, 2003, *The Secrets of the Vaulted Sky: Astrology and the Art of Prediction* (Harcourt Books), 16.

13. Genesis 11:4.

14. Isaiah 47:13.

15. Personal communications with Laith A. Jawad during 2002 and 2003. Jawad made this judgment from the position of the pelvic fin, which is clear at the center of the body, the size of the head and the shape and size of the caudal fin.

16. Jawad, Laith A., 1999, Shad of the Shatt Al-Arab River in Iraq, *Shad Journal* 4 (2).

Chapter 2 *The Journey of the Salmon*

1. Roper, Brett B., and Scarnecchia, Dennis L., 1999, Emigration of age-0 chinook salmon (*Oncorhynchus tshwytscha*) smolts from upper South Umpqua River basin, Oregon, U.S.A, *Canadian Journal of Fisheries and Aquatic Science* 56: 939-46.

2. Youngson, A. F., Buck, R. J. G., Simpson, T. H., and Hay, D. W., 1983, The autumn and spring emigrations of juvenile Atlantic salmon (*Salmo salar*) from the Girnock Burn, Aberdeen, Scotland, UK, environmental release of migration, *Journal of Fish Biology* 23 (6): 625-40.

3. Thorpe, J. E., Morgan, R. I. G., Pretswell, D., and Higgins, P. J., 1988, Movement rhythms in juvenile Atlantic salmon (*Salmo salar L*), *Journal of Fish Biology* 33 (6): 931-40.

4. Kuzishchin, K. V., Pavlov, D. S., Savvaitova, K. A., Gruzdeva, M. A, and Pustovit, O. P., 2001, Downstream migration of juvenile diadromous Kamchatka trout (*Parasalmo mykiss*) in the western Kamchatka rivers, *Journal of Ichthyology* 41 (3): 227-38, translated from 2001 *Voprosy Ikhtiologii* 41 (2): 220-31.

5. Brege, Dean A., Absolon, Randall F., and Graves, Ritchie J., Seasonal and diel passage of juvenile salmonids at John Day Dam on the Columbia River, 1996, *North American Journal of Fisheries Management* 16: 659-65.

6. "Space-time" is a term that I will use frequently throughout this book instead of "place and time," although they essentially mean the same. My definition differs from the more classical view of physicists.

7. There are other devices to keep the salmon from returning to the same time and place. They do not all return to their natal river. Often one cohort year will return as adults over more than one year.

8. Wagner, Harry, H., 1974, Photoperiod and temperature regulation of smolting in steelhead trout (*Salmo gairdneri*), *Canadian Journal of Zoology* 52: 219-34.

9. Giorgi, A. E., Muir, W. D., Zaugg, W. S., and McCutcheon, S., 1991, Biological Manipulation of Migration Rate: The Use of Advanced Photoperiod to Accelerate Smoltification in Yearling Chinook Salmon, Annual Report 1989, National Marine Fisheries Service, Contract No. DE-AI79-88BP50301, Project No. 88-141.

10. Nakari, T., Soivio, A., and Pesonen, S., 1986, Effects of advanced photoperiod cycle on the epidermis and gonadosomatic index of 2-year old rainbow trout, *Salmo gairdneri* R., reared at natural temperature, *Journal of Fish Biology* 29: 451-57.

11. In the more southern latitude rivers, which are warmer and support more prey, most of the juveniles tend to out-migrate within one year, but in northern climates where growth is slower, the migration may occur over two or more years.

12. Pickford, G. E., and Phillips, J. C., 1959, Prolactin, a factor in promoting survival of hypothysectomized killfish in freshwater, *Science* 130: 454-55.

13. Weber, Lavern J., and Smith, John R., Possible role of the pineal gland in migratory behavior of salmonids, *In Salmonid Ecosystems of the North Pacific*, ed. McNeil, William J., and Himsworth, Daniel C., 1980 (Oregon State University Press).

14. While it has proven to be much more difficult to determine in returning adults, it is thought that similar processes occur--leading the fish to "prefer" low-salinity water over high-salinity water. Thus, as the fish approach the coastlines they begin to turn into freshwater (inlets, estuaries, rivers). Juveniles migrating northward along the oceans show opposite preferences: They tend to shy away from low-salinity waters and stay the course in high-salinity ocean waters. Although biologists tend to think of smoltification being over once the fish have entered salt water, many of the driving forces continue to exert influence.

15. The southern limit of distribution of Pacific salmon appears to correspond roughly with the southern extent of Transition Domain across much of the North Pacific Ocean, although there are differences between species as to how far south they will be found. Populations from the central Oregon coast up to Alaska all pass through the fertile feeding grounds south of the Aleutian Islands and west of northern British Columbia. Stocks south of this line generally feed off the California

and southern Oregon coastlines. The dividing line for the two movements appears to be around Port Orford, Oregon, just north of the Rogue River. The division in migration can partly be explained by the divergence of these ocean currents. Migration work on stocks of steelhead trout from the west coast on Kamchatka similarly indicates that they travel eastward along the Pacific and sub-arctic currents, further supporting the hypothesis that salmonids use current to help set their course on the way out.

16. Reebs, Stephan, Sleep, inactivity and circadian rhythms in fish, In Ali, M. A, 1992, *Rhythms in Fishes* (Plenum Press), 127-35.

17. Brett, J. R., and Ali, M. A., 1958, Some observations on the structure and photochemical responses of the Pacific salmon retina, *Journal of the Fisheries Research Board of Canada* 15 (5): 815-29.

18. The physiochemical differences between the two classifications of fish were established in Hafeez, M. A., and Quay, W. B., 1970, Pineal acetylserotonin methyltransferase activity I the teleost fishes *Hesperoleucus symmetricus* and *Salmo gairdneri*, with evidence, *Comp. & Gen. Pharmacol.* 1: 257-62.

The predator-prey part of the hypothesis was demonstrated for the bass in Howick, G. L., and O'Brien, W. J., 1983, Piscivorous feeding behavior of largemouth bass: An experimental analysis, *Transactions of the American Fisheries Society* 112: 508-16.

19. Farbridge, K. J, and Leatherland, J. F., 1987, Lunar cycles of coho salmon, Oncorhynchus Kisutch, II, Scale amino acid update, nucleic acids, metabolic reserves and plasma thyroid hormones, *Journal of Exploratory Biology* 129: 179-89, and Farbridge, K. J., and Leatherland, J. F., 1987, Lunar periodicity of growth cycles in rainbow trout (*Salmo gairdneri*), Richardson, J., *Interdisc. Cycle Research* 18: 169-77.

20. Alldredge, A. L., and King, J. M., 1980, Effects of moonlight on the vertical migration patterns of demersal zooplankton, *Journal of Exploratory Biology and Ecology* 44 (2-3): 133-56.

21. The photoperiod varies with geography. Alaskans have endless summer days and winter evenings, while in more southerly latitudes there are shorter separations between day and night throughout the year. Alaskans are generally considered to be depressed during the winter as a result of the long evening lengths. This is probably a result of increased levels of melatonin. The production of melatonin is inhibited when light strikes the retina. Salmonids are also affected by these extremes in day and night lengths. Reduced light, such as during the winter months, depresses the locomotor activity in young salmon (Hoar, 1955). Increased day lengths induce the fish to be more chemically active during the sun-illuminated hours, which may reinforce the need to feed and possibly migrate out to sea (Weber and Smith, 1980).

The out-migration of juvenile salmonids south of the Arctic Circle starts to occur around the Vernal Equinox. In Oregon, the first peaks of coho fry and Chinook fingerlings occurred around the Vernal Equinox. Researchers have found increased levels of chemical plasma T4 in Pacific and Atlantic salmon associated with the New Moon nearest the Vernal Equinox. T4 is believed to be associated with a premigratory restlessness in salmon juveniles (Leatherland et al., 1992).

However, the shift in photoperiod is probably more important than the actual lengths of days and nights (Hoffnagle and Fivizzani, 1998) which is probably why we see the smolt out-migrations after the Vernal Equinox. All of the salmon and steelhead trout juveniles out-migrations I have observed below the Arctic Circle occurred after the Vernal Equinox and before the Summer Solstice. The Summer Solstice is the beginning of decreasing day lengths.

22. On Oregon and Washington rivers, spring Chinook generally enter first, followed by the summer steelhead trout, fall Chinooks, Coho, chums and then winter steelhead trout. In the Columbia River system there are three classes of Chinooks referred to as spring-run, summer-run and fall-run. In Alaska, the order is Chinook, pink, sockeye, chum, coho salmon and then steelhead trout. Prior to entering the rivers, winter and fall run salmonids have well-developed gonads in preparation for spawning, while spring and summer run fish mature in the freshwater environment and usually spawn just before the winter fish. All fish spawn in the same order. When there are two runs of fish within one species whose arrival timing are separated by more than five months, the ones that enter earlier usually have a longer distance to travel.

23. Chambers Creek steelhead trout have also been introduced throughout western Washington, including the Puget Sound region, and in tributaries of the lower Columbia River. As much as 90 percent of steelhead trout harvested from some western Washington streams can be attributed to Chambers Creek winter steelhead trout, through artificial and established natural production.

24. The wild fish start with the hatchery fish but end in March or April. These migration times are similar to other steelhead trout stocks in central to northern Oregon.

25. Though in some years stocks of coho may spawn in January.

26. Source: Data from the Washington Department of Fish and Wildlife. (Lunar phases added by author.)

27. This is not to say that the movement of salmonids is not affected by flow. During periods of lower than average seasonal flow, the river entry is closely associated with days when flow had increased since the previous day. However, during periods

of higher than average seasonal flow, river entry is not significantly associated with such periods of increased flow (Smith et al., 1994).

28. Temperature can have an effect on the speed of migration, although it cannot synchronize movements or events such as spawning. Dr. Douglas Workman from Michigan State University, in cooperation with Jim Dexter from the Michigan Department of Natural Resources, has done a great deal of research on the effect of temperature on salmonid's movement. Their work demonstrates that there is a strong relationship between temperature and the speed of movement (Workman, R. D, et al., 2002). Elevated water temperatures increase the metabolism of the fish, to a point, which in turn stimulates greater speed of migration. In some of the Great Lakes tributaries, there are extreme fluctuations in water temperature as a result of dam releases for power generation and the management of reservoirs. In the wintertime, these releases can sometimes drastically increase the water temperatures and greatly affect the movement of salmon and steelhead trout once they are in the river system.

29. Lorz, H. W., and Northcote, T. G., 1965, Factors affecting stream location, and timing and intensity of entry by spawning Kokanee (*Oncorhynchus nerka*) into an inlet of Nicola Lake, British Columbia, *Journal of the Fisheries Research Board of Canada* 22 (3): 665-87.

30. While magnetism and currents may lead the salmon and steelhead trout in a general direction, homing to a specific spot cannot be explained by these phenomena alone with the available data. We may be able to find part of the explanation to the precise positioning in the fish's olfactory system. If this is the mechanism that they use to home to a specific spot, it must be imprinted during the out-migration stage as smolts are often trucked from hatcheries and do not return. The amount of time required for acquisition of this home-stream response has been demonstrated to be as short as 36 hours (Jensen and Duncan, 1971). This ability is not too difficult to imagine; I live out in the country and commonly drive past cow pastures and other fragrant areas. They have a chemical signature that I can perceive, and I'm usually awakened by their presence. To the salmon, these scents would be of an even greater magnitude.

31. Chinook, coho and steelhead trout spawn in small to moderate sized gravel, Sockeye spawn in fine gravel and cobble in small creeks and large rivers. Chum and pinks generally spawn in the lower watershed, usually just outside tidewater in small to moderate-sized gravel.

32. Data supplied by the Oregon Department of Fish and Wildlife. (Lunar phase added by author.)

33. Each redd or nesting pocket may carry thousands of eggs. Small amounts of silt, detritus, or fine sand are removed by the female in the process of excavating the redd. She excavates the redd by vigorous upward and downward motions of her body, causing both the tail and water pressure to move the sand and gravel. When spawning occurs, the female places herself over the pocket, followed by a male a second or two later. Both fish lower their tails to bring their vents close together near the center of the pocket. Eggs and milt are then released, while the two fish remain over the pocket for up to 20 seconds while fertilization occurs. The female immediately buries the eggs after spawning. She may appear to stand guard on the "redd" against newly arriving females, seeking to lay their own eggs in the choice gravel, but perhaps she doesn't have any desire to go anywhere. In support of this hypothesis, steelhead trout, which can go back to sea, stay on redds for a shorter time after the peak redd counts than the other Pacific salmonids.

When spawning is complete, both males and females exhibit external physical deterioration in the form of frayed fins, skin loss, fungus, infections and, at times, blindness. While the decaying flesh may not be fragrant and pleasing to the eye, it is important to the ecosystem. It fertilizes the aquatic plant life on which the insects feed. It also provides food for a number of larger species, such as bear, that need this nourishment to survive the winter. The juvenile fish also feed directly on flesh and an increased amount of marine-derived nutrients turn up in terrestrial plants. The survival of a salmon run is not only critical for the preservation of their species, but also for numerous other life forms. Some Pacific coast conservation programs drop carcasses from hatcheries in rivers to increase their productivity. Internally, there is a degradation of the cardiovascular and endocrine systems, liver and stomach. The physical deterioration is not related to the rigors of their journeys and the salmon's commitment to this last act of perpetuating its kind. Great Lakes salmon exhibit similar decaying, yet they do not travel far. The only Pacific salmon that do not necessarily die after spawning are the steelhead trout and cutthroat trout (*Oncorhynchus clarki*), which can spawn more than once. However, most steelhead trout die after spawning unless they can regain condition following this event and successfully migrate downstream to the ocean.

The eggs begin the cycle again. The recently spawned and fertilized offspring will fight for survival, beginning in this egg sac and entombed in gravel. The development and initial survival of the sac fry is greatly influenced by water temperatures. Warmer waters will speed up growth while cooler ones will slow it down. The fragile and defenseless eggs that survive the silt and receding water flows will incubate and metamorphose into complex multi-celled vertebrates, with intricate organs and extensive nervous systems. They will be about the length of a pin, complete with gills and all organ systems. These small fish will remain in the gravel and will feed off their yolk sac.

34. Palmer, John D., and Goodenough, 1978, Mysterious monthly rhythms, *Natural History* 87 (10): 64-69.

Chapter 3 Interconnectedness

1. Nilsson, Martin P., 1920, *Primitive Time-Reckoning* (Lund).

2. Mars has two asteroids that are called "moons."

3. Anderson, Norman, 1966, Depressant effect of moonlight on activity of aquatic insects, *Nature* 209 (5020): 319-20.

4. Cowan, C. A., and Peckarsky, B. L., 1994, Diel feeding and positioning periodicity of a grazing mayfly in a trout stream and a fishless stream, *Canadian Journal of Fisheries and Aquatic Science* 51: 450-59.

5. The behavioral cascade part of this hypothesis was demonstrated in Romare, Pia, and Hansson, Lars-Anders, 2003, A behavioral cascade: Top-predator induced behavioral shifts in planktivorous fish and zooplankton, *Limnology and Oceanography* 48 (5). The authors studied the relationship between a predatory fish, roach (prey fish) and zooplankton. They found that the roach changed their behavior to the predator which in turn affected the zooplankton.

6. Morrison, D. W., 1978, Lunar phobia in a neotropical fruit bat, *Artibeus jamaicensis* (Chiroptera: Phyllostomidae), *Animal Behavior* 26: 852-55.

7. Todd, Martin, Richard Washington, Robert A. Cheke and Dominic Kniveton. 2002. Brown locust outbreaks and climate variability in southern Africa. *Journal of Applied Ecology.* 39: 31-42.

8. Exodus 10.

9. Hutchinson, G.E., 1967, *A Treatise on Limnology,* Vol. 2 (John Wiley & Sons, Inc.).

10. Luecke, C., and Wurtsbaugh, W., 1993, Effects of moon and daylight on hydroacoustic estimates of pelagic fish abundance, *Transactions of the American Fishery Society* 122: 112-20.

11. Gaudreau, Nathalie, and Boisclair, Daniel, 2000, Influence of moon phase on acoustic estimates of the abundance of fish performing daily horizontal migration in a small oligotrophic lake, *Canadian Journal of Fisheries and Aquatic Science* 57: 581-90.

12. Mackas, D. L., Goldblatt, R., and Lewis, A. G., 1998, Interdecadal variation in developmental timing of Neocalanus plumchrus populations at Ocean Station

P in the subarctic North Pacific, *Canadian Journal of Fisheries and Aquatic Science* 55: 1874-93. Additional years from 1996 provided by David Mackas.

13. Hartland-Rowe, R., 1955, Lunar rhythm in the emergence of an ephemeropteran, *Nature* 1976: 657.

14. Johannes, R. E., 1981, *Words of the Lagoon: Fishing & Marine Lore in the Palau District of Micronesia* (University of California Press).

15. Linkowski, T. B., 1996, Lunar rhythms of vertical migrations coded in otolith microstructure of North Atlantic lanternfishes, genus Hygophum (Myctophidae), *Marine Biology* 124: 495-508.

16. Baker, Gillian, and Dekker, Rene. 2000. Lunar synchrony in the reproduction of the Moluccan Megapode *Eulipoa wallacei* (Megapodiidae, Galliformes). *Ibis* 142: 382-88.

17. Archibald, H. L. 1976. Spring drumming patterns of ruffed grouse. *Auk* 93 (4): 808-29.

18. Morell, T.E., Yahner, R.H. & Harkness, W.L. 1991. Factors affecting detection of great horned owls by using broadcast vocalizations. *Wildlife Society, Bulletin* 19 (4): 481-88.

19. Pyle, Peter, Nur, Nadav, Henderson, R. Philip, and DeSante, David F. 1993. The effects of weather and lunar cycle on nocturnal migration of landbirds at Southeast Farallon Island, California. *The Condor* 95: 343-61.

Chapter 4 *The Harvest We Reap*

1. For the *Torah*, see Genesis 39-41 and for the *Qur'an*, see Chapter 12.

2. (*Sotah* 36b) tr. Neusner, Jacob, 1984, *The Talmud of Babylonia: An American Translation Xvii: Tractate Sotah* (Brown Judaic Studies, 72) (Scholars Press). The *Talmud* is a body of Jewish civil and religious law, including commentaries on the *Torah*. The teachings of the Babylonian Talmud were written by scholars between the 3rd century and the beginning of the 6th century.

3. This section and the one below are drawn from Swerdlow, N. M., 1998, *The Babylonian Theory of the Planets* (Princeton University Press). Swerdlow uses ARAK 82 referring to Hunger, H., *Astrological Reports to Assyrian Kings*.

4. For a review of this literature on this topic, see Palmer, John D., 2002, *The Living Clock: The Orchestrator of Biological Rhythms* (Oxford) and Bunning, E. 1956. Endogenous rhythms in plants. *Annual Review of Plant Physiology* 7: 71-90.

5. Refer to Appendix 2-5 for more information on the timing of moonrise and set.

6. Abrami, G., 1972, Correlations between lunar phases and the rhythmicities in plant growth under field conditions, *Canadian Journal of Botany* 50 (11): 2157-66.

7. Genesis 9:21.

8. Genesis 40:5-19.

9. Solomon 6:11.

10. Cox, Jeff, 1985, *From Vines to Wines* (Garden Way Publishing).

11. Graves, Ralph A., 1917, Fearful famines of the past, *National Geographic* (July): 68-90.

12. One approach to explain an El Niño is to look at the South Pacific Ocean under normal conditions. The ocean is relatively stable with warm waters flowing northwest towards Indonesia. Then, for unknown reasons, the trade winds slacken and change direction. This shift is what we view as the start of an El Niño event. During the 1997 El Niño, this change in movement caused the sea temperatures in the eastern Pacific to rise by almost 15 degrees Fahrenheit. The flow moves rapidly. The movements of these warm waters were clocked at almost 150 miles a day in one year. The pool of warm water modified wind patterns and affected climates around the world for more than a year. Such El Niño conditions have resulted in droughts in South Africa, over the Indian subcontinent, in Indonesia and Australia, while unusually fierce storms were experienced in North and South America. Nevertheless, El Niños are highly unpredictable. The same area can be wet in one event and dry the next, depending on the twists and turns of air currents disturbed by their forces.

13. Orlove, B. S., Chiang, J. C., and Cane, M. A., 2002, Ethnoclimatology in the Andes, *American Scientist* 90: 428-35.

14. Orlove, B. S., Chiang, J. C., and Cane, M. A., 2000, Forecasting Andean rainfall and crop yield from the influence of El Niño on Pleiades visibility, *Nature* 43: 68-71.

15. Job 9:8-9.

16. Job 38:31-33.

17. Amos 5:8.

18. Genesis 37:9.

19. The relationships between Mesopotamian and Canaanite myths is described in: Gray, John, 1969, *Near Eastern Mythology: Mesopotamia, Syria, Palestine* (The Hamlyn Publishing Group).

20. Ginzberg, Louis, 1920, *The Legends of the Jews: II, Bible Times and Characters from Joseph to the Exodus* (The Jewish Society of America).

21. Kolisko's findings were summarized by Drs. Klaus Peter Endres and Wolfgang Schad from University of Witten, Germany, in their book, *Moon Rhythms in Nature: How Lunar Cycles Affect Living Organisms* (2003).

22. Whiston, William. (trans.) 1960. *Josephus, Complete Works.* Kregel Publications. Book II, Chapter VII, Section 7.

Chapter 5 The Art of Time

1. Ibexes belong to the family Bovidae of the order Artiodactyla.

2. Redrawn from Ruspoli, Mario, 1986, *The Cave at Lascaux: The Final Photographs* (Harry N. Abrams, Inc.).

3. Redrawn from Ruspoli, Mario, 1986, *The Cave at Lascaux: The Final Photographs* (Harry N. Abrams, Inc.).

4. Redrawn from Ruspoli, Mario, 1986, *The Cave at Lascaux: The Final Photographs* (Harry N. Abrams, Inc.).

5. Redrawn from Ruspoli, Mario, 1986, *The Cave at Lascaux: The Final Photographs* (Harry N. Abrams, Inc.).

6. Rigaud, Jean-Philippe, 1988, Art treasures from the Ice Age: Lascaux Cave, *National Geographic* 174 (4): 482-99.

7. Price relates that roe deer are highly territorial. Done well, calling roe deer during the rut is a crafty business. The female gives a high pitched reedy note when in estrus to attract a buck (male), so unlike calling other deer that come mostly in response to a male challenge, roe come in to the call because they want to. Many times Price has had roe deer within five or six feet and several times had them actually jump over him as he sat calling for a client. The hide he uses is arranged on the spot. The bucks know their territory as we know our homes. They may come in very fast or slow like a cat. The best daytime calling conditions for roe are when scenting conditions are bad with little wind and there is no moon.

8. In all deer, Price has found that during the Full Moon there is usually less rutting activity observed during the day simply because the activity is too high those nights that the males are exhausted. He has watched and called deer under a Full Moon and they are very active if the weather is clear. Under these conditions, they are much more bold, having a sight and scent advantage, and can be see out on newly cut fields hundreds of yards away from cover.

9. Behrend, D. F., and McDowell, R. D., 1967, Antler shedding among white-tailed deer in Connecticut, *Journal of Wildlife Management* 31 (3): 588-90.

10. Antler growth and shedding has also been demonstrated to have a solar relationship. Researchers in Germany maintained five fallow deer in a barn with artificial light that was normal for the region but only lasted for six months. The increased number of photoperiods within 19 months produced three complete antler cycles (Schnare and Fischer, 1987). Elk and red deer trans-located across the equator change their seasonality to match the local light cycle.

11. Goss, Richard J., 1983, *Deer Antlers: Regeneration, Function, and Evolution* (Academic Press).

12. Bartos, Ludek; Perner, Vaclav; and Prochazka, Bohumir, 1987, On the relationship between social ranks during the velvet period and antler parameters in a growing red deer stag, *Acta Theriologica* 32 (24): 403-12.

13. Jacobson, H. A., and Waldhalm, S. J., Antler cycles of a white-tailed deer with congenital anophthalmia. In *The Biology of Deer*, ed. R. D. Brown (Springer-Verlag, 1992).

14. The date of death was April 14, 1990.

15. Redrawn from Ruspoli, Mario, 1986, *The Cave at Lascaux: The Final Photographs* (Harry N. Abrams, Inc.).

16. Sinclair, A. R. E., 1977, Lunar cycle and timing of mating season in Serengeti wildebeest, *Nature* 267: 832-33.

17. Cook, J. G., Johnson, B. K., Riggs, R. A., DelCurto, Bryant, L. D., and Irwin, L. L., 2002, Effects of summer-autumn nutritional and parturition date on reproduction and survival of elk: Final report, Oregon Department of Fish and Wildlife (La Grande, OR).

18. Guinness, F. E., Clutton-Brock, T. H., and Albon, S. D., 1978, Factors affecting calf mortality in red deer (*Cervus elaphus*), *Journal of Animal Ecology* 47: 817-32.

19. Redrawn from Laming, Annette, 1959, *Lascaux, Paintings and Engravings* (Pelican)

Chapter 6 *Patterning Plants and Animals*

1. Phelps, E. B., and Belding, D. L., 1931, *A Statistical Study of the Records of Salmon Fishing on the Restigouche River* (New York).

2. Redrawn from Phelps, E. B., and Belding, D. L., 1931, *A Statistical Study of the Records of Salmon Fishing on the Restigouche River* (New York). Lunar phases added by author.

3. See Bulmer, M. G., 1974, A statistical analysis of the 10-year cycle in Canada, *Journal of Animal Ecology* 43 (3): 701-18, for a review of this data.

4. Data Source: Statistics Canada (1958-2001) and Keith, Lloyd B., 1963, *Wildlife's Ten-Year Cycle* (University of Wisconsin Press, 1919-1957).

5. Gilg, Oliver, Hanski, Ilkka, and Sittler, Benoit, 2003, Cycle dynamics in a simple vertebrate predator-prey community, *Science* 302: 866-68.

6. Current crop estimates are made yearly by the U.S. Department of Agriculture (USDA) which is commissioned by the Hazelnut Marketing Board each year to estimate crop size before the nuts drop in order for the growers and producers to negotiate the price. The USDA sends teams of people into the orchards during the spring to survey the general health of the trees and choose limbs for a follow-up nut on the tree and inside meat count in August. The USDA's forecast generally comes within 10 percent of the actual harvest. Again, they are counting actual nuts just five weeks before they drop, so this is not a long-range forecasting tool. The estimate is useful for determining the price, helping farmers prepare for the harvest day and helping the industry to find places to channel excess nuts before the last minute, but in some respects we are living hand-to-mouth. The practice does not help us prepare for following years.

7. Germian, E., The reproduction of hazelnut (*Corylus avellana* L.): A review, in Me, Giovanni, and Radicati, Ludovico, 1994, Acta Horticulturae II International Congress on Hazelnut, *ISHS* 351 (January 1994): 195-209.

8. Hazelnuts have another peculiarity. Most female hazelnut tree flowers are not receptive to pollen from the same tree. Therefore, farmers must have at least two varieties of hazelnuts planted in their orchards to insure proper pollination. The most critical factor in choosing the mating trees is that the timing of the flower bloom and pollen shed from each species are in synchrony. The male pollinators account for 6 to 15 percent of the trees and are usually spaced within close proximity to the females. The predominant cultured varieties in Oregon are the Barcelona (*Corylus avellana* "barcelona") and Daviana (*Corylus avellana* "corylus"). The Barcelonas are round and generally referred to as the female, while the male Davianas are a longer and bigger nut. We also have the native *Corylus americana*, but they are not cultivated, usually growing like bushes along fencerows.

Chapter 7 *The Times of Our Lives*

1. For a review of papers on this subject, see: Endres, P., and Schad, W., 1997, *Moon Rhythms in Nature: How Lunar Cycles Affect Living Organisms* (Floris).

2. Stern, Kathleen, and McClintock, Martha K., 1998, Regulation of ovulation by human pheromones, *Nature* 392 (March 12).

3. For a review of papers published on this subject (trans. from German), see Endres, P., and Schad, W., 1997, *Moon Rhythms in Nature: How Lunar Cycles Affect Living Organisms* (Floris).

4. Sams, Jamie, 1994, *Earth Medicine: Ancestor's Ways of Harmony for Many Moons* (Harper).

5. Redrawn from Marshack, Alexander, 1971, *The Roots of Civilization: The Cognitive Beginnings of Man's First Art, Symbol, and Notation* (McGraw-Hill).

6. Blot, W. J., Fraumeni, J. F., and Stone, B. J., 1977, Geographic patterns of breast cancer in the United States, *Journal of the National Cancer Institute* 59: 1407-11.

7. Reynolds, P., Cone, J., Layefsky, M., Goldberg, D. E., and Hurley, S., 2002, Cancer incidence in California flight attendants (United States), *Cancer Causes and Control* 13: 317-24.

8. Davis, S., Mirick, D. K., and Stevens, R. G., 2001, Night shift work, light at night, and risk of breast cancer, *Journal of the National Cancer Institute* 93 (20): 1557-62.

9. Pukkala, E., Auvinen, A., and Wahlberg, G., 1995, Incidence of cancer among Finnish airline cabin attendants, 1967-92, *British Medical Journal* 311: 649-52.

10. Coleman, M. P., and Reiter, R. J., 1992, Breast cancer, blindness and melatonin, *European Journal of Cancer* 28: 501-03.

11. Verkasalo, P. K., Pukkala, E., Stevens, R. G., Ojamo, M., and Rudanko, S. L., 1999, Inverse relationship between breast cancer incidence and degree of visual impairment in Finland, *British Journal of Cancer* 80: 1459-60.

12. Cos, S., and Sánchez-Barceló, E. J., 1994, Differences between pulsatile or continuous exposure to melatonin on MCF-7 human breast cancer cell proliferation, *Cancer Letters* 85: 105-09.

13. Sánchez-Barceló, E. J., Cos, S., Fernández, R., and Mediavilla, M.D., 2003, Melatonin and mammary cancer: A short review, *Endocrine-Related Cancer* 10: 153-59.

14. Subramanian, A., and Kothari, L., 1991, Melatonin, a suppressor of spontaneous murine mammary tumors, *Journal of Pineal Research* 10: 136-40.

15. Willis, Judith L., 1990, Keeping in time to circadian rhythms, *FDA Consumer* (July/August).

16. It would be presumptuous to say that being out of rhythm for long periods of time is the only cause of breast cancer. There is a strong hypothesis that electric fields disrupt the pineal body and thereby distort the natural cycles (Stevens, et al.,

1977). The common ground between the electricity and rhythms hypotheses and that of the pineal body is affected.

17. Cohen, M., Lippman, M., and Chabner, B., 1978, Role of the pineal gland in the aetiology and treatment of breast cancer, *Lancet* 2: 814-16.

Chapter 8 Losing Our Place In Time

1. Part of this train of thought was presented in Leonard Mlodinow's book *Feynman's Rainbow* (2002). Dr. Mlodinow was a colleague of Feynman's at Caltech and had many thought-provoking conversations with him.

2. The return rates for adults that were barged as juveniles compared to those fish that passed through the system on their own volition range from 3:1 to 12:1 (Harmon, J. R., and Slatick, E., 1986).

3. Collis, Ken, and Adamany, Stephanie - Columbia River Inter-Tribal Fish Commission, Roby, Daniel D., Craig, David P., and Lyons, Donald E. - Oregon Cooperative Fish and Wildlife Research Unit, 2000, *Avian Predation on Juvenile Salmonids in the Lower Columbia River, 1998 Annual Report to Bonneville Power Administration, Portland, OR*, Contract No. 97B133475, Project No. 97-024-00, 101 electronic pages (BPA Report ODE/BP-33475.2).

4. The researchers who did the Caspian tern work also calculated that avian predation rates on hatchery-reared smolts was greater than those for wild smolts. The wild smolts probably fare better because they will migrate out more effectively once released, as they are physiologically ready and conditioned to avoid the predators by migrating during lower light. Similarly, part of the predation on the nonbarged salmonid juveniles in the main river is likely a result of the fish traveling during periods of illumination when they can be sighted by the northern squawfish, smallmouth bass and avian predators.

5. American Bird Conservancy. 2002. *Settlement a victory for beleaguered Caspian terns: Agreement protects world's largest colony of America's biggest tern.* Press release. March 8.

6. Kepler, Johannes. 1602. *Concerning the More Certain Fundamentals of Astrology.*

7. Genesis 1:16

Glossary of Terms

Adfluvial. Descriptive of migration patterns of fish species that spawn in a freshwater stream then migrate to a freshwater lake for growth.

Alevin. The lifestage of a salmonid between egg and fry. An alevin looks like a fish with a huge potbelly, which is the remaining egg sac. Alevin remain protected in the gravel riverbed, obtaining nutrition from the egg sac until they are large enough to fend for themselves in the stream.

Anadromous. A fish that spawns and spends its early life in fresh water, but moves into the ocean where it attains sexual maturity and spends most of its life.

Antler. A solid bony branched horn found in pairs on the head of animals, especially males, of the deer family including caribou and elk. Antlers are shed each year.

Arrhythmic. No regular pattern, due to an unchanging environment.

Autumnal Equinox. One of two times of the year when the sun's position makes day and night equal length in all parts of the earth. The Autumnal Equinox, which occurs around September 23, marks the beginning of the fall season in the Northern Hemisphere.

Bimodal. Relating to or consisting of a set of observations with two peaks, representing two values that occur with equal frequency and more often than any other value.

Biological Time. An organism's guidance by solar and lunar cues and the consequences from not being able to resynchronize them. The biological time of an organism is the main determinant of its position in time and space and survival rate/abundance. It helps the population to synchronize key events, find prey and avoid predators.

Bloom. The state of being in flower.

Blue Laws. A law regulating moral conduct; for example, a law prohibiting the sale of alcohol on Sunday.

Breast Cancer. Breast cancer is a malignant tumor in the glandular tissues of the breast. It falls in the category of carcinomas, which form when the processes that control normal cell growth break down, enabling an abnormal cell to multiply rapidly. The cancer tends to destroy an increasing portion of normal breast tissue over time and may spread to other parts of the body.

Brix. Measurement used to determine the sugar content of grapes and unfermented grape juice. An aid in determining the degree of ripeness. Most table wine grapes are picked at between 20 and 25 degrees Brix.

Bud Break. Term used to describe the unfurling of the grape buds on the vine.

Caddis. See *Trichoptera*.

Cancer. A malignant tumor or growth caused when cells multiply uncontrollably, destroying healthy tissue. The different forms are sarcomas, carcinomas, leukemias and lymphomas.

Cone Vision. The retina of the eye is made up of two types of cells: cones and rods. Cones are the nerve cells that are sensitive to light, detail and color.

Crepuscular. Event(s) occurring twice a day, i.e., at dawn and dusk.

Crescent. A curved shape like that of the Moon when it is less than half illuminated.

Crustaceans. Members of the class Crustacea, phylum Arthropoda; all have a hard exoskeleton. Includes crayfish, crabs, shrimp, zooplankton and others.

Cultivar. Horticulture shorthand for "cultivated variety."

Cycle. Same as Rhythm.

Daily. (Cycle) event(s) occurring on a 24-hour basis. Used synonymously with "diel."

Diel Periodicity. A 24-hour pattern of behavior in plants and animals; involved with many species of stream and lake invertebrates subject to migration and drift.

Diel Vertical Migration. Movements up and down that occur within intervals of 24 hours or less.

Drainage. An interconnected group of streams and tributaries forming a major river basin.

Drift. Movement of invertebrates in a moving body of water for migration, feeding or as a result of physical (e.g., high flow) or chemical (e.g., pollution) disturbances.

Ecology. The study of the relationship of plants and animals to their physical and biological environment. The physical environment includes light, heat or solar radiation, moisture, wind, oxygen, carbon dioxide, nutrients in soil, water and atmosphere. The biological environment includes organisms of the same kind, as well as other plants and animals.

El Niño. Oceanic and atmospheric phenomena in the Pacific Ocean, during which unusually warm ocean conditions appear along the western coast of Ecuador and Peru, causing climatic disturbances of varying severity. The term originally was used to describe the warm southward current that appears in the region every December, but it is now reserved for occurrences that are exceptionally intense and persistent. These occur approximately every three to seven years and can affect climates around the world for more than a year.

Emergence (insect). Metamorphosis of immature insects into flying adults; commonly called "the hatch."

Emergence (fish). The act of salmon fry leaving the gravel nest.

Endocrine System. Group of specialized organs and body tissues that produce, store and secrete chemical substances known as hormones.

Entrainment. To cause something to happen as a consequence of an action.

Ephemeroptera. Order of insects containing mayflies whose life cycle progression is the egg, nymph, emerger, adult and spinner. Mayflies are among the oldest insect groups and have been found as fossils dating from about 300 million years ago.

Extinct. No longer represented by living individuals anywhere within its former range; refers to species or other taxon.

Event. A point in space-time specified by its place and time.

Fertilization. The union of male and female reproductive cells (see Gametes) to produce a fertilized reproductive cell (zygote).

Fingerling. A small fish less than one year old, especially a salmon or trout.

Food Chain. Progression of feeding from prey to predators.

Food Web. Feeding pattern of predators and prey in a complex web of different forms.

Fry. A juvenile salmonid that has absorbed its egg sac and is rearing in the stream; the stage of development between an alevin (see Alevin) and a parr (see Parr).

Full Moon. The phase of the Moon when it is on the opposite side of the Earth from the Sun and receives sunlight across its entire face, forming a circle of light. At this point, the Moon is in opposition to the Sun. During the Full Moon period, the Moon rises approximately at sunset and sets around sunrise.

Gametes. Male or female cell: a specialized male or female cell with half the normal number of chromosomes that unites with another cell of the opposite sex in the process of sexual reproduction. Ova and spermatozoa are gametes that unite to produce a cell (zygote) that may develop into an embryo.

Gibbous. Used to describe the Moon or a planet before and after it is full, when it has more than half its disk illuminated.

Gonads. An organ that produces reproductive cells (gametes); for example, a testis or an ovary.

Gravity. One of the fundamental forces of nature, defined as the constant force of attraction between all objects in the universe. The gravitational force is inversely proportional to the square of the distance between the objects and proportional to the masses.

Gravitational Pull. See Tides.

Grouping. See Pre-spawn Grouping.

Half Moon. The Moon when only half its face is illuminated during the first or last quarter.

Homing. Relating to or possessing the ability to find the way home after traveling a long distance.

Host. A human, animal, plant or other organism in or on which another organism, especially a parasite, lives.

Ichthyology. The study of fishes.

Imprinting. A rapid and irreversible learning experience that provides fish with the ability to return to natal streams or a preselected site.

Kairomones. Chemical cues that animals of different species send to each other.

Kokanee. Landlocked Sockeye salmon (*Oncorhynchus nerka*).

Kype. The hooked jaw many male salmon develop during spawning.

Latitude. Lines of measurement around a planet or the Moon, parallel to its equator. These are measured in degrees, with the equator being 0 degrees and the poles being 90 degrees north or south.

Life Cycle. Sequence of life stages in an animal's existence.

Life History. Series of ecological events during major stages of life cycle.

Limnologists. Scientists who study Limnology.

Limnology. Study of the structural and functional interrelationships of organisms of inland waters as their dynamic physical, chemical and biotic environments affect them.

Longitude. Lines of measurement at right angles to the equator of a planet or the Moon. Measured in degrees of angle from a designated line of 0 degrees. On the Moon, 0 degrees longitude is at the center of the visible face, in the Sinus Medii.

Lunar Cycle. Events occurring either at a time basis of 29.53 days (synodic month, based on moon-phases resulting from orbital positions of Moon, sun and earth) or at a time basis of 27.32 days (sidereal Moon cycle around earth, relative to distant stars).

Magnetic Field. The field responsible for magnetic forces.

Mayfly. See Ephemeroptera.

Melanoma. Tumor of the skin. A malignant tumor, most often on the skin, that contains dark pigment and develops from a melanin-producing cell (melanocyte).

Melatonin. A naturally occurring hormone that is released into the bloodstream during the hours of darkness. Scientists believe this hormone (in humans) plays a role in the body's circadian rhythm. This rhythm regulates the physiological functions that occur in the body within a 24-hour period, such as sleep-wake cycles, fluctuations in body temperature, heart rate and blood pressure.

Menopause. The time in a woman's life when menstruation diminishes and ceases, usually between the ages of 45 and 50.

Menstruation. The monthly process of discharging blood and other matter from the womb that occurs between puberty and menopause in women and female primates who are not pregnant.

Metamorphosis. In complete metamorphosis, a clear distinction exists between the various stages of the animal's development. In the first phase, an embryo forms inside an egg. When the egg hatches, the animal is called a larva. During the next period, the larva changes into a pupa. At the end of the pupal stage, the adult emerges. Animals that grow in this way include many fishes, mollusks and insects.

Molecule. Smallest part of a chemical compound.

Moon. The natural satellite of the Earth or the natural satellite of any planet.

Moonlight. Sunlight reflected off the Moon that can be viewed from the dark side of the earth.

Moon Rise. The point in time when the upper limb of the Moon is even with the Earth's horizon as the Moon sets in the west.

Moon Set. The point in time when the upper limb of the Moon is even with the Earth's horizon as the Moon rises in the east.

Neap Tide. The lowest high tide of the lunar month, occurring near the first and last quarter Moon phases.

New Moon. One of the four phases of the Moon, during which it is directly between Earth and the Sun and invisible or seen only as a narrow crescent.

Nocturnal. Activity only during the hours of darkness.

Oligotrophic. Terms that refers to a low level of productivity. A nutrient-poor lake characterized by low production of plankton and fish and having considerable dissolved oxygen in the bottom waters (due to low organic content.)

Parr. Also known as fingerling. A large juvenile salmonid, between a fry and a smolt. The parr are designated by their colorful markings.

Periodicities. A recurrence at regular intervals.

Periphyton. Film of algae and other organisms on stones and other substrates on the streambed; the principal food of many benthic insects and other invertebrates.

PH. Term indicating the hydrogen ion (positively charged hydrogen atom) concentration of a solution, providing a measure of the solution's acidity.

Phases. The visible changes that the Moon goes through in every lunar month, caused by the changing angle of illumination from the Sun. There are four specific phases—New Moon, First Quarter Moon, Full Moon and Last Quarter Moon—and also nonspecific phase names such as Waxing Moon, Waning Moon, Gibbous Moon and Crescent Moon.

Pheromones. Chemical signals that animals within the same species send to one another.

Pituitary Gland. Master endocrine gland in vertebrate animals. The hormones secreted by the pituitary stimulate and control the functioning of almost all the other endocrine glands in the body. Pituitary hormones also promote growth and control the balance of water in the body.

Photoperiod. The daily cycle of light and darkness that affects the behavior and physiological functions of organisms.

Photosynthesis. The process by which green plants and certain other organisms use the energy of light to convert carbon dioxide and water into simple sugar glucose. Photosynthesis provides the basic energy source for virtually all organisms.

Phytoplankton. Minute plants, such as algae, which float or drift near the surface of a body of water; they are somewhat smaller than most zooplankton.

Piscivorous. Animals that feed on fish.

Pineal Gland. Small, cone-shaped projection from the top of the midbrain of most vertebrates. Photoreceptive structures linked with the pineal body are still observed in some higher vertebrates. A neural connection remains between the eyes and the gland. The functions of the pineal body in an animal are linked to surrounding light levels.

Plankton. Very small or microscopic plants and animals that swim passively or float near the surface of a body of water.

Planktivorous. Descriptive of animals that feed on plankton.

Predator. Animal that feeds on other animals.

Pre-Spawn Grouping. Pairing behavior of salmon that occurs during the Full Moon prior to spawning.

Prey Fish. Small fish upon which larger salmon feed, including kokanee, minnows, sculpins, shad, chubs, sticklebacks, shiners, smelt, alewife and sometimes smaller salmonids.

Prolactin. A hormone produced by the pituitary gland that controls the hydromineral balance in salmon and encourages them to migrate to or from the salt.

Quarter Moon. The phase of the Moon that can be either the first quarter moon or the last quarter moon. This phase occurs when the Moon is 90 degrees away from a line between the Sun and the Earth. In the Northern Hemisphere, the angle of illumination creates a half-circle picture of the Moon's surface, with the lighted half being on the right side during first quarter moon and on the left side for last quarter moon.

Racking. The processing of removing the deposits of sediment before barreling.

Redd. Spawning nest used by trout and salmon.

Resting Zones. Areas where the trout rest and digest. Usually cooler regions where there is sufficient oxygen.

Retinomotor Movement. Movement of the rods and cones within the retina of the eye.

Rhythm. Periodic recurrence of (an) event(s). Same as Cycle.

Riffle. A section of stream in which the water is usually shallower than in the connecting pools and over which the water runs more swiftly than it does in the pools. A riffle is shallower than a chute (run) and usually has at least some "white water" breaking over the substrate.

Rod Vision. Rods are one of the two types of cells in the retina. Cones are the second type of cell. Rods are designed for night vision and the detection of motion and objects. They also provide peripheral vision, but they do not see as acutely as cones. Rods are insensitive to color.

Run. Where a number of stocks can be grouped together on the basis of similar migration times.

Salmonid. Any member of the family Salmonidae, which includes the salmon, trout, chars, whitefishes, ciscoes, inconnu and grayling of North America.

Sexual Maturation. Age at the time of first spawning is the height of maturation. The maturation process occurs several months before spawning.

Shedding. Dropping of antlers, with respect to elk and deer.

Sidereal Month. A lunar month measured by a return to a specific position marked by a certain star: a period of 27.32166 days.

Smolt. Life cycle stage of a migratory fish, particularly salmonids, when they approach leaving their natal stream for the ocean.

Smolting. The preparation juveniles go through for the transition to saltwater.

Space-time. The four-dimensional space which has points that are events. The term is used in this book instead of time and place.

Spawning. Generally referred to as the period of time the salmon pair, build their redds, drop and fertilize the eggs.

Species. The fundamental taxonomic category; subdivision of a genus; group of organisms that naturally or potentially interbreed, are reproductively isolated from other such groups and are usually morphologically separable from them.

Spring Tide. The highest tides in a lunar month, occurring near New and Full Moons, when the Earth, Sun and Moon are aligned.

Starlight. Direct light from other suns.

Stock. The fish spawning in a particular lake or stream (or portion of it) at a particular season, which do not interbreed with any group spawning in a different place or at the same place in a different season.

Subspecies. A taxonomic subdivision of a species; a group of local populations inhabiting a geographic subdivision of the species range and differing taxonomically from other populations of the species.

Summer Solstice. The time of year in the Northern Hemisphere when the noon sun appears to be farthest north. The Summer Solstice occurs around June 21 and marks the beginning of the summer season in the Northern Hemisphere.

Sunlight. Direct light from our sun.

Synchronization. To make something work at the same time or the same rate as something else.

Synodic/Synodical. Relating to the alignment of celestial bodies or the interval between occasions when the same celestial bodies are aligned.

Synodic Period of Moon. Cycle of moon-phasing resulting from orbital positions of Earth, Moon and Sun—each 29.53 days.

Testosterone. A male steroid hormone produced in the testicles and responsible for the development of secondary sex characteristics.

Tides. The Moon, being much nearer to the Earth than the Sun, is the principal cause of tides. Because the force of gravity decreases with distance, the Moon exerts a stronger gravitational pull on the side of the earth that is closer to it and a weaker pull on the side farther from it. The world's oceans are liquid and can flow in response to the variation in the Moon's pull. On the side of the Earth facing the Moon, the Moon's stronger pull makes water flow toward it, causing a dome of water to rise on the Earth's surface directly below the Moon. On the side of the earth facing away from the Moon, the Moon's pull on the oceans is weakest. The water's inertia, or its tendency to keep traveling in the same direction, makes it want to fly off the Earth instead of rotate with the planet. The Moon's weaker pull doesn't compensate as much for the water's inertia on the far side, so another dome of water rises on this side of the Earth. The dome of water directly beneath the Moon is called direct tide and the dome of water on the opposite side of the Earth is called opposite tide. As the Earth rotates throughout the day, the domes of water remain aligned with the Moon and travel around the globe. When a dome of water passes a place on the Earth, that place experiences a rise in the level of the ocean water, known as high tide or high water.

Transition Periods. Long transition periods occur when the Moon rises before the sun sets or before the sun rises. Short transition periods are when the Moon rises after sunset or after the sun rises.

Tumor. An abnormal uncontrolled growth or mass of body cells, which may be malignant or benign and has no physiological function.

Vernal Equinox. One of two times of year when the sun's position makes day and night of equal length in all parts of the earth. The Vernal Equinox occurs around March 21 and marks the beginning of the spring season in the Northern Hemisphere.

Virus. A minute particle that lives as a parasite in plants, animals and bacteria and consists of a nucleic acid core within a protein sheath. Viruses can only replicate within living cells and are not considered to be independent living organisms.

Waning Moon. When the Moon is progressing from Full to New.

Watershed. Older term often used for valley or drainage basin.

Waxing Moon. When the Moon is progressing from New to Full.

Winter Solstice. The time of year in the Northern Hemisphere when the noon sun appears to be farthest south. The Winter Solstice occurs around December 21 and marks the beginning of the winter season in the Northern Hemisphere.

Zooplankton. Free-floating small crustaceans that inhabit lakes, ponds and oceans.

Bibliography

Abetti, Georgio. 1952. *The History of Astronomy.* Abelard-Schuman.

Abrami, G. 1972. Correlations between lunar phases and the rhythmicities in plant growth under field conditions. *Canadian Journal of Botany.* 50 (11):2157-66.

Alabaster, John S. 1970. River flow and upstream movement and catch of migratory salmonids. *Journal of Fish Biology* 2: 1-13.

Ali, M. A. 1975. *Vision in Fishes: New Approaches in Research.* Plenum Press.

———. 1979. *Environmental Physiology of Fishes.* Plenum Press.

———. 1992. *Rhythms in Fishes.* Plenum Press.

Alldredge, A. L. and King, J. M. 1980. Effects of moonlight on the vertical migration patterns of demersal zooplankton. *Journal of Exploratory Biology and Ecology* 44 (2-3):133-56.

American Bird Conservancy. 2002. *Settlement a victory for beleaguered Caspian terns: Agreement protects world's largest colony of America's biggest tern.* Press release. March 8.

Anderson, Norman. 1966. Depressant effect of moonlight on activity of aquatic insects. *Nature* 209 (5020): 319-20.

Antonsson, Thorolfur, and Sigurdur Gudjohsson. 2002. Variability in timing and characteristics of Atlantic salmon smolt in Icelandic rivers. *Transactions of the American Fisheries Society* 131: 643-55.

Archibald, H. L. 1976. Spring drumming patterns of ruffed grouse. *Auk* 93 (4): 808-29.

———. 1977. Is there a ten-year wildlife cycle induced by a lunar cycle? *Wildlife Society Bulletin* 5 (3): 126-29.

Auerbach, Leo. 1944. *The Babylonian Talmud: In Selection.* Philosophical Library.

Baggerman, B. 1960. Salinity preference, thyroid activity and the seaward migration of four species of Pacific salmon (*Oncorhynchus*). *Journal of Fisheries Research Board of Canada* 17: 295-322.

Bailey, J. E., and S. G. Taylor. 1974. Salmon fry production in a gravel incubator hatchery, Auke Creek, Alaska, 1971-72. *National Oceanic and Atmospheric Administration Technical Memorandum,* National Marine Fisheries Service ABFL-3, Auke Bay, Alaska, USA.

Bailey, J. E., J. J. Pella, and S. G. Taylor. 1976. Production of fry and adults of the 1972 brood of pink salmon, *Oncorhynchus gorbuscha*, from gravel incubators and natural spawning at Auke Creek, Alaska. *U.S. National Marine Fisheries Service Fishery Bulletin* 74: 961-71.

Baker, Gillian, and Rene Dekker. 2000. Lunar synchrony in the reproduction of the Moluccan Megapode *Eulipoa wallacei* (Megapodiidae, Galliformes). *Ibis* 142: 382-88.

Balch, W. M. 1981. An apparent lunar tidal cycle of phytoplankton blooming and community succession in the Gulf of Maine. *J. Exp. Mar. Biol. Ecol.* 55: 65-77.

Bams, R. A. 1969. Adaptations of sockeye salmon associated with incubation in stream gravels. In T. G. Northcote (ed.) symposium on salmon and trout in streams, *H. R. McMillan Lectures in Fisheries.* Inst. Fish, UBC, Vancouver, 71-87.

——. 1972. A quantitative evaluation of survival to the adult stage and other characteristics of pink salmon (*Oncorhynchus gorbuscha*) produced by a revised hatchery method which simulates optimal natural conditions. *Journal of Fisheries Research Board of Canada* 29: 1151-67.

——. 1974. Gravel incubators: a second evaluation on pink salmon (*Oncorhynchus gorbuscha*) including adult returns. *Journal of the Fisheries Research Board of Canada* 31: 1379-85.

Banks, J. W. 1969. A review of the literature on the upstream migration of adult salmonids. *Journal of Fish Biology* 1: 85-136.

Barrett, J. D., G. D. Grossman, and J. Rosenfeld. 1992. Turbidity induced changes in reactive distance in rainbow trout (*Oncorhynchus mykiss*). *Transactions of the American Fisheries Society* 121: 437-43.

Bartos, Ludek, Vaclav Perner, and Bohumir Prochazka. 1987. On the relationship between social rank during the velvet period and antler parameters in a growing red deer stag. *Acta Theriologica* 32 (24): 403-12.

Beamish, Richard J., and Conrad Mahnken. 2001. A critical size and period hypothesis to explain natural regulation of salmon abundance and the linkage to climate and climate control. *Progress in Oceanography* 49: 423-37.

Beamish, Richard J., and Donald J. Noakes. 2002. The role of climate in the past, present, and future of Pacific salmon fisheries off the west coast of Canada. *American Fisheries Society Symposium* 32: 231-44.

Beckman, Brian R., Donald A. Larsen, Beeda Lee-Pawlak, and Walton W. Dickhoff. 1998. Relation of fish size and growth rate to migration of spring Chinook salmon smolts. *North American Journal of Fisheries Management* 18: 537-46.

Behnke, R. J. 1992. *Native Trout of Western North America.* American Fisheries Society Monograph 6.

———. 2002. *Trout and Salmon of North America.* The Free Press.

Behrend, D. F. and R. D. McDowell. 1967. Antler shedding among white-tailed deer in Connecticut. *Journal of Wildlife Management* 31 (3): 588-90.

Berlinski, David. 2003. *The Secrets of the Vaulted Sky: Astrology and the Art of Prediction.* Harcourt Books.

Bjornn, T. C., P. J. Keniry, K. R. Tolotti, J. P. Hunt, and R. R. Ringe. 1998. *Effects of Zero Versus Normal Flow at Night Passage of Steelhead in Summer and Fall: Part VII of Final Report for Migration of Adult Chinook Salmon and Steelhead Past Dams and Through Reservoirs in the Lower Snake River and into Tributaries.* U.S. Army Corps of Engineers and Bonneville Power Administration.

Black, Geoff, A. and J. Brian Dempson. 1986. A test of the hypothesis of pheromone attraction in salmonid migration. *Environmental Biology of Fishes* 15 (3): 229-35.

Blackwell, Harold. 2002. Telephone interview by author while at the Warm Springs Tribe.

Blakemore, R. P., R. B. Frankel, and A. J. Kalmijin. 1980. South-seeking magneto-tactic bacteria in the Southern Hemisphere. *Nature* 286: 384.

Blot, W. J., J. F. Fraumeni, and B. J. Stone. 1977. Geographic patterns of breast cancer in the United States. *Journal of the National Cancer Institute* 59: 1407-11.

Boetius, J. 1967. Experimental indication of lunar activity in European silver eels, *Anguilla anguilla* (L.) *Meddr. Danm Fisk Havunders* 6: 16.

Brege, Dean A., Randall F. Absolon, and Ritchie J. Graves. 1996. Seasonal and diel passage of juvenile salmonids at John Day Dam on the Columbia River. *North American Journal of Fisheries Management* 16: 659-65.

Brett, J. R., and M. A. Ali. 1958. Some observations on the structure and photo-chemical responses of the Pacific salmon retina. *Journal of the Fisheries Research Board of Canada* 15 (5): 815-29.

Briggs, J. C. 1953. The behaviour and reproduction of salmonid fishes in a small coastal stream. *California Department of Fish and Game Fish Bulletin* 94.

British Broadcasting Corporation. 2001. *The Blue Planet, Seas of Life.* Video series.

Bronowski, J. 1973. *The Ascent of Man.* Little Brown and Company.

Bubenik, George A., and Anthony B. Bubenik (ed.). 1990. Horns, *Pronghorns and Antlers.* Springer-Verlag.

Bulmer, M. G. 1974. A statistical analysis of the 10-year cycle in Canada. *Journal of Animal Ecology* 43 (3): 701-18

Bunning, E. 1956. Endogenous rhythms in plants. *Annual Review of Plant Physiology* 7: 71-90

Burger, Carl V., R. L. Wilmot, and D. B. Wangaard. 1985. Comparison of spawn-ing areas and times of two runs of Chinook salmon (*Oncorhynchus tshawytscha*) in the Kenai River, Alaska. *Canadian Journal of Fisheries and Aquatic Science* 42: 693-700.

Burger, Carl V., R. L. Wilmot, D. B. Wangaard, and A. N. Palmisano. 1982. Salmon investigations in the Kenai River, Alaska. U.S. Fish and Wildlife Service, National Fishery Research Center, Seattle, Washington, and the Alaska Field Station, Anchorage, Alaska.

Carpenter, J. A., S. Gautam, R. R. Freedman, and M. Andrykowski. 2001. Circadian rhythm of objectively recorded hot flashes in postmenopausal breast cancer survivors. *Menopause: The Journal of the North American Menopause Society* 8 (3): 181-88.

Casteret, Norbert. Lascaux cave, cradle of world art. *National Geographic* 94 (6): 771-94.

Chadwick, M., and A. Sinclair. 1991. Fisheries production in the Gulf of St. Lawrence. In *The Gulf of St. Lawrence: Small Ocean or Big Estuary?*, ed. J. C. Therriault, Department of Fisheries and Oceans, *Can. Spec. Publ. Fish. Aquat. Sci.* 113: 125-36.

Chaney, William R. *Does Night Lighting Harm Trees?* Forestry and Natural Resources. Purdue University. FNR-FAQ-17.

Chilcote, M. W., S. A. Leider, R. P. Jones. 1980. *Kalama River Salmonid Studies, 1980 Progress Report*. Washington Department of Fish and Game.

Cohen, M., M. Lippman, and B. Chabner. 1978. Role of the pineal gland in the aeticolgy and treatment of breast cancer. *Lancet* 2: 814-16.

Coleman, M. P., and R. J. Reiter. 1992. Breast cancer, blindness and melatonin. *European Journal of Cancer* 28: 501-03.

Collis, Ken, Stephanie Adamany – Columbia River Inter-Tribal Fish Commission, Daniel D. Roby, David P. Craig, and Donald E. Lyons – Oregon Cooperative Fish and Wildlife Research Unit. 2000. *Avian Predation on Juvenile Salmonids in the Lower Columbia River, 1998 Annual Report to Bonneville Power Administration, Portland, OR*. Contract No. 97B133475, Project No. 97-024-00, 101 electronic pages (PBA Report ODE/BP-33475. 2).

Columbia River Intertribal Fish Commission (CRITFC). 2003. "Seeing sunspots." *Wana Chinook Tymoo.* Winter, p. 27.

Cook, J. G., B. K. Johnson, R. A. Riggs, Bryant L. D. DelCurto, and L. L. Irwin. 2002. Effects of summer-autumn nutritional and parturition date on reproduction and survival of elk. *Final Report*. Oregon Department of Fish and Wildlife. La Grande, Oregon.

Cooke, Fred, Robert F. Rockwell, and David B. Lank. 1995. *The Snow Geese of La Pérouse Bay.* Oxford University Press.

Copernicus, Nicolaus. 1543. *The Revolution of the Heavenly Orbs.*

Cos, S., and E. J. Sánchez-Barceló. 1994. Differences between pulsatile or continuous exposure to melatonin on MCF-7 human breast cancer cell proliferation. *Cancer Letters* 85: 105-09.

Couper-Johnston, Ross. 2001. *El Nino: The Weather Phenomenon That Changed the World.* Coronet Books.

Cowan, C. A., and B. L. Peckarsky. 1994. Diel feeding and positioning periodicity of a grazing mayfly in a trout stream and a fishless stream. *Canadian Journal of Fisheries and Aquatic Science* 51: 450-59.

Cox, Jeff. 1985. *From Vines to Wines.* Garden Way Publishing.

Coyne, G. V., M. A. Hoskin, and O. Pedersen (ed.). 1983. *Gregorian Reform of the Calendar: Proceedings of the Vatican Conference to Commemorate its 400th Anniversary, 1582-1992.* Vatican City: Pontifical Academy of Sciences, Specolo Vaticano.

D'Aleo, Joseph S. 2002. *The Oryx Resource Guide to El Niño and La Niña.* Oryx Press.

Dalke, P. D., Beeman, R. D., Kindel, F. J., Robel, R. J., and Williams, T. R. 1965. Seasonal movements of elk in the Selway River Drainage, Idaho. *Journal of Wildlife Management* 29 (2): 333-38.

Danilkin, A. 1996. *Behavioral Ecology of Siberian and European Roe Deer.* Chapman & Hall.

Darwin, Charles. 1859. *The Origin of Species: By Means of Natural Selection or The Preservation of Favoured Races in the Struggle for Life.* Random House, 1999.

———. 1881. *The Power and Movement of Plants.* D. Appleton & Co.

Davis, S., D. K. Mirick, and R. G. Stevens. 2001. Night shift work, light at night, and risk of breast cancer. *Journal of the National Cancer Institute* 93 (20): 1557-62.

Diamond, Jared. 1999. *Guns, Germs, and Steel.* W. W. Norton and Company.

Douglas, R. H., and M. B. A. Djamgoz. 1990. *The Visual System of Fish.* Chapman Hall.

Dronia, Horst. 1967. *Der Einfluss des Mondes auf die Witterung.* Broschiert – 78 Seiten-Reimer.

Duncan, David Ewing. 1998. *Calendar: Humanity's Epic Struggle to Determine a True and Accurate Year.* Bard.

Egan, T. 1990. *The Good Rain: Across Time and Terrain in the Pacific Northwest.* Alfred A. Knopf.

Einstein, Albert. 1993. *The World As I See It.* Carol Publishing Group.

Endres, P., and W. Schad. 1997. *Moon Rhythms in Nature: How Lunar Cycles Affect Living Organisms.* Floris.

Everest, Fred H., Jr. An ecological and fish cultural study of summer steelhead in the Rogue River, Oregon. *Annual Progress Report Anadromous Fish Project.* AFS-31. Oregon State Game Commission.

Ewing, R. D., M. D. Evenson, E. K. Birks, E. K., and A. R. Hemmingsen. 1984. Indices of parr-smolt transformation in juvenile steelhead trout (*Salmo gairdneri*) undergoing volitional release at Cole Rivers Hatchery, Oregon. *Aquaculture* 40: 209-21.

Fang, Sheng-chung. 1948. *Physical, Chemical and Biological Investigations of the Barcelona and the Du Chilly Filbert Nuts.* Thesis. Oregon State College.

Farbridge, K. J., and J. F. Leatherland. 1987. Lunar cycles of coho salmon, *Oncorhynchus Kisutch*: I. Growth and Feeding. *Journal of Exploratory Biology* 129: 165-78.

———. 1987. Lunar cycles of coho salmon, Oncorhynchus Kisutch: II. Scale amino acid update, nucleic acids, metabolic reserves and plasma thyroid hormones. *Journal of Exploratory Biology* 129: 179-89.

———. 1987. Lunar periodicity of growth cycles in rainbow trout, Salmo gairdneri Richardson, *J. Interdisc. Cycle Research* 18: 169-77.

Favorite, F., A. J. Dodimead, and K. Nasu. 1976. Oceanography and the subarctic Pacific Region, 1960-71. *International North Pacific Fish Commission Bulletin* 11: 57-72.

Feychting, M., B. Osterlund, and A. Ahlbom. 1998. Reduced cancer incidence among the blind. *Epidemiology* 9: 490-94.

Fladmark, K. R. 1986. *British Columbia Prehistory.* The Runge Press.

Flint, S. J., L. W. Enquist, R. M. Krug, V. R. Racaniello, and A. M. Skalka. 2000. *Principles of Virology: Molecular Biology, Pathogenesis, and Control.* ASM Press.

Foerster, R. E. 1968. The sockeye salmon, Oncorhynchus nerka. *Bulletin of the Fisheries Research Board of Canada 162.*

Frankel, R. B., R. P. Blakemore, F. F. Torres de Araujo, E. M. S. Esquivel, and J. Danon. 1981. Magnetotactic bacteria at the geomagnetic equator. *Science* 212: 1269.

Freeland, H. J., K. L. Denman, C. S. Wond, F. Whitney, and R. Jacques. 1997. Evidence of change in the winter mixed layer in the northeast Pacific Ocean. *Deep-Sea Research* 44: 2117-29.

Frost, W. E. 1950. The eel fisheries of the River Bann. *J. Cons. Perm. Int. Explor. Mer* 16: 358-83.

Fuss, Howard, and Jim Byrne. 2002. Differences in survival and physiology between Coho salmon reared in seminatural and conventional ponds. *North American Journal of Aquaculture* 64: 267-77.

Gaudreau, Nathalie, and Daniel Boisclair. 2000. Influence of moon phase on acoustic estimates of the abundance of fish performing daily horizontal migration in a small oligotrophic lake. *Canadian Journal of Fisheries and Aquatic Science* 57: 581-90.

Germian, E. 1994. The reproduction of hazelnut (*Corylus avellana* L.): A review. IN: Me, Giovanni and Radicati, Ludovico. Acta Horticulturae II International Congress on Hazelnut. *ISHS*, no. 351: January, 195-209.

Gern, W. A., S. S. Greenhouse, J. M. Nervina, and P. J. Gasser. 1992. The Rainbow trout pineal organ: An endocrine photometer. *In Rhythms in Fishes*, ed. M. A. Ali. Plenum Press.

Gibson, R. N. 1978. Lunar and tidal rhythms in fish. In *Rhythmic Activity of Fishes*, ed. J. E. Thorpe. Academic Press.

Gilg, Oliver, Ilkka Hanski, and Benoit Sittler. 2003. Cycle dynamics in a simple vertebrate predator-prey community. *Science* 302: 866-68.

Gillian, Baker and Rene Dekker. 2000. Lunar synchrony in the reproduction of the Moluccan Megapode *Megapodius wallacei. Ibis* 142: 382-88.

Ginetz, R. M., and P. A. Larkin. 1973. Choice of colors of food items by rainbow trout (*Salmo gairdneri*). *Journal of the Fisheries Research Board of Canada* 30: 229-34.

Ginzberg, Louis. 1920. *The Legends of the Jews: II, Bible Times and Characters from Joseph to the Exodus.* The Jewish Society of America.

Giorgi, A. E., W. D. Muir, W. S. Zaugg, and S. McCutcheon. 1991. Biological manipulation of migration rate: the use of advanced photoperiod to accelerate smoltification in yearling Chinook salmon. Annual Report 1989. National Marine Fisheries Service. Contract No. DE-AI79-88BP50301. Project No. 88-141.

Godfrey, Harold, MS. 1969. Chinook and coho salmon hatchery evaluation studies: 8th Progress Report. *Fisheries Research Board of Canada* MS Report (1053): 42.

Godin, J-G. J. 1981. Migrations of salmonid fishes during early life history phases: Daily and annual timing, pp. 22-50. In *Proceedings of the salmon and trout migratory behavior symposium, School of Fisheries,* ed. E. L. Brannon and E. O. Salo. Seattle: University of Washington.

Goss, Richard J. (1969a). Photoperiodic control of antler cycles in deer. Vol. 1. Alteration in amplitude, phase shift and frequency changes. *Journal of Exploratory Zoology* 171: 223-34.

——. (1969a). Photoperiodic control of antler cycles in deer. Vol. 1. Phase shift and frequency changes. *Journal of Exploratory Zoology* 170: 311-24.

——. 1983. *Deer Antlers: Regeneration, Function, and Evolution.* Academic Press.

Graves, Ralph A. 1917. Fearful famines of the past. *National Geographic* (July): 68-90.

Gray, John. 1969. *Near Eastern Mythology: Mesopotamia, Syria, Palestine*. The Hamlyn Publishing Group.

Groot, C., and L. Margolis (ed.). 1991. *Pacific Salmon Life Histories*. UBC Press.

Groot, C., L. Margolis, and R. Bailey. 1984. Does the route of seaward migration of Fraser River Sockeye salmon (*Oncorhunchus nerka*) smolts determine the route of return migration of the adults? In *Mechanisms of Migration in Fishes*, ed. Arnold McCleave and Neill Dodson. Plenum Press.

Gross, M. R., R. M. Coleman, and R. M. McDowall. 1988. Aquatic productivity and the evolution of diadromous fish migration. *Science* 239: 1291-93.

Guinness, F. E., T. H. Clutton-Brock, and S. D. Albon. 1978. Factors affecting calf mortality in red deer (*Cervus elaphus*). *Journal of Animal Ecology* 47: 817-32.

Guinness, F. E., R. M. Gibson, and T. H. Clutton-Brock. 1978. Calving times of red deer (*Cervus elaphus*) on Rhum. *Journal of Zoology* 185: 105-14.

Gwinner. 1986. Internal rhythms in bird migration. *Scientific American* 254 (April): 84.

Hafeez, M. A. 1970. Effect of melatonin on body coloration and spontaneous swimming activity in rainbow trout (*Salmo gairdneri*). *Comp. Biochem. Physiol.* 36: 639-56.

Hafeez, M. A., and W. B. Quay. 1970. Pineal acetylserotonin methyltransferase activity I the teleost fishes Hesperoleucus symmetricus and Salmo gairdneri, with evidence. *Comp. and Gen. Pharmacol.* 1: 257-62.

Hager, R. C., and R. E. Noble. 1976. Relation of size at release of hatchery-reared Coho salmon to age, size and sex composition of returning adults. *The Progressive Fish-Culturist* 38 (3): 144-47.

Hammarstrom, S. L. 1981. Evaluation of Chinook salmon fisheries of the Kenai Peninsula. *Alaska Department of Fish and Game Annual Report, 1980-1981*. Project F-9-13, 22 (G-II-L): 39-66.

———. 1997. Stock assessment of the return of early-run Chinook salmon to the Kenai River, 1996. *Alaska Department of Fish and Game Fishery Data Series* No. 97-10.

———. 1997. Stock assessment of the return of late-run Chinook salmon to the Kenai River, 1996. *Alaska Department of Fish and Game Fishery Data Series* No. 97-11.

Harmon, Jerrel R., and Emil Slatick. 1986. Use of a fish transportation barge for increasing returns of steelhead imprinted for homing: Annual Report of

Research 1986. Prepared for U.S. Department of Energy, Bonneville Power
Administration, Division of Fish and Wildlife, Project 82-2.

Hartland-Rowe, R. 1955. Lunar rhythm in the emergence of an ephemeropteran.
Nature (1976): 657.

———. 1983. The adaptive value of synchronous emergence in the tropical mayfly
Povilla Adjusta: a preliminary investigation. In *Proceedings of the Fourth
International Conference on Emphemeroptera, Bechyne, September 4-10, 1983*, ed.
Vladimir Landa, Tomas Soldan, and Martin Tonner. Institute of Entomology,
Czechoslovak Academy of Sciences.

Hawking, Stephen. 2001. *The Universe in a Nutshell.* Bantam.

Heath, D. D., J. W. Heath, and G. K. Iwama. 1991. Maturation in Chinook salmon,
Oncorhynchus tshawytscha (Walbaum): Early identification based on the development of a bimodal weight-frequency distribution. *Journal of Fish Biology* 39:
565-75.

Heinen, John M. 1998. Light control for fish tanks. *The Progressive Fish-Culturist* 60:
323-30.

Hendry, M. A, J. K. Wenburg, K. W. Myers, and A. P. Hendry. 2002. Genetic and
phenotypic variation through the migratory season provides evidence for multiple populations of wild steelhead in the Dean River, British Columbia.
Transactions of the American Fishery Society 131: 418-34.

Hernandez-Leon S., C. Almeida, L. Yebra, and J. Aristegui. 2002. Lunar cycle of
zooplankton biomass in subtropical waters: biogeochemical implications. *Journal
of Plankton Research* 24 (9): 935-39.

Hicks, Jim. 1975. *The Emergence of Man: The Persians.* Time Life Books.

Hinch, S. G., and P. S. Rand. 1998. Swim speeds and energy use of upriver-migrat-
ing sockeye salmon (*Oncorhynchus nerka*): role of local environment and fish
characteristics. *Canadian Journal of Fisheries and Aquatic Sciences* 55: 1821-31.

Hoar, W. S. 1955. Phototactic and pigmentary responses of sockeye salmon smolts
following injury to the pineal organ. *Journal of the Fishery Research Board of Canada*
12: 178-85.

Hobson, L. A. 1980. Primary productivity of the north Pacific Ocean – A Review.
In *Salmonid Ecosystems of the North Pacific*, ed. William J. McNeil and Daniel C.
Himsworth. Oregon State University Press.

Hoffnagle, Timothy L., and Albert J. Jr. Fivizzani. 1998. Effect of three hatchery
lighting schemes on indices of smoltification in Chinook salmon. *The Progressive
Fish Culturist* 60: 179-91.

Howick, G. L., and W. J. O'Brien. 1983. Piscivorous feeding behavior of largemouth bass: An experimental analysis. *Transactions of the American Fisheries Society* 112: 508-16.

Huntington, Ellsworth. 1931. The Matamek conference on biological cycles. *Science* 74 (1914): 229-35.

Hutchinson, G. E. 1967. *A Treatise on Limnology*. Vol. 2. John Wiley & Sons, Inc.

Hsu, Ying-chou. 1982. *Yami Fishing Practices: Migratory Fish*. Taipei: Southern Materials Center.

Ibrahim, A. A., and F. A. Huntingford. 1988. Foraging efficiency in relation to within-species variation in morpholoty in three-spined sticklebacks (*Gasterosteus aculeatus*). *Journal of Fish Biology* 33: 823-24.

———. 1989. Laboratory and field studies on diet choice in three-spined sticklebacks (*Gasterosteus aculeatus*) in relation to profitability and visual features of prey. *Journal of Fish Biology* 34: 245-57.

———. 1989. The role of visual cues in prey selection in three-spined sticklebacks (*Gasterosteus aculeatus*). *Ethology* 81: 265-72.

International Game Fish Association. 2002. *World Record Game Fishes*.

Jacobson, H. A., and S. J. Waldhalm. 1992. Antler cycles of a white-tailed deer with congenital anophthalmia. In *The Biology of Deer*, ed. R. D. Brown. Springer-Verlag.

Jawad, Laith A. 1999. Shad of the Shatt Al-Arab River in Iraq. *Shad Journal* 4 (2).

Jenkins, K., K. Cooper, and Starkey. 1988. *Ecology of Elk Inhabiting Crater Lake National Park and Vicinity*. National Park Service Report.

Jensen, A. L., and R. N. Duncan. 1971. Homing of transplanted Coho salmon. *Progressive Fish Culturist* 33: 216-18.

Jensen, A. L., T. G. Heggberget, and B. O. Johnsen. 1986. Upstream migration of adult Atlantic salmon (*Salmo salar* L.) in the River Vefsna, northern Norway. *Journal of Fish Biology* 29: 459-65.

Johannes, R. E. 1981. *Words of the Lagoon: Fishing & Marine Lore in the Palau District of Micronesia*. University of California Press.

Jonsson, Nina. 1991. Influence of water flow, water temperature and light on fish migration in rivers. *Nordic Journal of Freshwater Research* 66: 20-35.

Jordan, D. S. 1904. The salmon of the Pacific. *Pacific Fisherman* 2: 1.

Keith, Lloyd, B. 1963. *Wildlife's Ten-Year Cycle*. The University of Wisconsin Press.

Kenaston, K. R., R. B. Lindsay, and R. K. Schroeder. 2001. Effect of acclimation on the homing and survival of hatchery steelhead. *North American Journal of Fisheries Management* 21: 765-73.

Kepler, Johannes. 1602. *Concerning the More Certain Fundamentals of Astrology.*

Kesner, William D., and Roger A. Barnhart. 1972. Characteristics of the fall-run steelhead trout (*salmo gairdneri*) of the Klamath River system with emphasis on the half-pounder. *California Fish and Game* 58 (3): 204-20.

Kirschvink, J. L. 1980. South-seeking magnetic bacteria. *Journal of Experimental Biology* 86: 345.

Kirschvink, J. L., and J. W. Hagadorn. 2000. A grand unified theory of biomineralization. In *Biomineralization*, ed. E. Bauerlein. *Wiley-VCH Verlag GmbH*: 139-50.

Kirschvink, J. L., M. M. Walker, and C. Deibel. 2001. Magnetite-based magnetoreception. *Current Opinion in Neurobiology* 11: 462-67.

Koestler, Arthur. 1960. *The Watershed.* Doubleday & Co.

Koski, K. V. 1975. "The survival and fitness of two stocks of chum salmon (*Oncorhynchus keta*) from egg deposition to emergence in a controlled-stream environment at Big Beef Creek." Ph.D. thesis. Seattle: University of Washington.

Kosisky, Susan E., and Gary B. Carpenter. 1997. Predominant tree aeroallergens of the Washington, DC area: A six year survey (1989-1994). *Ann Allergy Asthma Immunology* 78: 381-92.

Kroeber, A. L., and E. W. Gifford. 1949. World renewal, a cult system of native northwest California. *Anthropological Records* 13 (1).

Krupp, E. C. 1984. *Echoes of the Ancient Skies: The Astronomy of Lost Civilizations.* Meridian.

———. 1991. *Beyond the Blue Horizon: Myths and Legends of the Sun, Moon, Stars, and Planets.* Harper Collins.

———. 1997. *Skywatchers, Shamans & Kings.* Wiley.

———. 2001. *Astronomical Babel. Sky and Telescope* (November): 93-96.

Kuzishchin, K. V., D. S. Pavlov, K. A. Savvaitova, M. A. Gruzdeva, and O. P. Pustovit. 2001. Downstream migration of juvenile diadromous Kamchatka trout Parasalmo mykiss in the western Kamchatka rivers. *Journal of Ichthyology* 41 (3): 227-38. Trans. from *Voprosy Ikhtiologii* 41 (2), 2001, 220-31.

Laming, Annette. 1959. *Lascaux, Paintings and Engravings.* Pelican.

Leach, E. R. 1950. Primitive Calendars. *Oceania* 20 (4): 245-62.

Leatherland, J. F., K. J. Farbridge, and T. Boujard. 1992. Lunar and semi-lunar rhythms in fishes. In *Rhythms in Fishes*, ed. M. A. Ali. Plenum Press.

Leiber, Arnold L. 1978. *The Lunar Effect.* Dell.

Leider, Steven A. 1985. Precise timing of upstream migrations by repeat steelhead spawners. *Transactions of the American Fisheries Society* 114: 906-08.

Leider, S., M. Chilcote, and John Loch. 1984. Spawning characteristics of sympatric populations of steelhead trout (*Salmo gairdneri*): evidence for partial reproductive isolation. *Canadian Journal of Fisheries and Aquatic Sciences* 41: 1454-62.

———. 1986. Comparative life history characteristics of hatchery and wild steelhead trout (*Salmo gairdneri*) of summer and winter races in the Kalama River, Washington. *Canadian Journal of Fisheries and Aquatic Science* 43: 1398-1409.

———. 1986. Movement and survival of presmolt steelhead in a tributary and the main stem of a Washington river. *North American Journal of Fisheries Management* 6: 526-31.

Lewis, Gary. 2003. *Deer Hunting: Tactics for Today's Big-Game Hunter.* Gary Lewis Outdoors.

Lichatowich, Jim. 1999. *Salmon Without Rivers: A History of the Pacific Salmon Crisis.* Island Press.

Lima-de-Faria, A. (ed.). 1995. *Biological Periodicity.* JAI Press Inc.

Linkowski, T. B. 1996. Lunar rhythms of vertical migrations coded in otolith microstructure of North Atlantic lanternfishes, genus Hygophum (*Myctophidae*). *Marine Biology.* 124: 495-508.

Lorz, H. W., and T. G. Northcote. 1965. Factors affecting stream location, and timing and intensity of entry by spawning Kokanee (*Oncorhynchus nerka*) into an inlet of Nicola Lake, British Columbia. *Journal of the Fisheries Research Board of Canada* 22 (3): 665-87.

Luecke, C. 1986. A change in the pattern of vertical migration of Chaoborus flavicans after the introduction of trout. *Journal of Plankton Research* 8: 649-57.

Luecke, C., and W. Wurtsbaugh. 1993. Effects of moon and daylight on hydroacoustic estimates of pelagic fish abundance. *Transactions of the American Fishery Society* 122: 112-20.

Lythgoe, J. N. 1979. *The Ecology of Vision.* Oxford.

Mackas, D. L., R. Goldblatt, and A. G. Lewis. 1998. Interdecadal variation in developmental timing of *Neocalanus plumchrus* populations at Ocean Station P in the subarctic North Pacific. *Canadian Journal of Fisheries and Aquatic Science* 55: 1874-93.

Malthus, Thomas. 1978. *Essay on the Principle of Population.*

Mann, S., N. H. C. Sparks, M. M. Walker, and J. L. Kirschvink. 1988. Ultrastructure, morphology and organization of biogenic magnetite from sockeye salmon, *Oncorchynchus Nerka*: Implications for magnetoreception. *Journal of Experimental Biology* 140: 35-49.

Marine, Keith, and David Vogel. 2000. Lower Mokelumne River fisheries monitoring program, 1999-2000. *A Technical Report on Upstream Migration Monitoring at Woodbridge Dam During August 1999 through March 2000.* Red Bluff, CA: Natural Resource Scientists, Inc.

Marshack, Alexander. 1971. *The Roots of Civilization: the Cognitive Beginnings of Man's First Art, Symbol, and Notation.* McGraw-Hill.

———. 1975. Exploring the mind of Ice Age man. *National Geographic* 147 (1): 62-89.

Matson, R. G., and G. Coupland. 1995. *The Prehistory of the Northwest Coast.* Academic Press.

Mayama, Hiroshi. 1988. Efficient techniques for producing Masu salmon smolt and improving adult returns from outplantings, pp. 1-8. In *Marine Ranching: Proceedings of the Seventeenth U.S.-Japan Meeting on Aquaculture Ise, Mie Prefecture, Japan,* ed. R. S. Svrjcek. October 16, 17, and 18, 1988; Satellite Symposium: October 20. U.S. Department of Commerce.

———. 1989. Masu salmon management in Hokkaido: A review of smolt and fingerling release experiments. *Physiology Ecology Japan Spec.* 1: 673-82.

McAlpine, Robert Gooding. 1973. *American Sycamore.* U.S. Department of Agriculture, Forest Service.

McCleave, Arnold, and Neill Dodson. 1984. *Mechanisms of Migration in Fishes.* Plenum Press.

McKinley, Timothy. 2002. Telephone interviews with author at the Alaska Department of Fish and Wildlife.

McMillan, Bill. 2001. *Males as Vectors to Hatchery/Wild Spawning Interactions and the Reshaping of Wild Steelhead/Rainbow Populations Through Fishery Management.* Washington Trout.

McNeil, William J., and Daniel C. Himsworth. 1980. *Salmonid Ecosystems of the North Pacific.* Oregon State University Press.

Meeus, Jean, and Denis Savoie. 1992. The history of the tropical year. *Journal of the British Astronomical Association* 102 (1): 40-42

Microsoft. 2003. *Encarta Encyclopedia Deluxe.*

Miller, Harald. 2004. Star search. *National Geographic* 205 (1): 76-87.

Minard, R. E., M. Alexandersdottir, and S. Sonnichsen. 1992. Estimation of abundance, seasonal distribution, and size and age composition of Rainbow trout in the Kvichak River, Alaska, 1986-1991. Alaska Department of Fish and Wildlife, Fishery Data Series No. 92-51.

Mohr, Hans and Peter Schopfer. 1995. *Plant Physiology.* Springer.

Morell, T.E., Yahner, R.H. & Harkness, W.L. 1991. Factors affecting detection of great horned owls by using broadcast vocalizations. *Wildlife Society, Bulletin* 19 (4): 481-88.

Morrison, D. W. 1978. Lunar Phobia in a neotropical fruit bat, Artibeus jamaicensis (*Chiroptera: Phyllostomidae*). *Animal Behavior* 26: 852-55.

Muller, Karl. Locomotor activity of fish and environmental oscillations. In *Rhythmic Activity of Fishes*, ed. J. E. Thorpe, 1978. Academic Press.

Myers, Ransom A., and Boris Worm. 2003. Rapid worldwide depletion of predatory fish communities. *Nature* 423 (May 15): 280-83.

Nakari, T., A. Soivio, and S. Pesonen. 1986. Effects of advanced photoperiod cycle on the epidermis and gonadosomatic index of 2-year old rainbow trout (*Salmo gairdneri R.*), reared at natural temperature. *Journal of Fish Biology* 29: 451-57.

National Audubon Society. 1991. *Field Guide to the Night Sky*. Alfred A. Knopf.

National Freshwater Fishing Hall of Fame. 2002. *Official World and USA State Freshwater Angling Records*.

Neal, Joseph C. 1998. *Postemergence, Non-Selective Herbicides for Landscapes and Nurseries*. North Carolina Cooperative Extension Service. Horticulture Information Leaflet 648.

Neusner, Jacob (trans.). 1984. *The Talmud of Babylonia: An American Translation Xvii: Tractate Sotah* (Brown Judaic Studies, 72). Scholars Press.

Nilsson, Martin P. 1920. *Primitive Time-Reckoning*. Lund.

NOAA-NWFSC Tech Memo-27: *Status Review of West Coast Steelhead*.

Northwest Power and Conservation Council. 2003. *Artificial Production Review and Evaluation. Draft Basin-Level Report*. Document 2003-17. Oct. 7.

NOVA. 1998. *Chasing El NiNo*. Video.

Ogura, M., M. Kato, N. Arai, T. Sasada, and Y. Sakaki. 1992. Magnetic particles in chum salmon (*Oncorhynchus keta*): Extraction and transmission electron microscopy. *Canadian Journal of Zoology* 70: 874.

O'Leary, J. A. 1984. "Characteristics of the downstream migration of juvenile American Shad (*Alosa sapidissima*) and Blueback Herring (*Alosa aestivalis*) in the Connecticut River." Master's thesis. University of Massachusetts.

Olsson, Ivan C., and Larry A. Greenberg. 2001. Effect of an artificial pond on migrating brown trout smolts. *North American Journal of Fisheries Management* 21: 498-506.

Oregon Department of Fish and Wildlife. 2001. *Summary of Habitat and Fish Monitoring Data from East Fork and Upper Mainstem Lobster Creeks: 1988-2001*.

Orlove, B. S., Chiang, J. C., and Cane, M. A. 2000. Forecasting Andean rainfall and crop yield from the influence of El Niño on Pleiades visibility. *Nature* 43: 68-71.

———. 2002. Ethnoclimatology in the Andes. *American Scientist* 90: 428-35.

Osborne, Harold. 1968. *South American Mythology*. The Hamlyn Publishing Group.

Palmer, John D. 1973. Tidal rhythms: the clock control of the rhythmic physiology of marine organisms. *Biology Review* 48: 377-418.

———. 1976. *An Introduction to Biological Rhythms.* Academic Press.

———. 1982. Biorhythms bunkum. *Natural History* 91 (10): 90-97.

———. 1995. *The Biological Rhythms and Clocks of Intertidal Animals.* Oxford University Press.

———. 2002. *The Living Clock: The Orchestrator of Biological Rhythms.* Oxford.

Palmer, John D., and Goodenough. 1978. Mysterious monthly rhythms. *Natural History* 87 (10): 64-69.

Papi, F. (ed.). 1992. *Animal Homing.* Chapman and Hall.

Pascual, M., P. Bentzen, C. R. Rossi, G. Mackey, M. T. Kinnison, and R. Walker. 2002. First documented case of anadromy in a population of introduced rainbow trout in Patagonia, Argentina. *Transactions of the American Fisheries Society* 130 (1): 53-67.

Parkinson, E. A. 1984. Genetic variation in populations of steelhead trout (*Salmo gairdneri*) in British Columbia. *Canadian Journal of Fisheries and Aquatic Sciences* 41: 1412-20.

Pauley, G. B., R. Risher, and G. L. Thomas. 1989. Species profiles: Life histories and environmental requirements of coastal fishes and invertebrates (Pacific Northwest). *Biological Report 82* (11. 116) TR EL-82-4. U.S. Department of the Interior, Fish and Wildlife Service.

Pentateuch, O. T. 1992. *The Torah, The Five Books of Moses.* The Jewish Publication Society.

Petersen, James H., and Thomas P. Poe. 1993. System-wide significance of predation on juvenile salmonids in Columbia and Snake River Reservoirs. *Report to Bonneville Bower Administration*, Contract No. DE-AI79-90BP07096, Project No. 90-078 (BPA Report DOE/BP-33299-1B).

Petersen, James H., Richard A. Hinrichsen, Dena M. Gadomski, Daniel H. Feil, and Dennis W. Rondorf. 2003. American Shad in the Columbia River. *American Fisheries Society Symposium.*

Phelps, E. B., and D. L. Belding. 1931. *A Statistical Study of the Records of Salmon Fishing on the Restigouche River.* New York.

Pickford, G. E., and J. C. Phillips. 1959. Prolactin, a factor in promoting survival of hypothysectomized killfish in freshwater. *Science* 130: 454-55.

Ptolemy, Claudius. 2nd Century. *Phases of the Fixed Stars and Collection of Weather Signs.*

Pukkala, E., A. Auvinen, and G. Wahlberg. 1995. Incidence of cancer among Finnish airline cabin attendants, 1967-92. *British Medical Journal* 311: 649-52.

Pyle, Peter, Nadav Nur, R. Philip Henderson, and David F. DeSante. 1993. The effects of weather and lunar cycle on nocturnal migration of landbirds at Southeast Farallon Island, California. *The Condor* 95: 343-61.

Pyper, B. J., R. M. Peterman, M. F. Lapointe, and C. J. Walters. 1999. Patterns of covariation in length and age at maturity of British Columbia and Alaska sockeye salmon (*Oncorhynchus nerka*) stocks. *Canadian Journal of Fisheries and Aquatic Science* 56: 1046-57.

Quinn, Thomas P. 1984. An experimental approach to fish compass and map orientation. In *Mechanisms of Migration in Fishes*, ed. Arnold McCleave and Neill Dodson. Plenum Press.

———. 1984. Homing and straying in Pacific salmon. In *Mechanisms of Migration in Fishes*, ed. J. D. McCleave, G. P. Arnold, J. J. Dodson, and W. H. Neill, pp. 357-62. Plenum Press.

Quinn, Thomas P., Ronald T. Merrill, and Ernest L. Brannon. 1981. Magnetic field detection in sockeye salmon. *The Journal of Experimental Zoology* 217: 137-42.

Ransom, A. Myers and Boris Worm. 2003. Rapid worldwide depletion of predatory fish communities. *Nature* 423 (May 15): 280-83.

Ratliff, Don. 1974. *Pelton Project – Deschutes River Adult Summer Steelhead, 1970-1974.* Prepared for Portland General Electric.

Reebs, Stephan. 1992. Sleep, inactivity and circadian rhythms in fish. In *Rhythms in Fishes*, M. A. Ali, pp. 127-35. Plenum Press.

Reeves, Gordon. 2000. *Salmon Life History in Fresh Water.* Oregon State University.

Reisenbichler, R. R., and J. D. McIntyre. 1977. Genetic differences in growth and survival of juvenile hatchery and wild steelhead trout (*Salmo gairdneri*). *Journal of the Fisheries Research Board of Canada* 34: 123-28.

Reynolds, P., J. Cone, B. Layefsky, D. E. Goldberg, and S. Hurley. 2002. Cancer incidence in California flight attendants (United States). *Cancer Causes and Control* 13: 317-24.

Ricker, W. E. 1970. Heredity and environmental factors affecting certain salmonid populations. In The stock concept in Pacific salmon, *H. R. MacMillian Lectures in Fisheries*, University of British Columbia, pp. 27-160.

Rigaud, Jean-Philippe. 1988. Art treasures from the Ice Age: Lascaux cave. *National Geographic* 174 (4): 482-99.

Rojas-Burke, Joe. 2003. "Salmon plant faulty, judge rules," *The Oregonian* (May 8): A1 and A16.

Romare, Pia, and Lars-Anders Hansson. 2003. A behavioral cascade: Top-predator induced behavioral shifts in planktivorous fish and zooplankton. *Limnology and Oceanography* 48 (5).

Roper, Brett B., and Dennis L. Scarnecchia. 1999. Emigration of age-0 Chinook salmon (*Oncorhynchus tshwytscha*) smolts from upper South Umpqua River basin, Oregon, U.S.A. *Canadian Journal of Fisheries and Aquatic Science* 56: 939-46.

Rottiers, D. V., and L. A. Redell. 1993. Volitional migration of Atlantic salmon from seasonal holding ponds. *North American Journal of Fisheries Management* 13: 238-52.

Ruggerone, G. T, T. P. Quinn, I. A. McGregor, and T. D. Wilkinson. 1990. Horizontal and vertical movements of adult steelhead trout, *Oncorhynchus mykiss*, in the Dean and Fisher Channels, British Columbia. *Canadian Journal of Fisheries and Aquatic Sciences* 47: 1963-69.

Ruspoli, Mario. 1986. *The Cave at Lascaux. The Final Photographs.* Harry N. Abrams, Inc.

Safarik, Ivo, and Mirka Safarikova. 2002. Magnetic nanoparticles and biosciences. *Monatshefte fur Chemie* 133: 737-59.

Sagan, Carl. 2002. *Cosmos.* Random House.

Sagan, Carl, and Ann Druyan. 1992. *Shadows of Forgotten Ancestors, A Search for Who We Are.* Random House.

Saggs, H. W. F. 1965. *Everyday Life in Babylonia and Assyria.* Dorset Press.

———. 2000. *Babylonians: Peoples of the Past.* University of California Press.

Sams, Jamie. 1994. *Earth Medicine: Ancestor's Ways of Harmony for Many Moons.* Harper.

Sánchez-Barceló, E. J., S. Cos, R. Fernández, and M. D. Mediavilla. 2003. Melatonin and mammary cancer: a short review. *Endocrine-Related Cancer* 10: 153-59.

Schnare, H., and K. Fischer. 1987. Secondary sex characteristics and connected physiological value in male fallow-deer (*Dama dama L.*) and their relationship to changes in the annual photoperiod: doubling the frequency. *Journal of Experimental Zoology* 244: 463-71.

Schreck, Carl B., Hiram W. Li, Randy C. Hjort, Cameron Sharpe. 1984. Stock identification of Columbia River Chinook salmon and steelhead trout, Annual Progress Report, Report to Bonneville Power Administration., Contract No. 1983BP13499, Project No. 198345100. Oregon Cooperative Fisheries Research Unit, Oregon State University. 68 electronic pages (BPA Report DOE/BP-13499-1).

Schroeder, Kurt. 2002. Telephone interview while he was at the Oregon Department of Fish and Wildlife with author regarding sexual development of riverine trout and steelhead on the Deschutes River.

Schroeder, R. K., K. R. Kenaston, and R. B. Lindsay. 2001. *Spring Chinook Salmon in the Willamette and Sandy Rivers: Annual Progress Report.* Portland, OR: Oregon Department of Fish and Wildlife.

Seelbach, Paul W. 1985. Smolt migration of wild and hatchery-raised Coho and Chinook salmon in a tributary of Northern Lake Michigan. *Fisheries Research Report No. 1935.* Michigan Department of Natural Resources.

Sinclair, A. R. E. 1977. Lunar cycle and timing of mating season in Serengeti wildebeest. *Nature* 267: 832-33.

Sinclair, A. R. E., and Peter Arcese (ed.). *Serengeti II: Dynamics, Management, and Conservation of an Ecosystem: Dynamics.* University of Chicago Press.

Sinclair, A. R. E., and M. Norton-Griffiths (ed.). 1979. *Serengeti: Dynamics of an Ecosystem.* University of Chicago Press.

Slatick, Emil, Lyle G. Gilbreath, Jerrel R. Harmon, Clinton S. McCutcheon, Ted C. Bjornn, and R. R. Ringe. Imprinting salmon and steelhead trout for homing. *Annual Report to Bonneville Power Administration* (Contract DE-A179-82BP39646). Portland, OR.

Smith, Douglas C. 1998. *The Yami of Lan-yu Island: Portrait of a Culture in Transition.* Phi Delta Kappa Educational Foundation.

Smith, G. C. 1990. Factors influencing egg laying and feeding in black-naped terns Sterna sumatrana. *Emu* 90 (2): 88-96.

Smith, G. W., I. P. Smith, and S. M. Armstrong. 1994. The relationship between river flow and entry to the Aberdeenshire Dee by returning adult Atlantic salmon. *Journal of Fish Biology* 45: 953-60.

Smith, R. J. F. 1985. *The Control of Fish Migration.* Springer-Verlag.

Smoker, William W., Anthony J. Gharrett, and Michael S. Stekoll. 1998. Genetic variation of return date in a population of pink salmon: A consequence of fluctuating environment and dispersive selection? *Alaska Fishery Research Bulletin* 5 (1): summer.

Solazzi, M. F. 2001. *Summary of Habitat and Fish Monitoring Data from East Fork and Upper Mainstem Lobster Creeks: 1988-2001.* Oregon Department of Fish and Wildlife.

Solazzi, M. F., S. L. Johnson, B. Miller, T. Dalton, and K. A. Leader. 2003. Salmonid life-cycle monitoring project 2002. *Oregon Plan for Salmon and Watersheds Monitoring*, Report No. OPSW-ODF&W-2003-2. February 14.

Stearley, R. F. 1992. Historical ecology of Salmonidae, with special reference to *Oncorhynchus*. In *Systematics, Historical Ecology, and North American Freshwater Fishes*, ed. R. L. Mayden, pp. 622-58. Stanford University Press.

Stern, Kathleen, and Martha K. McClintock. 1998. Regulation of ovulation by human pheromones. *Nature* 392: March 12.

Stevens, R. G., B. W. Wilson, and L. E. Anderson (ed.). 1977. *The Melatonin Hypothesis*. Battelle Press.

Subramanian, A., and L. Kothari. 1991. Melatonin, a suppressor of spontaneous murine mammary tumors. *Journal of Pineal Research* 10: 136-40.

Susac, G. L., and S. E. Jacobs. 1999. *Evaluation of Spawning Ground Surveys for Indexing the Abundance of Adult Winter Steelhead in Oregon Coastal Basins: Annual Progress Report Fl45-R-08*. Portland, OR: Oregon Department of Fish and Wildlife.

Sweka, J. A., and K. L. Hartman, K. L. 2001. Effects of turbidity on prey consumption and growth in brook trout and implications for biogenetics modeling. *Canadian Journal of Fisheries and Aquatic Sciences* 59 (2): 386-93.

———. 2001. Influence of turbidity on brook trout reactive distance and foraging success. *Transactions of the American Fisheries Society* 130: 138-46.

Swerdlow, N. M. 1998. *The Babylonian Theory of the Planets*. Princeton University Press.

Swetz, Frank J. 1994. *From Five Fingers to Infinity*. Open Court.

Swift, D. R. 1974. Activity cycles in brown trout. *Journal of the Fisheries Research Board of Canada* 21: 133-38.

Tarling, G., F. Buchholz, and J. Matthews. 1999. The effect of lunar eclipse on the vertical migration behaviour of *Meganyctiphanes norvegica* (Crustacea: Euphausiacea) in the Ligurian Sea. *Journal of Plankton Research* 21: 1475-88.

Taylor, Bernie. 2002. *Big Trout*. The Lyons Press.

Taylor, Malcolm H. 1984. Lunar synchronization of fish reproduction. *Transactions of the American Fisheries Society* 113: 484-93.

Taylor, Sidney G. 1980. Marine survival of pink salmon fry from early and late spawners. *Transactions of the American Fisheries Society* 109: 79-82.

Thomas, W. K., R. E. Withler, and A. T. Beckenbach. 1986. Mitochondrial DNA analysis of Pacific salmonid evolution. *Canadian Journal of Zoology* 64: 1058-64.

Thorpe, J. E. 1978. *Rhythmic Activity of Fishes*. Academic Press.

———. 1984. Downstream movements of juvenile salmonids: a forward speculative view. In *Mechanisms of Migration in Fishes*, ed. Arnold McCleave and Neill Dodson. Plenum Press.

Thorpe, J. E., R. I. G. Morgan, D. Pretswell, D., and P. J. Higgins. 1988. Movement rhythms in juvenile Atlantic salmon (*Salmo salar L*). *Journal of Fish Biology* 33 (6): 931-40.

Tinbergen, N. 1951. *The Study of Instinct*. Oxford University Press.

Todd, Martin, Richard Washington, Robert A. Cheke and Dominic Kniveton. 2002. Brown locust outbreaks and climate variability in southern Africa. *Journal of Applied Ecology*. 39: 31-42.

Townsend, Bill. 2003. Telephone interview with author while the Hatchery Manager at Troutlodge, Inc., Summer, Washington.

Tsuchida, Shigeru, Yukihiro Yamada, and Tsunekazu Moriguchi. 1987. *Lists of Selected Words of Batanic Languages*. University of Tokyo.

U.S. Department of Agriculture. 1980. *Sycamore: Platanus occidentalis*.

Varanelli, Carole C., and James D. McCleave. 1974. Locomotor activity of Atlantic salmon parr (*Salmo salar L.*) in various light conditions and in weak magnetic fields. *Animal Behavior* 22: 178-86.

Verkasalo, P. K., E. Pukkala, R. G. Stevens, M. Ojamo, and S. L. Rudanko. 1999. Inverse relationship between breast cancer incidence and degree of visual impairment in Finland. *British Journal of Cancer* 80: 1459-60.

Videgar, D. T. 2000. "Population estimates, food habits and estimates of consumption of selected predatory fishes in Lake Pend Oreille, Idaho." Master's thesis. University of Idaho.

von Gaertner, T., and E. Braunroth. 1935. Uber den Einflub des Mondlichtes auf den Bluhtermin der Lang-und Kurztagspflanzen. *Beihefte zum Botanischen Zentralblatt* 53: 554-63.

Wagner. Harry H. 1974. Photoperiod and temperature regulation of smolting in steelhead trout (*Salmo gairdneri*). *Canadian Journal of Zoology* 52: 219-34.

Walcott, C. 1978. Anomalies in the earth's magnetic field increase the scatter of pigeon's vanishing bearings. In *Animal Migration, Navigation and Homing*, ed. K. Schmidt-Koenig and W. T. Keeton, pp. 143-51. Springer-Verlag.

Walcott, C., and R. P. Green. 1974. Orientation of homing pigeons altered by a change in the direction of an applied magnetic field. *Science* 184, 180-82.

Walker, B. W. 1949. Periodicity of spawning by the grunion, *Leuresthes tenuis*, an atherine fish. Doctoral dissertation. Los Angeles: University of California.

Walker, Michael M. 1984. Learned magnetic field discrimination in yellowfin tuna, Thunnus albacares, *Journal of Comparative Physiology* A155: 673-79.

———. 1984. Magnetic sensitivity and its possible physical basis in the Yellowfin Tuna, Thunnus Albacares. In *Mechanisms of Migration in Fishes*, ed. Arnold McCleave and Neill Dodson.. Plenum Press.

Walker, Michael M., and M. E. Bitterman. 1985. Conditioned responding to magnetic field discrimination by honeybees. *Journal of Comprehensive Physiology* 157: 61-71.

———. 1989. Attached magnets impair magnetic field discrimination by honeybees. *Journal of Exploratory Biology* 141: 447-51.

Walker, Michael M., D. L. Baird, and M. E. Bitterman. 1989. Failure of stationary but not of flying honeybees to respond to magnetic field stimuli. *Journal of Comprehensive Physiology* 103: 62-69.

Walker, Michael M., J. L. Kirschvink, G. Ahmed, and A. E. Diction. 1992. Evidence that fin whales respond to the geomagnetic field during migration. *Journal of Exploratory Biology* 171: 67-78.

Walker, Michael M., C. E. Diebel, C. V. Haugh, P. M. Pankhurst, J. C. Montgomery, and C. R. Green. 1997. Structure and function of the vertebrate magnetic sense. *Nature* 390: 371.

Wallis, J. 1963. *An evaluation of the Alsea River Salmon Hatchery, Oregon Fish Commission Research Laboratory, 1961.* Clackamas, OR.

———. 1964. *An evaluation of the Bonneville Salmon Hatchery, Oregon Fish Commission Research Laboratory, 1961.* Clackamas, OR.

Ward, B. R., and P. A. Slaney. 1988. Life history and smolt-to-adult survival of Keogh River steelhead trout (*Salmo gairdneri*) and the relationship to smolt size. *Canadian Journal of Fisheries and Aquatic Sciences* 45: 1110-22.

———. 1990. Returns of pen-reared steelhead from riverine, estuarine, and marine releases. *Transactions of the American Fisheries Society* 119 (3): 492–99.

Waterman, T. T., and A. L. Kroeber. 1938. *The Kepel Fish Dam.* University of California Press.

Watson, Rupert. 1999. *Salmon, Trout and Charr of The World: A Fisherman's Natural History.* Swan Hill Press.

Weber, Lavern J., and John R. Smith. 1980. Possible role of the pineal gland in migratory behavior of salmonids. In *Salmonid Ecosystems of the North Pacific*, ed. William J. McNeil and Daniel C. Himsworth. Oregon State University Press.

Welch, D. W., B. R. Ward, S. D. Batten, and G. W. Boehlert. Early ocean survival and comparative marine movements of hatchery and wild juvenile steelhead, as determined by an acoustic array: Queen Charlotte Straight, British Columbia.

Whalen, K. G., D. L. Parrish, and S. D. McCormick. Migration timing of Atlantic salmon smolts relative to environmental and physiological factors. *Transactions of the American Fisheries Society* 128: 289-301.

Whenham, Gordon J. 1987. *World Biblical Commentary.* Vol. 1, Genesis 1:15. Word Books.

Whiston, William. (trans.) 1960. *Josephus, Complete Works.* Kregel Publications.

Whitney, F. A., C. S. Wong, and P. W. Boyd. 1998. Interannual variability in nitrate supply to surface waters of the Northeast Pacific Ocean. *Mar. Ecol. Prog. Ser.* 170: 15-23.

Whitney, Frank, David Mackas, David Welch, and Marie Robert. Impact of the 1990s' El Niños on nutrient supply and productivity of Gulf of Alaska Waters. *PICES Scientific Report*, no. 10: 59-62.

Williams, J. G., S. G. Smith, and W. D. Muir. 2001. Survival estimates for downstream migrant yearling juvenile salmonids through the Snake and Columbia Rivers Hydropower System, 1996-1980 and 1993-1999. *North American Journal of Fisheries Management* 21: 310-17.

Willis, Judith L. 1990. Keeping in time to circadian rhythms. *FDA Consumer*: July/August.

Wilson, Alistair Macintosh. 1995. *The Infinite in the Finite.* Oxford University Press.

Wiltschko, R., and W. Wiltschko. 1995. *Magnetic Orientation in Animals.* Springer.

Windels, Fernand. 1949. *The Lascaux Cave Paintings.* Faber and Faber Ltd.

Withler, I. L. 1966. Variability in life history characteristics of steelhead trout (*Salmo gairdneri*) along the Pacific Coast of North America. *Journal of the Fisheries Research Board of Canada* 23 (3): 365-92.

Workman, R. D., D. B. Hayes, and T. G. Coon. 2002. A model of steelhead movement in relation to water temperature in two Lake Michigan tributaries. *Transactions of the American Fisheries Society* 131: 463-75.

Young, Kyle A. 1999. Environmental correlates of male life history variation among Coho salmon populations from two Oregon coastal basins. *Transactions of the American Fisheries Society* 128: 1-16.

Youngson, A. F., R. J. G. Buck, T. H. Simpson, and D. W. Hay. 1983. The autumn and spring emigrations of juvenile Atlantic salmon (*Salmo salar*) from the Girnock Burn, Aberdeen, Scotland, UK, environmental release of migration. *Journal of Fish Biology* 23 (6): 625-40.

Zabel, R. W., S. G. Smith, W. D. Muir, D. M. Marsh, and J. G. Williams — Northwest Fisheries Science Center, National Marine Fisheries Service. 2002. Survival estimates for the passage of spring-migrating juvenile salmonids through

Snake and Columbia River dams and reservoirs, 2001. Report to Bonneville Power Administration, Contract No. 00004922, Project No. 199302900, 143 electronic pages (BPA Report DOE/BP-00004922-1).

Zimmerman, Christian E., and Gordon H. Reeves. 1999. Steelhead and resident Rainbow trout: Early life history and habitat use in the Deschutes River, Oregon. Pelton Round Butte Hydroelectric Project FERC No. 2030. Prepared for Portland General Electric Company by Oregon State University Department of Fisheries and Wildlife.

Index